The 1st International Conference on Computational Engineering and Intelligent Systems

The 1st International Conference on Computational Engineering and Intelligent Systems

Editors

Abdelmadjid Recioui
Hamid Bentarzi
Fatma Zohra Dekhandji

MDPI • Basel • Beijing • Wuhan • Barcelona • Belgrade • Manchester • Tokyo • Cluj • Tianjin

Editors

Abdelmadjid Recioui
University of Boumerdes
Algeria

Hamid Bentarzi
University of Boumerdes
Algeria

Fatma Zohra Dekhandji
University of Boumerdes
Algeria

Editorial Office
MDPI
St. Alban-Anlage 66
4052 Basel, Switzerland

This is a reprint of articles from the Proceedings published online in the open access journal *Engineering Proceedings* (ISSN 2673-4591) (available at: https://www.mdpi.com/2673-4591/14/1).

For citation purposes, cite each article independently as indicated on the article page online and as indicated below:

LastName, A.A.; LastName, B.B.; LastName, C.C. Article Title. *Journal Name* **Year**, *Volume Number*, Page Range.

ISBN 978-3-0365-3701-6 (Hbk)
ISBN 978-3-0365-3702-3 (PDF)

© 2022 by the authors. Articles in this book are Open Access and distributed under the Creative Commons Attribution (CC BY) license, which allows users to download, copy and build upon published articles, as long as the author and publisher are properly credited, which ensures maximum dissemination and a wider impact of our publications.

The book as a whole is distributed by MDPI under the terms and conditions of the Creative Commons license CC BY-NC-ND.

Contents

About the Editors ix

Preface to "The 1st International Conference on Computational Engineering and Intelligent Systems" xi

Abdelmadjid Recioui
Statement of Peer Review
Reprinted from: *Eng. Proc.* 2022, 14, 25, doi:10.3390/engproc2022014025 1

Fatma Zohra Dekhandji and Abdelmadjid Recioui
An Investigation into Pricing Policies in Smart Grids
Reprinted from: *Eng. Proc.* 2022, 14, 15, doi:10.3390/engproc2022014015 3

Khaled Dassa and Abdelmadjid Recioui
Demand Side Management and Dynamic Economic Dispatch Using Genetic Algorithms
Reprinted from: *Eng. Proc.* 2022, 14, 12, doi:10.3390/engproc2022014012 7

Cilina Touabi and Hamid Bentarzi
Photovoltaic Panel Parameters Estimation Using GreyWolf Optimization Technique
Reprinted from: *Eng. Proc.* 2022, 14, 3, doi:10.3390/engproc2022014003 15

Mohamed Cherif Rais, Fatma Zohra Dekhandji, Abdelmadjid Recioui, Mohamed Sadek Rechid and Lahcen Djedi
Comparative Study of Optimization Techniques Based PID Tuning for Automatic Voltage Regulator System
Reprinted from: *Eng. Proc.* 2022, 14, 21, doi:10.3390/engproc2022014021 25

Djamila Talah and Hamid Bentarzi
Frequency Control System Effectiveness in a Combined Cycle Gas Turbine Plant
Reprinted from: *Eng. Proc.* 2022, 14, 1, doi:10.3390/engproc2022014001 31

Mohamed Mezaache, Omar Fethi Benaouda, Saad Chaouch, Badreddine Babes and Rachid Amraoui
Optimizing MAG Welding Input Variables to Maximize Penetration Depth Using Particle Swarm Optimization Algorithm
Reprinted from: *Eng. Proc.* 2022, 14, 5, doi:10.3390/engproc2022014005 39

Mohammed Tsebia and Hamid Bentarzi
Sub-Synchronous Torsional Interaction Study and Mitigation Using a Synchro-Phasors Measurement Unit
Reprinted from: *Eng. Proc.* 2022, 14, 8, doi:10.3390/engproc2022014008 49

Abdelkarim Ammar, Kahina Hamraoui, Moufida Belguellaoui and Aissa Kheldoun
Performance Enhancement of Photovoltaic Water Pumping System Based on BLDC Motor under Partial Shading Condition
Reprinted from: *Eng. Proc.* 2022, 14, 22, doi:10.3390/engproc2022014022 57

Hocine Khati, Hand Talem, Mohand Achour Touat, Rabah Mellah and Said Guermah
Online Adaptation of a Compensatory Neuro-Fuzzy Controller Parameters Using the Extended Kalman Filter: Application on an Inverted Pendulum
Reprinted from: *Eng. Proc.* 2022, 14, 11, doi:10.3390/engproc2022014011 67

Ali Saibi, Razika Boushaki and Hadjira Belaidi
Backstepping Control of Drone
Reprinted from: *Eng. Proc.* **2022**, *14*, 4, doi:10.3390/engproc2022014004 75

Achouri Mourad and Youcef Zennir
Fuzzy-PI Controller Tuned with HBBO for 2 DOF Robot Trajectory Control
Reprinted from: *Eng. Proc.* **2022**, *14*, 10, doi:10.3390/engproc2022014010 85

Achouri Mourad and Zennir Youcef
Adaptive Sliding Mode Control Improved by Fuzzy-PI Controller: Applied to Magnetic Levitation System
Reprinted from: *Eng. Proc.* **2022**, *14*, 14, doi:10.3390/engproc2022014014 93

Remus Pusca, Salim Sbaa, Noureddine Bessous, Raphaël Romary and Radouane Bousseksou
Mechanical Failure Detection in Induction Motors Using Stator Current and Stray Flux Analysis Techniques
Reprinted from: *Eng. Proc.* **2022**, *14*, 19, doi:10.3390/engproc2022014019 103

Halima Boussadia, Arezki Mohamed Si Mohammed, Nabil Boughanmi and Abdelkrim Meche
Sliding Mode Control Based on Backstepping Approach for Microsatellite Attitude Pointing
Reprinted from: *Eng. Proc.* **2022**, *14*, 24, doi:10.3390/engproc2022014024 113

Bouhamdi Merzoug, Mohamed Ouslim, Lotfi Mostefai and Mohamed Benouis
Evaluation of Dimensionality Reduction Using PCA on EMG-Based Signal Pattern Classification
Reprinted from: *Eng. Proc.* **2022**, *14*, 23, doi:10.3390/engproc2022014023 123

Naceur Aounallah
Performance Enhancement of Capon's DOA Algorithm Using Covariance Matrix Decomposition
Reprinted from: *Eng. Proc.* **2022**, *14*, 7, doi:10.3390/engproc2022014007 133

Khalfa Ali, Amardjia Nourredine and Kenane Elhadi
Blind Image Separation Using the JADE Method
Reprinted from: *Eng. Proc.* **2022**, *14*, 20, doi:10.3390/engproc2022014020 141

Warda Amalou and Merouane Mehdi
An Approach to Mitigate DDoS Attacks on SIP Based VoIP
Reprinted from: *Eng. Proc.* **2022**, *14*, 6, doi:10.3390/engproc2022014006 149

Youssouf Zemam, Noureddine Boukli Hacene and Yamina Belhadef
Hilbert Fractal PIFA Antenna for DCS, PCS, UMTS and WiMAX Wireless Applications
Reprinted from: *Eng. Proc.* **2022**, *14*, 2, doi:10.3390/engproc2022014002 155

Yamina Belhadef, Fatima Zohra Moussa and Souheyla Ferouani
Design of a Miniature Dual-Band Patch Antenna Based on Meta-Materials for 5G and Wi-Fi Applications
Reprinted from: *Eng. Proc.* **2022**, *14*, 13, doi:10.3390/engproc2022014013 161

Mohamed Amine Ouamri, Marius-Emil Oteşteanu, Gordana Barb and Cedric Gueguen
Coverage Analysis and Efficient Placement of Drone-BSs in 5G Networks
Reprinted from: *Eng. Proc.* **2022**, *14*, 18, doi:10.3390/engproc2022014018 169

Ali Houadef and Boualem Djezzar
UIS Characterization of LOCOS-Based LDMOS Transistor Fabricated by 1 µm CMOS Process
Reprinted from: *Eng. Proc.* **2022**, *14*, 16, doi:10.3390/engproc2022014016 . . . . **177**

Nabila Belkhelfa and Rafik Serhane
Process and Device Simulation of SAW Temperature Sensors Compatible with 1 µm CMOS Technology
Reprinted from: *Eng. Proc.* **2022**, *14*, 9, doi:10.3390/engproc2022014009 . . . . **185**

Ali Houadef and Boualem Djezzar
Design of an LDMOS Transistor Based on the 1 µm CMOS Process for High/Low Power Applications
Reprinted from: *Eng. Proc.* **2022**, *14*, 17, doi:10.3390/engproc2022014017 . . . . **195**

About the Editors

Abdelmadjid Recioui (Prof. Dr.) is a professor at the Institute of Electrical Engineering and Electronics at the University of Boumerdes, Algeria. He obtained a PhD degree in electrical and electronic engineering option telecommunications from the Institute of Electrical Engineering and Electronics, University of Boumerdes, in 2011. He also holds a master's (Magister) degree in electronic system engineering, which was achieved at the Institute of Electrical Engineering and Electronics, University of Boumerdes, in 2006. In June 2002, he finished his engineering studies at the Institute of Electrical Engineering and Electronics, University of Boumerdes. He has been a research assistant at a laboratory for signals and systems since January 2008 (Laboratory: signals and systems, Inst. of Electrical Engineering and electronics, University of Boumerdes). His research interests include: antennas, wireless communication systems, antenna array synthesis and design, capacity enhancement, system optimization, smart antennas, power system protection, power system optimization, and power system communications.

Hamid Bentarzi (Prof. Dr.) has been a faculty member at the Institute of Electrical and Electronic Engineering (IGEE), University M'hamed Bougara, Boumerdes, Algeria, since 1998. He received a bachelor's and M. Phil degrees from INELEC, Boumerdes, in 1989 and 1992, respectively, in applied electronics. In 2004, he also obtained a PhD degree at the ENP, Algiers. From 1993 to 1998, he was a lecturer at INELEC. Currently, he is a full-time professor. His research activities are centered around control and protection system reliability enhancements using recent technologies. He has been the author and coauthor of more than a hundred papers.

Fatma Zohra Dekhandji (Dr.) has been a faculty member at the Institute of Electrical and Electronic Engineering (IGEE), University M'hamed Bougara, Boumerdes, Algeria, since 2007, where she also obtained her PhD degree in 2016. She received an engineering degree from IGEE in 2003 in power engineering and drives. Currently, she holds the rank of associate professor. Her research activities are centered around power quality enhancements in smart grids. She has authored and coauthored many journal and conference papers.

Preface to "The 1st International Conference on Computational Engineering and Intelligent Systems"

In this Special Issue of Engineering Proceedings, we present a collection of papers presented at the 1st International Conference on Computational Engineering and Intelligent Systems (ICCEIS 2021), held online on 10–12 December 2021 via the Jitsi Meet platform.

This conference aimed to assemble scientists, research individuals and industrials to share knowledge and findings regarding the topics within its scope. ICCEIS 2021 is a platform for the possible collaboration and exchange of ideas towards the advancement of the proliferating topic of computational engineering, artificial intelligence and smart systems.

ICCEIS 2021 contributions were accentuated around: biomedical engineering and applications; the computational study of biological systems; climate modeling; energy systems; modeling and simulation; multiphysical models and cosimulation; cybersecurity; data science and engineering; high-performance computing; optimization; multiagent systems; evolutionary computation; artificial intelligence; complex systems; computation intelligence and soft computing; intelligent control; advanced control technology; robotics and applications; intelligent information processing; iterative learning control; machine learning; smart grids and systems.

Forty-two technical contributions and one keynote presentation were received and underwent a peer-review process performed through the Microsoft CMT toolkit. Twenty-five papers were successfully presented.

We would like to express our warm thanks to all contributors of ICCEIS 2021, with special thanks to prof. Youcef Zennir, Prof. Mohamed Belkhiri and Dr. Riad Bendib for their support in the organization of ICCEIS 2021. We are also grateful to MDPI for accepting to publish ICCEIS 2021 proceedings, and in particular Christian Liang for his patience and guidance.

Abdelmadjid Recioui, Hamid Bentarzi and Fatma Zohra Dekhandji
Editors

Editorial
Statement of Peer Review †

Abdelmadjid Recioui

Institut de Génie Electrique et Electronique, University of Boumerdes, Boumerdes 35000, Algeria; rec79dz2002@yahoo.com

† Presented at the 1st International Conference on Computational Engineering and Intelligent Systems, Online, 10–12 December 2021.

In submitting conference proceedings to *Engineering Proceedings*, the volume editors of the proceedings certify to the publisher that all papers published in this volume have been subjected to peer review administered by the volume editors. Reviews were conducted by expert referees to the professional and scientific standards expected of a proceedings journal.

- Type of peer review: single-blind; double-blind; triple-blind; open; other (please describe): Single Blind
- Conference submission management system: Microsoft CMT
- Number of submissions sent for review: 42
- Number of submissions accepted: 24
- Acceptance rate (number of submissions accepted/number of submissions received): 57%
- Average number of reviews per paper: 2
- Total number of reviewers involved: 19

Citation: Recioui, A. Statement of Peer Review. *Eng. Proc.* **2022**, *14*, 25. https://doi.org/10.3390/engproc2022014025

Published: 23 March 2022

Publisher's Note: MDPI stays neutral with regard to jurisdictional claims in published maps and institutional affiliations.

Copyright: © 2022 by the author. Licensee MDPI, Basel, Switzerland. This article is an open access article distributed under the terms and conditions of the Creative Commons Attribution (CC BY) license (https://creativecommons.org/licenses/by/4.0/).

Proceeding Paper

An Investigation into Pricing Policies in Smart Grids †

Fatma Zohra Dekhandji and Abdelmadjid Recioui *

Laboratory of Signals and Systems, Institute of Electrical and Electronic Engineering, University M'hamed Bougara of Boumerdes, Boumerdes 35000, Algeria; fzdekhandji@univ-boumerdes.dz
* Correspondence: a_recioui@univ-boumerdes.dz
† Presented at the 1st International Conference on Computational Engineering and Intelligent Systems, Online, 10–12 December 2021.

Abstract: One achievement in smart grids is the construction of smart cities. In this kind of city houses are equipped with smart meters that can record electric energy as well as transmit and accept data regarding energy utilization and prices to consumers. Additionally, new methods, known as real-time pricing of electricity, have been introduced in which energy prices change based on an hourly timeline and depend on consumers' energy requests. Due to the production of electricity by PV panels, a smart grid will share the surplus of the energy provided by the panels to the grid. These pricing policies will force and encourage consumers to track their power consumption and use renewable energies. In this paper, the impacts of pricing policy on the reduction in consumers' power consumption are investigated. A small-scale smart city is presented and a policy is applied to it. Additionally, an implementation through a simulation of some houses equipped with renewable energy sources is done to study their effect on the grid performance.

Keywords: smart grids; smart meters; smart cities; pricing policies

Citation: Dekhandji, F.Z.; Recioui, A. An Investigation into Pricing Policies in Smart Grids. *Eng. Proc.* **2022**, *14*, 15. https://doi.org/10.3390/engproc 2022014015

Academic Editor: Hamid Bentarzi

Published: 10 February 2022

Publisher's Note: MDPI stays neutral with regard to jurisdictional claims in published maps and institutional affiliations.

Copyright: © 2022 by the authors. Licensee MDPI, Basel, Switzerland. This article is an open access article distributed under the terms and conditions of the Creative Commons Attribution (CC BY) license (https:// creativecommons.org/licenses/by/ 4.0/).

1. Introduction

Emerging smart grid technology has been introduced to help utilities conserve energy; reduce costs, and increase grid transparency, sustainability, and efficiency. In addition, this introduction aims at captivating consumer attention via one important aspect of smart grids, which is demand-side management (DSM) [1–3]. Dynamic pricing is one of the emerging areas and is a DSM approach that is able to cut the overstress in energy requests through assigning various pricing at variable time intervals depending on energy requests [4]. The common practices in the electricity markets are that prices remain unchanged irrespective of demand (flat pricing) or that the kilowatt price of energy will be raised or lowered with the growing portions of electricity consumption (block pricing) [5].

A variety of research has dealt with dynamic pricing and found it to quite effective in stimulating a high level of demand response. Customers are more likely to reduce electricity usage than postpone. Users with large electricity demand and in hot regions tend to adhere better to this program. Modern technology facilitates the realization of this dynamic pricing. Faruqui et al. [6] analyzed five dynamic pricing programs in the USA and demonstrated that users react completely to pricing irrespective of where electricity service is located. The deployment of facilitating equipment allows a better likelihood of a positive request pricing reaction. Zhou and Teng [7] discovered cheap pricing and revenue flexibility of demand in city housing consumption in China. The standard of living and population growth parameters turn out to have a significant impact on explaining electricity demand. Faruqui et al. [8] have shown that customers' reactions to dynamic pricing increases according to the facilitating equipment. The reaction to pricing is larger in hot regions. Users in housing areas are more likely to react to dynamic pricing compared to business and small industrial users. Users with lower revenue react to a lesser extent as their utilization is weak and essential, causing them to have no chance to lessen their utilization any more. Pagani and Aiello [9] established a practical scheme to reasonably motivate dynamic pricing with smart grid benefits based on statistics of general sales and renewable energy deployment in the Netherlands. In-lab tests are being deployed more and more to advertise community plans and in-societal discipline in general [10]. Despite their probability of being "hypothetically biased", hypothetical actions of favoritism and motivation to pay [11] in addition to procedures of ability are probably more consistent and can be motivated through incentives [12]. Investigative set-ups that evaluate the precision of resolution-taking at diverse phases of procurement turned out to be victorious in suggesting a broad collection of perspectives in all community plan areas, such as in the ruling of automobile economics [13].

2. Case Study

In Algeria, the company SONELGAZ, which is a state-owned utility in charge of electricity and natural gas distribution, has employed different pricing policies for its consumers. These are summarized in Tables 1–4.

Table 1. Tariffs for code 51M.

Tariff Code	Peak Hours	Middle	Night
51M	17–21 h 81,147 DA	6–17 h and 21–22 h 30 min 21,645 DA	22 h 30 min–6 h 12,050 DA

Table 2. Tariffs for code 52M.

Tariff Code	Peak Hours	Off-Peak Hours
52M	17–21 h 81,147 DA	21–17 h 17,807 DA

Table 3. Tariffs for code 53M.

Tariff Code	Night	Day
53M	22 h 30 min–6 h 12,050 DA	6–22 h 30 min 48,698 DA

Table 4. Tariffs for code 54M.

Tariff Code	For Consumption per Quarter
54M	First section: from 0 to 125 kWh: 17,787 DA Second section: more than 125 until 250 kWh: 41,789 DA Third section: more than 250 until 1000 kWh: 48,120 DA Fourth section: more than 1000 kWh: 54,796 DA

As an illustration of the use of this policy, we suppose a smart city containing 12 houses; 10 of them are not equipped with PV panels (renewable energy) and the rest are not equipped with this system. The pricing policy in Table 5 is adopted for the entire city:

Table 5. The applied tariffs for the proposed policy.

	High Tariff (17–21 h)	Low Tariff (21–17 h)	In the Case of a PV
Cost for 1 kWh (DA)	81,147	17,807	30

Figure 1 illustrates the power consumption profile for the 12 houses with the tariffs used by SONELGAZ (Tables 1–4). The loads used have been turned on based on a pattern to produce peak load consumption.

We observe that for the power consumption curve in Figure 1, there exist two peak values at 12 h (4.0122 kWh) and 20 h (4.23621 kWh). After applying the proposed pricing policy, we notice in Figure 2 that the curve shows only one peak value at 20 h (3.9822 kWh); this is due to the pricing policy we have implemented for this city.

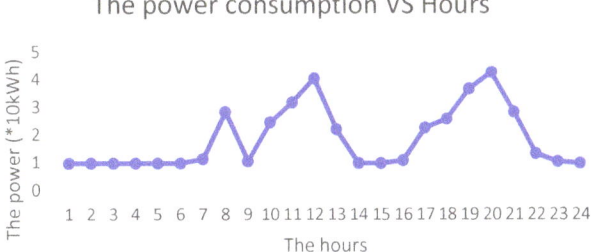

Figure 1. The consumption of power before applying the proposed policy.

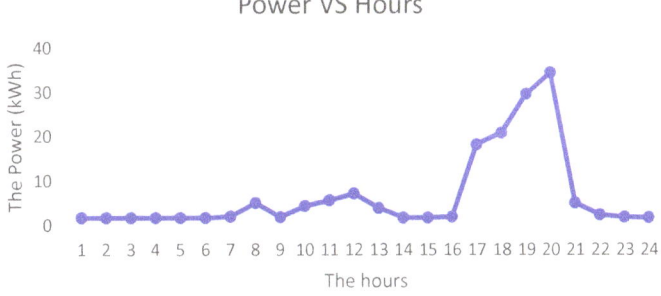

Figure 2. The profile after applying the pricing.

3. Conclusions

In this work, the impact of a pricing policy on the power consumption in a smart city has been illustrated. If a client consumes much energy at peak hours, the tariffs will be large. The implementation of smart meters in houses will help a consumer control and track his power consumption as well as the associated cost. A consumer can choose to use power at different periods of time (during a low-tariff period). This will also help relieve the stress on power plants as well as the entire network. The use of renewable energy will further help in the production of power, as the system will use the power produced by the panels.

Author Contributions: Conceptualization, A.R.; methodology, F.Z.D.; software, F.Z.D.; validation, A.R. and F.Z.D.; formal analysis, A.R.; investigation, F.Z.D.; resources, F.Z.D.; data curation, F.Z.D.; writing—original draft preparation, F.Z.D.; writing—review and editing, A.R.; visualization, F.Z.D.; supervision, A.R.; project administration, A.R.; funding acquisition, A.R. All authors have read and agreed to the published version of the manuscript.

Funding: No external funds were received to perform this research.

Institutional Review Board Statement: Not applicable.

Informed Consent Statement: Not applicable.

Data Availability Statement: No new data were created or analyzed in this study. Data sharing is not applicable to this article.

Conflicts of Interest: The authors declare no conflict of interest.

References

1. Recioui, A.; Bentarzi, H. *Optimizing Smart Grid Operation and Control*; IGI Global: Hershey, PA, USA, 2021.
2. Recioui, A.; Djemai, H.; Boucenna, F. A Smart Metering Simulation in LABVIEW. *Alg. J. Sig. Syst.* **2019**, *4*, 89–100.
3. Recioui, A. Home Load-Side Management in Smart Grids Using Global Optimization. In *Research Anthology on Multi-Industry Uses of Genetic Programming and Algorithms*; IGI Global: Hershey, PA, USA, 2021.
4. Dekhandji, F.Z. Smart Metering and Pricing Policy in Smart Grids. In *Optimizing and Measuring Smart Grid Operation and Control*; IGI Global: Hershey, PA, USA, 2021.
5. Simshauser, P.; Downer, D. On the inequity of flat-rate electricity tariffs. In *AGL Applied Economic and Policy Working Paper*; 41 AGL Energy Ltd.: Brisbane, Australia, 2014.
6. Faruqui, A.; Hledik, R.; Sergici, S. Piloting the smart grid. *Electricity J.* **2009**, *22*, 55–69. [CrossRef]
7. Zhou, S.; Teng, F. Estimation of urban residential electricity demand in China using household survey data. *Energy Policy* **2013**, *61*, 394–402. [CrossRef]
8. Faruqui, A.; Sergici, S.; Akaba, L. The impact of dynamic pricing on residential and small commercial and industrial usage: New experimental evidence from Connecticut. *Energy J.* **2014**, *35*, 137–160. [CrossRef]
9. Pagani, G.; Aiello, M. Generating realistic dynamic prices and services for the smart grid. *IEEE Syst. J.* **2015**, *9*, 191–198. [CrossRef]
10. Falk, A.; Heckman, J.J. Lab experiments are a major source of knowledge in the social sciences. *Science* **2009**, *326*, 535–538. [CrossRef] [PubMed]
11. Harrison, G.W.; Rutström, E.E. Experimental evidence on the existence of hypothetical bias in value elicitation methods. *Handb. Exp. Econ. Results* **2008**, *1*, 752–767.
12. Lunn, P.D.; Choisdealbha, Á.N. The case for laboratory experiments in behavioural public policy. *Behav. Public Policy* **2018**, *2*, 22–40. [CrossRef]
13. McElvaney, T.J.; Lunn, P.D.; McGowan, F.P. Do consumers understand PCP car finance? An experimental investigation. *J. Consum. Policy* **2018**, *41*, 229–255. [CrossRef]

Proceeding Paper

Demand Side Management and Dynamic Economic Dispatch Using Genetic Algorithms [†]

Khaled Dassa and Abdelmadjid Recioui *

Laboratory of Signals and Systems, Institute of Electrical and Electronic Engineering, University M'hamed Bougara of Boumerdes, Boulevard de L'indépendance, Boumerdes 35000, Algeria; k.dassa@univ-boumerdes.dz
* Correspondence: a_recioui@univ-boumerdes.dz
† Presented at the 1st International Conference on Computational Engineering and Intelligent Systems, Online, 10–12 December 2021.

Abstract: The purpose of this work is to find the optimal energy management mix in order to maximize the benefit for the client by minimizing the bill and reducing losses by optimizing the energy distribution in the network. There exist two smart grid management problems: demand side management (DSM) and dynamic economic dispatch (DED). DSM consists of modifying electricity consumption patterns with reference to the overall consumption picture, consumption time profile, and contractual supply parameters in order to achieve savings in electricity charges. DED aims at providing the ideal share of electricity produced corresponding to the overall energy request of users and the generated power. Research works in the literature dealt with DSM or DED issues independently. In this work, genetic algorithms will be used to solve DSM and DED problems, considering them as two complementary stages in the optimization process.

Keywords: smart grids; energy management; optimization; genetic algorithms

1. Introduction

Smart grid is a modernized electricity network that functions based on a two-way communication link. Smart grids, in addition to supporting utility companies in preserving energy, lowering expenditures, and raising network intelligibility, durability and effectiveness, encourage user involvement. Smart power managing encompasses the plan–control–optimize energy acts via intelligent responses or sophisticated equipment with the final goal to enhance production and ease, as well as to lessen the electricity price and emissions [1].

Demand side management (DSM) refers to plan and control actions that would in one way or another influence the end customer request in energy. The aim of the DSM plan is to reduce costs of electricity, which in turn restricts the need for building more transmission and distribution networks [2]. Various DSM strategies have been suggested and implemented. These include—energy conservation and energy efficiency, energy consumption optimization and scheduling, demand response, distributed generation, and energy storage [3,4]. To shape the end used energy consumption profile, a lot of mechanisms exist. Practical approaches are comprised of peak clipping, basin fill up, intentional preservation, consumption transferring, and time-reallocation [5,6].

With the advances in computers, computing techniques have been applied to the DSM problem. These techniques include artificial neural network, fuzzy logic and metaheuristic computation [7]. A user-adapted scheme is built up to tune the consumer's altering favorites in [8]. An HVAC system has been managed via fuzzy logic concepts with the efficacy contrasted with the traditional on–off counterpart in [9]. An intelligent HEMS using fuzzy logic to control storage and demand is proposed in [10]. An hourly energy consumption predictor [11] is developed using a multilayer perceptron. Artificial neural networks were deployed to predict DR and electricity request profile to sustain an intelligent house that is energetically efficient [12–14]. An optimized electricity planner for consumption reliability was studied with the optimization task resolved via PSO [15]. An online energy organizer for intelligent house electricity management, considering renewable sources and battery systems, was built up in [16]. A consumption prediction for a whole day was assumed prior to optimized planning with a joint Harmony Search-PSO approach via an HMI, inner manager, and various consumption levels [17]. A two-stage profound strengthening training strategy for domestic device planning besides incorporating charging and discharging schedules of energy storage and EV has been presented in [18]. On the other hand, economic dispatch refers to the share of total energy generation within existing distributed generators. Online active planning refers to online dynamic economic dispatch (DED) of energy and aims at minimizing the overall operating fuel cost and fulfilling the energy request in each time interval. Optimization techniques for solving the DED problem have been applied in the literature. Examples include artificial immune system algorithm [19], genetic algorithms [20], artificial bee colony [21], and particle swarm optimization [22,23].

The purpose of this paper is to illustrate Smart Grid management problems in order to maximize the benefit for the consumer. The aim is to minimize the bill and reduce losses. We will be using genetic algorithms to solve DSM and DED problems by considering them as two complementary stages in the optimization process.

2. DSM Optimization (First Stage)

Demand side management is one of the main elements in smart grids and has many advantages to both utility and users. Its goal is to wisely employ the existing electricity to enhance the financial matters of the grid. Controlling the energy profile may cut down on the maximum energy request, and hence enhance the efficacy of the power system, lowering hazardous emissions and energy cost for consumers.

Here, a DSM approach utilizing load shifting method considering several kinds of domestic devices at different time slots in order to minimize a cost function, along with the equality and inequality restraints to reach energy bill maximum and decrease the Max to Typical Quotient. The load scheduling problem is formulated as follows:

$$min\ f = \sum_{t=1}^{t=24} \sum_{a=1}^{n} \sum_{b=1}^{m} Xab(t) * Eab(t) * EP(t) \qquad (1)$$

$$min\ f = \sum_{t=1}^{t=24} \sum_{a=1}^{n} \sum_{b=1}^{m} Xab(t) * Eab(t) \leq L(t) \qquad (2)$$

$ma = 24 - la;\ Yab = 0 \forall 24 - li > ma;\ Yab > 0 \forall a, b$

$$\sum_{t=1}^{24} Ctbab \leq A(t) \qquad (3)$$

where: 't' represents time slots; 'a' is the number of appliances. 'b' is the type of appliance; 'Xab' is ON/OFF state of appliance of type 'b', 'Eab' is the energy consumption of appliance 'a' of type 'b', 'EP' is the electricity price at time slot 't', ma is maximum permissible delay of appliance b. la is the Number of ON request of appliances, i.e., length of operation time. L(t) is maximum power limit at time slot t; and Yab is controllable appliance of type b.

A(t) is set of controllable appliances at time slot b.

To illustrate the efficacy of the adopted approach, the scheme is applied on two unlike regions: residential and commercial areas. The regions have diverse kinds of controllable appliances, as detailed in Tables 1 and 2.

Table 1. Controllable devices in residential area.

Device	Power Consumption (kWh)	Number of Devices
Dryer	1.2	189
Dish Washer	0.7	288
Wshing Machine	0.5	268
Oven	1.3	279
Iron	1.0	340
Vacuum Cleaner	0.4	158
Fan	0.2	288
Kettle	2.0	406
Toaster	0.9	48
Rice-Cooker	0.85	59
Hair Dryer	1.5	58
Blender	0.3	68
Frying Pan	1.1	101
Cofee Maker	0.8	56
Total	–	2604

Table 2. Controllable devices in commercial area.

Device	Power Consumption (kWh)	Number of Devices
Water Heater	12.5	39
Welding Machine	25	35
Fan/AC	30	16
Arc Furnace	50	8
Induction Motor	100	5
DC motor	150	6
Total	–	109

It is clear from Figure 1a that the peak load of the residential area has been reduced by about 21.04%. Residential users schedule their maximum load where the price is low, which leads to minimize the electricity bill, as shown in Figure 1c. Indeed, the electricity bill has been reduced from 311,290 $ to 257,940 $ per day, which accounts for about a 17.1382% reduction.

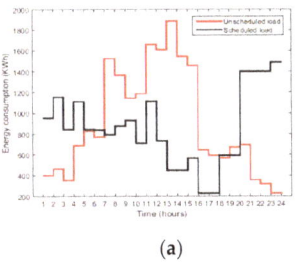
(a)

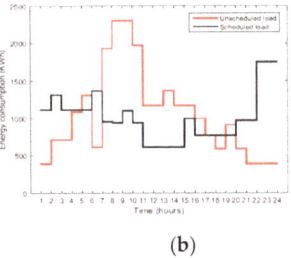
(b)

Figure 1. *Cont.*

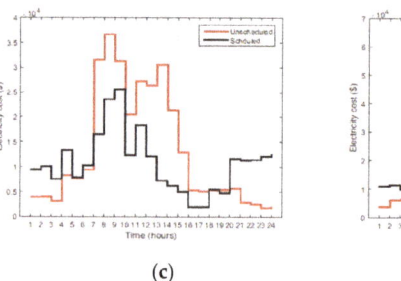
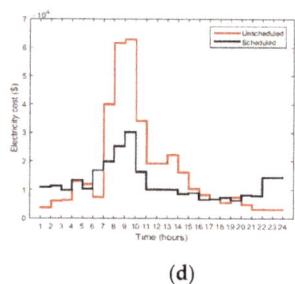

(c)   (d)

Figure 1. Optimization results: (**a**) Residential area daily energy consumption. (**b**) Commercial area daily energy. (**c**) Residential area daily electricity bill. (**d**) Commercial area daily electricity bill.

For the commercial area, peak load is reduced, where it used to be 1752 kW, it is now 2301 kW, which means a reduction of about 23.85% in max. consumption, as shown in Figure 1c. The electricity bill used to be 380,650 $ and has been lowered to 297,040 $ a day, which translates to about a 21.9647% reduction in the electricity bill per day as seen in Figure 1d.

3. ED Optimization (Second Stage)

This stage will use the best adequate sharing of appliances utilized by consumers at various time intervals obtained from the 1st optimization stage. To keep the price and electricity simultaneously at their minimum values, this second phase considers the following cost function:

$$min\ f2 = \sum_{i=1}^{t}(\sum_{u=1}^{m}(\sum_{s=1}^{S}\left(X(s)_{i,u} \times E_s(i) \times C_s(i) \times d_{u,s}\right))). \qquad (4)$$

where: $X(s)_{i,u}$ is the share of electricity obtained from generator 's' to consumer 'u' during inteval 't'. $E_s(i)$ is the electricity from source 's' in the interval 'i' (kWh). $C_s(i)$ is the corresponding price ($/kWh). $d_{u,s}$ is a parameter to account for losses due to the Joule effect and depends on the relative location of consumer and electricity generator.

The equality constraint equation is defined by:

$$\sum_{s=1}^{S} X(s)_{i,u} \times E_s(i) = \sum_{a=1}^{n} \left(y(i)_{a,u} \times P_{shif}(i)_{a,u} \times \Delta t_{a,u} + P_{unshift}(i)_{a,u} \times T\right). \qquad (5)$$
$$\forall\ i\ \epsilon\{1,2\ldots t\}\ and\ \forall\ u\ \epsilon\{1,2\ldots m\}$$

where: n is the number of electrical devices. $P_{shif}(i)_{a,u}$ and $P_{unshift}$ are the energy consumed by scheduled and nonscheduled appliances, respectively, in (kW). $\Delta t_{a,u}$ is the time of use for appliance 'a' utilized by consumer 'u' in the interval multiplied by 'i' (hours). $\Delta t_{a,u}$ can take values smaller or equal to the time length T.

In this section, we took 5 users, 5 devices, 32 total device numbers, 4 slots of time and 3 different energy sources.

Step 1 (selection): introducing the required input data randomly, generating the initial population of chromosomes that is called parents that contribute to the population of the next generation. Evaluate the equality constraint, if any chromosome violates the problem's constraints, it will be replaced by another randomly selected one.

Step 2 (fitness selection): This step concerns the objective function calculation for the potential solutions in the chosen group. The smallest objective function value with respect to the evaluation obtained in the preceding iterations is regarded as a first best result of the optimization process. More fit individuals are more likely to be selected.

The optimized energy profile for each consumer at each time interval will be fulfilled by three unlike generators: PV, wind and fossil fuel energy, for the sake of establishing in each time interval the best combination with respect to the share of each power generator to fulfill each consumer in the time interval, all at the lowest price with the least electricity losses in the network.

In the foremost time interval, the share of each generator to fulfill each consumer is presented in Figure 2. In this time interval, electricity is delivered to consumers 1, 3, 4 and 5 from the wind generator and the grid, as no electricity is supplied from generator 1 (PV), at a relatively smaller importance for the grid generator, as it is cheaper compared to the wind generation in this time interval.

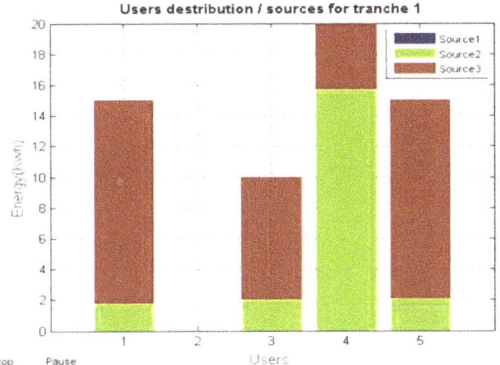

Figure 2. Share of electricity generation for various consumers for time interval 1 (tranch '$i = 1$').

For the second time interval, Figure 3 illustrates the generated electricity for each consumer using the three generators and PV and grid generators show dominance. This is because the electricity generation prices of these generators are at (0.5$/kWh), which makes them cheaper than the cost of electricity generated by wind (0.7$/kWh).

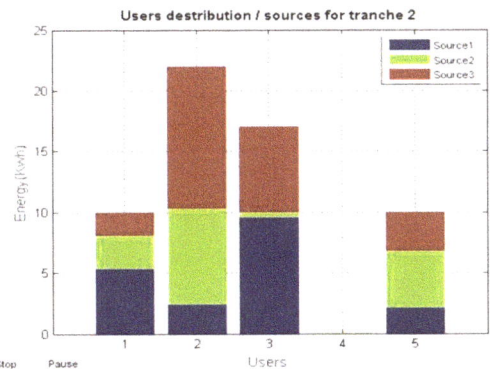

Figure 3. Share of electricity generation for various consumers in time interval 2 (tranch '$i = 2$').

In the time interval 3, the price of electricity from the wind generator is lower than that of the PV generator, causing the dominance of the wind and grid generators as shown in Figure 4.

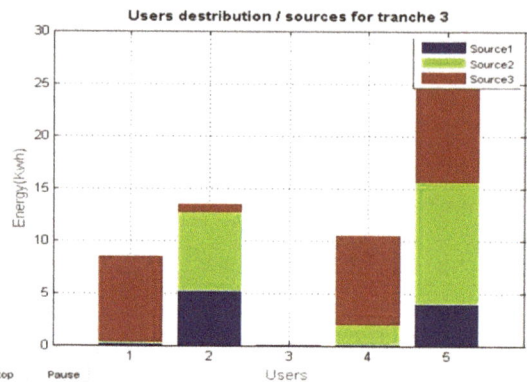

Figure 4. Share of electricity generation for various consumers in time interval 3 (tranch '$i = 3$').

Finally, the best share for the time interval 4 is related to consumer 5 only, who is fed from the wind and grid generators at a remarkable dominance of the wind generator, as shown in Figure 5. It is worth noting that these findings concern not only the electricity price, but also the cost of electricity losses while transmitting from generators to consumers via the distance parameters as well.

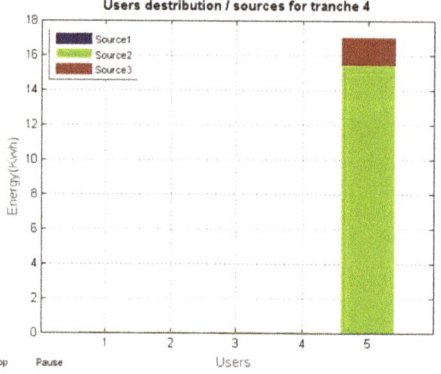

Figure 5. Share of electricity generation for various consumers in time interval 4 (tranch '$i = 4$').

4. Conclusions

This work considers a set of users in two different regions employing many scheduled electrical appliances and supplied from various electricity generators. These generators exhibit variable electricity and production cost patterns at four daily time intervals. The planned electricity usage pattern for each region is dealt with separately for the sake of obtaining the best share of appliance usage time at various intervals to keep away from excessive consumption situation. At this situation, maximum values for the cost coefficient are adopted. The findings are then blended by computing the share of each power generator at each time interval. The results demonstrate the practicability of the adopted procedure with respect to the traditional non-planned techniques when considering both DSM and DED problems.

Author Contributions: Conceptualization, A.R.; methodology, K.D.; software, K.D.; validation, A.R., and K.D.; formal analysis, A.R.; investigation, K.D.; resources, K.D.; data curation, K.D.; writing—original draft preparation, K.D.; writing—review and editing, A.R.; visualization, K.D.; supervision,

A.R.; project administration, A.R.; funding acquisition, A.R. All authors have read and agreed to the published version of the manuscript.

Funding: This research received no external funding.

Institutional Review Board Statement: Not applicable.

Informed Consent Statement: Not applicable.

Data Availability Statement: No new data were created or analyzed in this study. Data sharing is not applicable to this article.

Conflicts of Interest: The authors declare no conflict of interest.

References

1. Ahmad, Z.; Abbasi, M.H.; Khan, A.; Mall, I.S.; Khan, M.F.N.; Sajjad, I.A. Design of IoT Embedded Smart Energy Management System. In Proceedings of the 2020 International Conference on Engineering and Emerging Technologies (ICEET), Lahore, Pakistan, 22–23 February 2020; pp. 1–5.
2. Recioui, A.; Bentarzi, H. *Optimizing Smart Grid Operation and Control*; IGI Global: Hershey, PA, USA, 2021.
3. Recioui, A.; Djemai, H.; Boucenna, F. A Smart Metering Simulation in LABVIEW. *Alg. J. Sig. Syst.* **2019**, *4*, 89–100. [CrossRef]
4. Recioui, A.; Dekhandji, F.Z. Implementation of Load Control for Smart Metering in Smart Grids. In *Optimizing and Measuring Smart Grid Operation and Control*; IGI Global: Hershey, PA, USA, 2021.
5. Azzougui, Y.; Recioui, A. Hardware and software load power control in smart home applications based on Taguchi optimisation technique. *Int. J. Intell. Syst. Des. Comput. Indersci.* **2018**, *2*, 203–223.
6. Recioui, A. Home Load-Side Management in Smart Grids Using Global Optimization. In *Research Anthology on Multi-Industry Uses of Genetic Programming and Algorithms*; IGI Global: Hershey, PA, USA, 2021.
7. Vesselényi, T.; Moldovan, O.; Bungau, C.; Csokmai, L. A survey on soft computing techniques used in intelligent building control. *Recent Innov. Mechatron.* **2014**, *1*. [CrossRef]
8. Keshtkar, A.; Arzanpour, S. An adaptive fuzzy logic system for residential energy management in smart grid environments. *Appl. Energy* **2017**, *186*, 68–81. [CrossRef]
9. Anastasiadi, C.; Dounis, A.I. Co-simulation of fuzzy control in buildings and the HVAC system using BCVTB. *Adv. Build. Energy Res.* **2018**, *12*, 195–216. [CrossRef]
10. Krishna, P.N.; Gupta, S.R.; Shankaranarayanan, P.; Sidharth, S.; Sirphi, M. Fuzzy Logic Based Smart Home Energy Management System. In Proceedings of the 2018 9th International Conference on Computing, Communication and Networking Technologies (ICCCNT), Bengaluru, India, 10–12 July 2018; pp. 1–5.
11. Wahid, F.; Ghazali, R.; Fayaz, M.; Shah, A.S. Statistical Features Based Approach (SFBA) for Hourly Energy Consumption Prediction Using Neural Network. *Int. J. Inf. Technol. Comput. Sci.* **2017**, *9*, 23–30. [CrossRef]
12. Lu, R.; Hong, S.H.; Yu, M. Demand Response for Home Energy Management Using Reinforcement Learning and Artificial Neural Network. *IEEE Trans. Smart Grid.* **2019**, *10*, 6629–6639. [CrossRef]
13. Hafeez, G.; Alimgeer, K.S.; Wadud, Z.; Khan, I.; Usman, M.; Qazi, A.B.; Khan, F.A. An Innovative Optimization Strategy for Efficient Energy Management With Day-Ahead Demand Response Signal and Energy Consumption Forecasting in Smart Grid Using Artificial Neural Network. *IEEE Access* **2020**, *8*, 84415–84433. [CrossRef]
14. Yousefi, M.; Hajizadeh, A.; NorbakhshSoltani, M.; Hredzak, B. Predictive Home Energy Management System with Photovoltaic Array, Heat Pump and Plug-in Electric Vehicle. *IEEE Trans. Ind. Inf.* **2020**, *17*, 430–440. [CrossRef]
15. Ren, Y.; Wu, H.; Yang, H.; Yang, S.; Li, Z. A Method for Load Classification and Energy Scheduling Optimization to Improve Load Reliability. *Energies* **2018**, *11*, 1558. [CrossRef]
16. Li, S.; Yang, J.; Song, W.; Chen, A. A Real-Time Electricity Scheduling for Residential Home Energy Management. *IEEE Internet Things J.* **2019**, *6*, 2602–2611. [CrossRef]
17. Zhang, Z.; Wang, J.; Zhong, H.; Ma, H. Optimal scheduling model for smart home energy management system based on the fusion algorithm of harmony search algorithm and particle swarm optimization algorithm. *Sci. Technol. Built Environ.* **2020**, *26*, 42–51. [CrossRef]
18. Lee, S.; Choi, D.H. Energy Management of Smart Home with Home Appliances, Energy Storage System and Electric Vehicle: A Hierarchical Deep Reinforcement Learning Approach. *Sensors* **2020**, *20*, 2157. [CrossRef] [PubMed]
19. Hatata, A.Y.; Hafez, A.A. Ant lion optimizer versus particle swarm and artificial immune system for economical and eco-friendly power system operation. *Int. Trans. Electr. Energy Syst.* **2019**, *29*, e2803. [CrossRef]
20. Zou, D.; Li, S.; Kong, X.; Ouyang, H.; Li, Z. Solving the combined heat and power economic dispatch problems by an improved genetic algorithm and a new constraint handling strategy. *Appl. Energy* **2019**, *237*, 646–670. [CrossRef]
21. Secui, D.C. A new modified artificial bee colony algorithm for the economic dispatch problem. *Energy Convers. Manag.* **2015**, *89*, 43–62. [CrossRef]

22. Mahdi, F.P.; Vasant, P.; Watada, J.; Kallimani, V.; Abdullah-Al-Wadud, M. A quantum-inspired particle swarm optimization approach for environmental/economic power dispatch problem using cubic criterion function. *Int. Trans. Electr. Energy Syst.* **2018**, *28*, e2497. [CrossRef]
23. Elsayed, W.T.; Hegazy, Y.G.; El-Bages, M.S.; Bendary, F.M. Improved Random Drift Particle Swarm Optimization with Self-Adaptive Mechanism for Solving the Power Economic Dispatch Problem. *IEEE Trans. Ind. Inform.* **2017**, *13*, 1017–1026. [CrossRef]

Proceeding Paper

Photovoltaic Panel Parameters Estimation Using Grey Wolf Optimization Technique [†]

Cilina Touabi and Hamid Bentarzi *

Laboratory Signals and Systems (LSS), IGEE, University M'hamed Bougara Boumerdes (UMBB), Boumerdes 35000, Algeria; lss@univ-boumerdes.dz
* Correspondence: h.bentarzi@univ-boumerdes.dz
† Presented at the 1st International Conference on Computational Engineering and Intelligent Systems, Online, 10–12 December 2021.

Abstract: In different photovoltaic PV applications, it is very important to model the PV cell. However, the model parameters are usually unavailable in the datasheet provided by the manufacturers and they change due to degradation. This paper presents a method for identifying the optimal parameters of a PV cell. This method is based on the one diode model using the grey wolf algorithm as well as datasheets. An algorithm is implemented in a SIMULINK simulator for making the I-V and P-V characteristics. This approach is found to be useful for designers due to its simplicity, fastness, and accuracy. The final results are compared to demonstrate the efficiency and accuracy of the proposed method.

Keywords: PV cell; one diode model; model parameters; grey wolf optimization algorithm

Citation: Touabi, C.; Bentarzi, H. Photovoltaic Panel Parameters Estimation Using Grey Wolf Optimization Technique. *Eng. Proc.* **2022**, *14*, 3. https://doi.org/10.3390/engproc2022014003

Academic Editors: Abdelmadjid Recioui and Fatma Zohra Dekhandji

Published: 25 January 2022

Publisher's Note: MDPI stays neutral with regard to jurisdictional claims in published maps and institutional affiliations.

Copyright: © 2022 by the authors. Licensee MDPI, Basel, Switzerland. This article is an open access article distributed under the terms and conditions of the Creative Commons Attribution (CC BY) license (https://creativecommons.org/licenses/by/4.0/).

1. Introduction

Among all renewable energy sources, solar energy has acquired the highest growth rate worldwide in recent years. The major application of solar energy is photovoltaic (PV) power generation, which saw growth of more than 22% in 2019 and is predicted to output over 720 TWh [1]. PV systems are easy to install, noise-free, and can directly convert solar energy to electrical energy. For an accurate study in different PV applications, it is very important to model the basic device of the PV cell. However, the model parameters are usually unavailable in the datasheet provided by the manufacturers and their values change over time due to the PV degradation [2]. Thus, how to estimate appropriate parameters is of high importance and has attracted immense interest among researchers.

The one diode model (ODM) is considered the most suitable model used to characterize the solar cells/modules [3–7] in comparison to the double diode model (DDM) and the three-diode model (TDM) as it has a minimum number of parameters and a good level of accuracy. The five electrical parameters of the ODM are: photocurrent (I_{ph}), diode ideality factor (n), reverse saturation current (I_0), shunt resistance (R_{sh}), and series resistance (R_S).

Several methods have been developed to extract the ODM parameters which are classified into three main categories [5,7]:

- Analytical methods [7]
- Numerical methods [3–6]
- Artificial intelligence or optimization methods [8–10]

Numerical methods are widely used in the literature since they provide a good compromise between speed of calculation, simplicity, and accuracy. These numerical methods are utilized to solve a system of a few non-linear equations related with the PV cell.

The objective of this work is to simulate the I-V and P-V characteristics using a one diode model (ODM) associated with a developed algorithm that permits finding the appropriate value of the ideality factor and hence extracting the other needed parameters simply from datasheet information provided by the manufacturer.

2. Photovoltaic Cell

A PV cell is basically a semiconductor diode, as shown in Figure 1. According to the principle theory of photoelectric effect, for any material exposed to light generating charge carriers, when sunlight that is basically photons of different frequencies and energies hits the solar cell surface and is absorbed by a semiconducting material, such as silicon, electrons will be excited from atoms, making them free and ready to move.

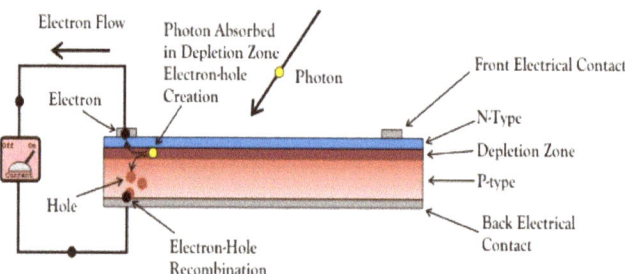

Figure 1. Photo electric effect of PV cell.

Solar cells produce electricity with very small voltage. For the common single junction silicon solar cell, it is approximately 0.5–0.6 volts. They are available in the form of modules or panels to provide sufficient voltage and current for real life applications.

2.1. Characteristics of the PV Cell

Electrical characteristics of PV modules are given by the producers under precise conditions that are known as standard test conditions (STC). Such conditions are defined by the ambient temperature $T_{STC} = 25\ °C$, irradiation level $G_{STC} = 1000\ W/m^2$, and the air mass value AM = 1.5. However, in the working field, PV modules operate at higher temperatures and somewhat lower insulation conditions. In order to determine the power output of the solar cell, it is important to know the expected operating temperature. The nominal operating cell temperature (NOCT) is defined as the temperature reached by open circuited cells in a module under the conditions: solar irradiance $G = 800\ w/m^2$, air temperature $T_{ambiant} = 20\ °C$, and wind speed = 1 m/s. Then, the cell temperature can be calculated by the following equation:

$$T_{cell} = T_{ambiant} + \left(\frac{NOCT - 20}{800}\right) \times G \qquad (1)$$

where G is taken in (w/m^2).

The typical I-V and P-V characteristics of a photovoltaic cell are shown in Figure 2. The main three significant parameters on the photovoltaic characteristics are open circuit voltage (V_{oc}), short circuit current (I_{sc}), and maximum power point at (V_{mpp}, I_{mpp}).

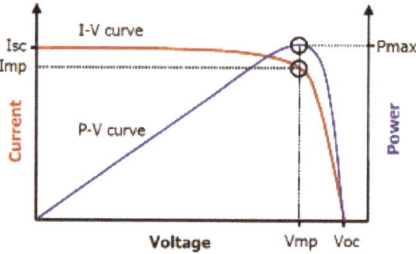

Figure 2. Typical I-V and P-V characteristics of PV cell.

The maximum current in photovoltaic cell is produced when there is a short circuit between its positive and negative terminals and it is denoted as I_{sc}. As $I = I_{sc}$, the voltage in the circuit is zero. The maximum voltage, denoted as V_{oc}, occurs when there is a break in the circuit.

The maximum power achieved from a photovoltaic cell occurs at a point on the bend in the I-V curve known as the maximum power point (MPP), which can be found at voltage and current points designated as V_{mpp} and I_{mpp}.

Generally, these parameters are provided in the datasheet by manufacturers of a particular photovoltaic cell or module. When the PV cell is connected to an external load, the electrical characteristics of the load determine the actual point on the I-V curve at which the photovoltaic cell operates.

2.2. Single Diode Model of PV Cell

To analyze characteristics of solar cells, electrical equivalent circuits are needed and hence modeled using simulation software. Researchers have developed mathematical models to understand and predict the effect of changing conditions on photovoltaic electrical output. The lumped parameter model is one of these models classified based on the number of diodes. It is widely used and has proven to be more successful. The lumped parameter models can take the form of a one diode model, double diode model, or three diode model. Although the accuracy of the characteristics of the model improves as the number of diode increases, the required mathematical expression to obtain the output characteristics become more complex. For simplicity, in this work, the one diode model known as the five parameter model is chosen for the identification of photovoltaic cell parameters.

The complete governing equation for the one diode model is given as [3]:

$$I = I_{ph} - I_s \left[e^{\left(\frac{V + I*R_s}{n*V_t}\right)} - 1 \right] - \frac{V + I \times R_s}{R_{sh}} \quad (2)$$

where V_t is the thermal voltage.

Then, the five parameters of one diode model are: (1) I_s: Diode saturation current (A), (2) n: Diode ideality factor (1 < n < 2), (3) R_s: Series resistance (Ω), (4) R_{sh}: Shunt resistance (Ω), and (5) I_{ph}: Photocurrent (A).

The one-diode model takes into account different properties of solar cell: R_s is introduced as to consider the voltage drops and internal losses due to flow of current, and R_{sh} takes into account the leakage current to the ground when the diode is reverse biased. However, this model has neglected the recombination effect of the diode. Therefore, it is still not the most accurate model.

3. Identification of PV Cell Parameters

The current versus voltage relationship of the single diode PV cell model (Figure 3) is presented in Equation (2). It can be noticed that the equation of the I-V curve is nonlinear, which is difficult to solve by the analytical methods. Due to this difficulty, scientists have developed several algorithms in order to solve this equation to determine the parameters of the solar cell. In this work, metaheuristic methods, which can be adapted to solve a wide range of optimization problems, are used. These methods are designed to find a good solution among a large set of feasible solutions with less computational effort than other optimization techniques.

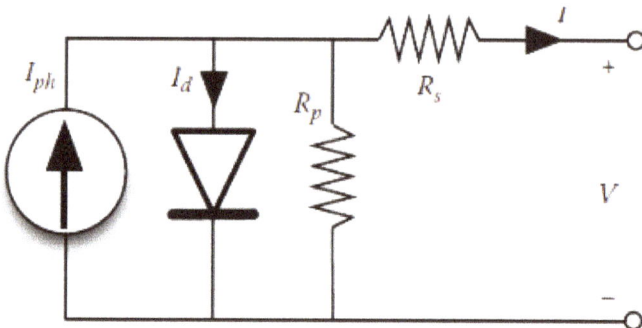

Figure 3. One-diode Model of PV cell.

3.1. Grey Wolf Optimization Technique

Grey wolf optimization (GWO) is a population-based meta-heuristic optimization method inspired by grey wolves (Canis lupus). The GWO algorithm mimics the leadership hierarchy and hunting mechanism of grey wolves in nature. The pack is classified into four groups, alpha, beta, delta, and omega, for simulating the leadership hierarchy. Alpha is the first level and is the leader of the pack. Beta is the second level on the hierarchy of wolves, as they help alpha wolves to make a decision. Delta represents the third level in the pack, as members have to succumb to alpha and beta, however they dominate omega. Omega wolves have the lowest position in the pack, having to succumb to all other dominant wolves. Figure 4 shows the grey wolf social hierarchy [11,12].

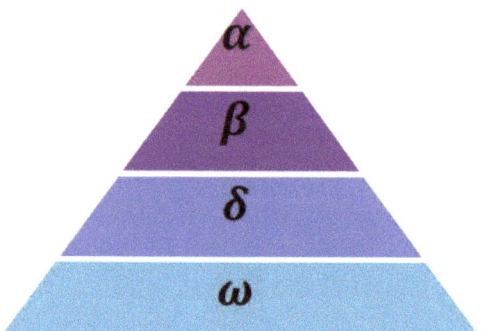

Figure 4. Hierarchy of grey wolf.

In addition to the social hierarchy of wolves, group hunting is another interesting social behavior of grey wolves. According to Muro et al. [13], the main phases of grey wolf hunting are as follows:

- Tracking, chasing, and approaching the prey.
- Following, encircling, and harassing the prey until it stops moving.
- Attacking the target.

Wolves encircle the target during the chase. The encircling is modeled by the Equations (7) and (8) [13]:

$$\vec{D} = |\vec{C}\vec{X}_p(t) - \vec{X}(t)| \qquad (3)$$

$$\vec{X}(t+1) = \vec{X}_p(t)\vec{A}.\vec{D} \qquad (4)$$

where t represents the current iteration, $\vec{A}, \vec{C}$, and $\vec{D}$ are coefficient vectors, $\vec{X_p}$ is the position vector of the victim, and $\vec{X}$ is the position vector of a grey wolf $\vec{A}$ and $\vec{C}$, as computed through these two equations:

$$\vec{A} = 2\vec{a}\vec{r_1} - \vec{a} \tag{5}$$

$$\vec{C} = 2\vec{r_2} \tag{6}$$

Components of $\vec{a}$ linearly reduce from 2 to 0 through the iterations and $\vec{r_1}$ and $\vec{r_2}$ as random vectors in [0, 1].

The pursuit is habitually directed by the leader alpha (α) followed by beta (β) and delta (δ) which can sometimes contribute in chasing. (δ) and (ω) look after the injured wolves in the group. Alpha (α) is considered the best result owing to the best information of the place of the target, while beta (β) and delta (δ) are the second and the third best solutions respectively in designing GWO. (ω) is the last best. Therefore, the first three best solutions obtained so far are saved and the other search agents (including ω) are obliged to update their positions according to the position of the best search agent. When the prey stops moving, the wolves terminates the chase by attacking it, as shown in Figure 5.

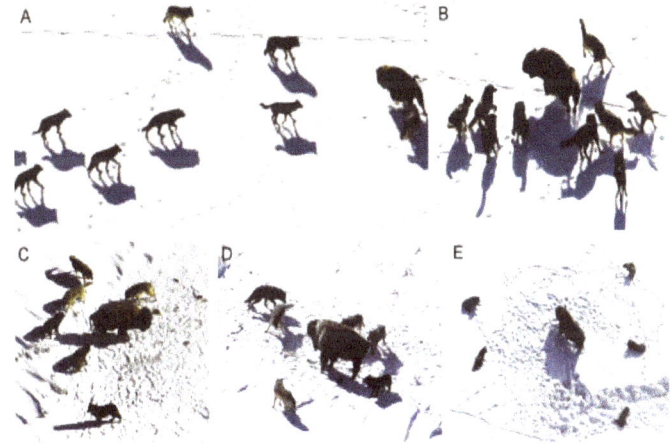

Figure 5. Hunting conduct of grey wolves: (**A**) approaching and pursuing target, (**B–D**) following, encircling and disturb the target, (**E**) attacking the target [13].

In this regard, the following formulas are applied:

$$\begin{cases} \vec{D_\alpha} = |\vec{C_1} \cdot \vec{X_\alpha}(t) - \vec{X}(t)| \\ \vec{X_1} = \vec{X_\alpha}(t) - \vec{A_1} \cdot \vec{D_\alpha} \end{cases} \tag{7}$$

$$\begin{cases} \vec{D_\beta} = |\vec{C_2} \cdot \vec{X_\beta}(t) - \vec{X}(t)| \\ \vec{X_2} = \vec{X_\beta}(t) - \vec{A_2} \cdot \vec{D_\beta} \end{cases} \tag{8}$$

$$\begin{cases} \vec{D_\delta} = |\vec{C_3} \cdot \vec{X_\delta}(t) - \vec{X}(t)| \\ \vec{X_3} = \vec{X_\delta}(t) - \vec{A_3} \cdot \vec{D_\delta} \end{cases} \tag{9}$$

$$\vec{X}(t+1) = \frac{\vec{X_1} + \vec{X_2} + \vec{X_3}}{3} \tag{10}$$

19

3.2. ODM Parameters Extraction Using a GWO Method

The proposed five-parameter estimation method is based on the three points that characterize the I-V curve, which are the maximum power point (V_{mpp}, I_{mpp}), short circuit point (0, I_{sc}), and open circuit point (V_{oc}, 0). These data can be provided in the datasheet or extracted from the experiments.

Like any optimization algorithm, an objective function F(X) should first be set. F(X) is based on the one diode Equation (2). For the identification of PV module parameters, the number of series connected cells N_s is considered. Thus, the objective function is:

$$\begin{cases} F(X) = I - I_{ph} - I_s \left[e^{\left(\frac{V+I \times R_s}{n \times N_s \times V_t}\right)} - 1 \right] - \frac{V+I \times R_s}{R_{sh}} \\ X = \{I_{ph}, I_s, R_s, n, R_{sh}\} \end{cases} \quad (11)$$

The fitness function that needs to be minimized in order to quantify the error is the root main square error (RMSE) between the approximated values in the datasheet I_{mpp}, I_{sc} and I = 0 at open circuit condition and the calculated ones.

$$\text{Fitness} = \text{RMSE} = \sqrt{\frac{1}{3} \sum_1^3 (I_{Datasheet} - I_{calculated})^2} \quad (12)$$

Then, the NRMSE error is calculated as follows:

$$\text{NRMSE} = \frac{\text{RMSE}}{\sqrt{\frac{1}{3} \times \sum_1^3 I_{Datasheet}^2}} \times 100 \quad (13)$$

The pseudo code of the proposed algorithm is presented in Algorithm 1.

Algorithm 1 GWO

1: Input: T, N_s, V_{mpp}, I_{mpp}, V_{oc}, I_{sc}
2: Output: X_α
3: Initialize the grey wolf population Xi (i = 1, 2, ... n)
4: Initialize a, A, and C
5: Calculate the fitness of each search agent by Equation (12)
6: X_α = the best search agent
7: X_β = the second best search agent
8: X_δ = the third best search agent
9: **while** (t < Max number of iterations)
10: **for** each search agent
11: X_δ = the third best search agent
12: **while** (t < Max number of iterations)
13: **for** each search agent
14: **Update** the position of current search agent by Equation (10)
15: **end for**
16: Update a, A, and C
17: Calculate the fitness of all search agents by Equation (12)
18: Update X_α, X_β and X_δ
19: t = t + 1
20: **end while**
21: return X_α
22: Calculate NRMSE using Equation (13)
23: **end procedure**

---

4. Test Results and Discussion

The proposed algorithm GWO is used to extract the parameters of the ODM based on curve fitting method. The algorithm is tested on two PV modules and compared with other algorithms to prove its effectiveness. The simulator is developed using MATLAB R2016a and executed on a PC with Intel® Core™ i5-2450M CPU processor @ 2.50 GHz, 4 GB RAM, under Windows 10 64-bit OS.

The search ranges used in the optimization of the five parameters are given Table 1. However, the GWO parameters are given in Table 2. The datasheet parameters of used PV modules are presented in Table 3.

Table 1. ODM parameter search ranges.

Parameter	Search Range
I_{ph}	$[0.95 \times I_{sc}, 1.05 \times I_{sc}]$
I_s	$[1\ \mu A, 5\ \mu A]$
n	$[1, 2]$
R_{sh}	$\left[\dfrac{V_{mpp}}{I_{sc} - I_{mpp}}, 1500\ \Omega\right]$
R_s	$\left[0, \dfrac{V_{mpp} - V_{oc}}{I_{mpp}}\right]$

Table 2. GWO parameters.

Parameters	Value
Random values r1, r2	[0, 1]
No. of search agents	30
Maximum iteration	1000

Table 3. Datasheet Parameters under STC (T = 25 °C, G = 1000 W/m^2).

Module	Type	Parameters				
		$V_{mpp}[V]$	$I_{mpp}[A]$	$V_{oc}[V]$	$I_{sc}[A]$	N_s
STP050D-12/MEA	Poly-crystalline	17.4	2.93	21.8	3.13	36

Case Study #1: KC200GT

The polycrystalline module KC200GT ODM parameters are extracted to draw the I-V and P-V characteristics using the developed PV simulator, as shown in Figure 6. The results obtained at STC are presented in Table 4. The GWO results for the KC200GT module are compared with other published optimization methods results to prove its efficiency.

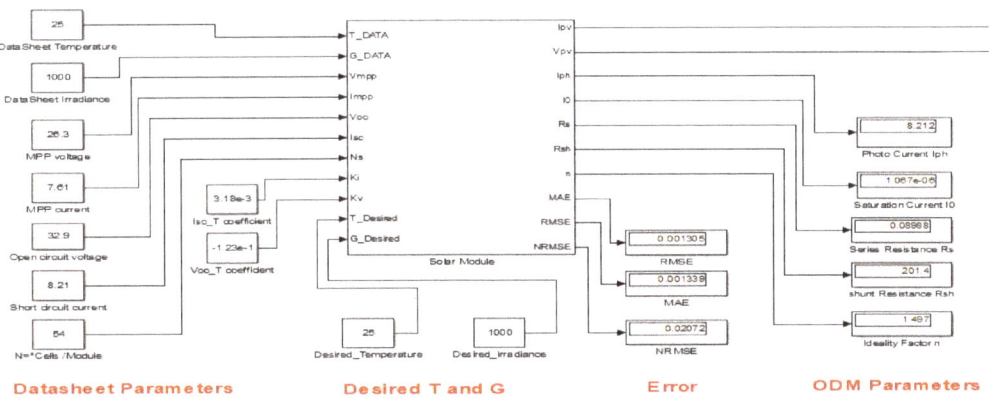

Figure 6. GWO based ODM PV simulator.

Table 4. KC200GT parameters at STC achieved by different methods.

Methods	Parameters					Error	
	$I_{ph}[A]$	$I_s[\mu A]$	n	$R_s[\Omega]$	$R_{sh}[\Omega]$	RMSE [A]	NRMSE [%]
Villalva [3]	8.193	0.08520	1.300	0.13870	466.0	2.3×10^{-1}	3.02
Accarino [3]	8.193	0.00200	1.079	0.23630	204.0	1.1×10^{-1}	1.49
Stornelli [3]	8.220	0.00514	1.120	0.26560	144.9	1.2×10^{-1}	1.53
GWO *	8.212	1.06700	1.497	0.08988	201.4	1.305×10^{-4}	2.072×10^{-2}

* Proposed method.

As given in Table 4, the normalized mean absolute error NRMSE obtained by the proposed method (0.02072%) is the lowest, which proves the effectiveness of this technique in extracting the unknown PV parameters. Moreover, the convergence using this method is very fast, where the simulation execution time is less than 7 s.

Case Study #2: STP050D-12/MEA

The PV characteristics of the poly-crystalline STP050D-12/MEA module are simulated at T = 45.57 °C and G = 632 w/m² using the GWO based ODM PV simulator as shown in Figure 6. The obtained results are given in Table 5 and Figure 7. The computed errors are: RMSE = 1.327×10^{-3} and NRMSE = 7.282×10^{-2}. The simulated characteristics are compared with the module's experimental data obtained in our research laboratory [14]. The comparison results are presented in Figure 8 and Table 6.

Table 5. STP050D-12/MEA extracted parameters.

T [°C]	G [w/m²]	Parameters				
		$I_{ph}[A]$	$I_s[A]$	n	$R_s[\Omega]$	$R_{sh}[\Omega]$
45.57	632	1.986	1.326	1.497	0.1024	1497

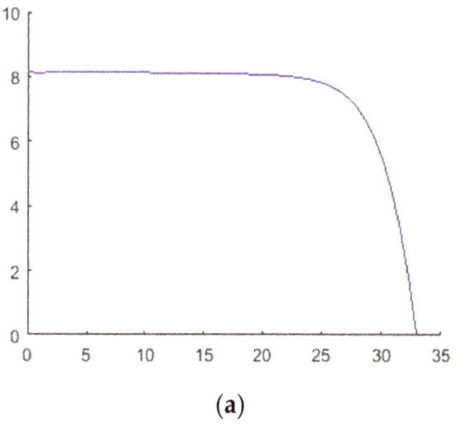
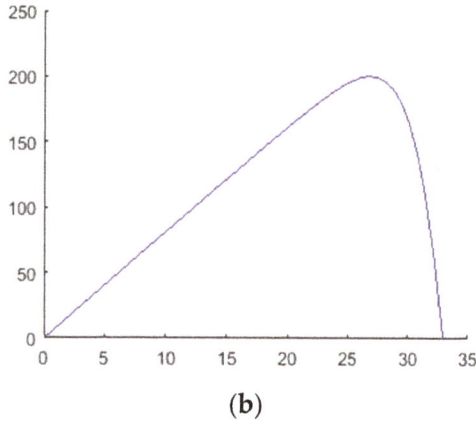

(a) (b)

Figure 7. (a) I-V and (b) P-V characteristics of KC200GT at STC.

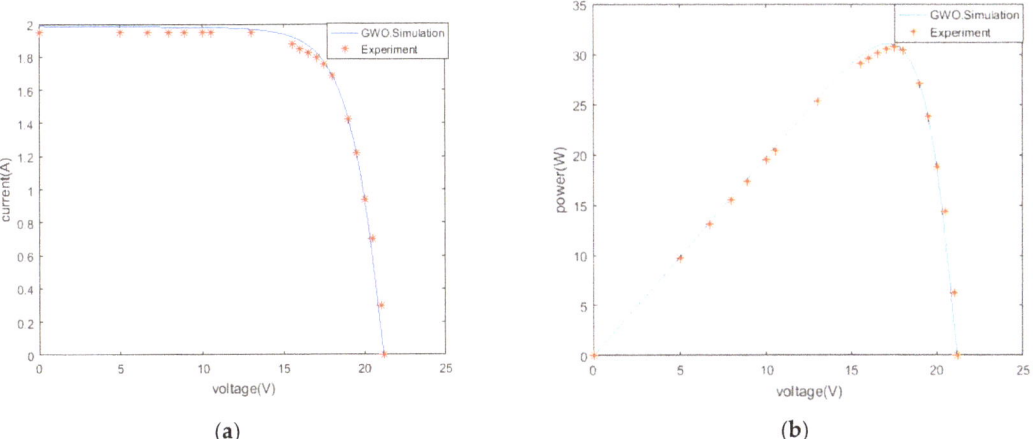

Figure 8. (a) Experimental versus Simulation I-V and, (b) Experimental versus Simulation P-V characteristics of STP050D-12/MEA at T = 45.57 °C and G = 632 w/m^2.

Table 6. Comparison of Experimental and simulation model values.

Parameters	Experimental Data	Simulation Data	Relative Error (%)
V_{mpp}[V]	17.591	17.16	2.450116537
I_{mpp}[A]	1.76824	1.8138	2.576573316
P_{max}[W]	31.1052	31.1242	0.06108303435
V_{oc}[V]	21.1435	21.15	0.03074230851
I_{sc}[A]	1.94817	1.9926	2.280601796

It can be noticed that the measured data points obtained in our laboratory for the STP050D-12/MEA module highly agreed with the simulated curves. Thus, the obtained I-V and P-V characteristics for the STP050D-12/MEA module based only on the datasheet information using the GWO based ODM PV simulator gives good results.

5. Conclusions

PV cell characterization is a hot research topic in the field of renewable energy. Obtaining the most accurate I-V and P-V characteristics has been the main purpose of this research work. This was attempted by finding an efficient method based on the one diode model using the information provided by the manufacturers. However, not all (five) parameters are available in the datasheet. Thus, the simulation has been associated with the developed algorithm that permits finding the appropriate value of the needed parameters. Grey wolf optimization (GWO) has been implemented using SIMULINK for extracting the five parameters based only on the three critical I-V points information provided in the datasheet, namely the open circuit point (0, V_{oc}), the short circuit point (I_{sc}, 0), and the maximum power point (I_{mpp}, V_{mpp}). Furthermore, this method has been enhanced to provide the parameters under different environmental conditions. The developed ODM-GWO simulation was tested for various PV modules, under different temperatures and irradiances. The obtained I-V and P-V curves were compared to the characteristics provided in the datasheet. Moreover, the BP MSX 120 multi-crystalline module simulated curves were compared to the experimental I-V data. The measured data points conformed to the obtained curves. Thus, the good accuracy of the developed PV simulator was demonstrated.

Adding to the fact that these proposed algorithms have provided optimal results with an acceptable accuracy, the time taken by the ODM-GWO simulation execution is less than 10 s.

Author Contributions: Conceptualization, C.T. and H.B.; methodology, C.T. and H.B.; validation, C.T. and H.B.; formal analysis, C.T. and H.B.; investigation, C.T. and H.B.; writing—original draft preparation, H.B.; writing—review and editing, H.B.; visualization, H.B.; supervision, H.B.; project administration H.B.; funding acquisition, H.B. All authors have read and agreed to the published version of the manuscript.

Funding: This research received no external funding.

Institutional Review Board Statement: Not applicable.

Informed Consent Statement: Not applicable.

Data Availability Statement: The data presented in this study are available on request from the corresponding author. The data are not publicly available due to the data may involve confidential information of our research group.

Conflicts of Interest: The authors declare no conflict of interest.

References

1. International Energy Agency. 2020. Available online: https://www.iea.org/reports/solar-pv (accessed on 13 September 2021).
2. Xiong, G.; Zhang, J.; Shi, D.; He, Y. Parameter extraction of solar photovoltaic models using an improved whale optimization algorithm. *Energy Convers. Manag.* **2018**, *174*, 388–405. [CrossRef]
3. Stornelli, V.; Muttillo, M.; de Rubeis, T.; Nardi, I. A New Simplified Five-Parameter Estimation Method for Single-Diode Model of Photovoltaic Panels. *Energies* **2019**, *12*, 4271. [CrossRef]
4. Silva, E.A.; Bradaschia, F.; Cavalcanti, M.C.; Nascimento, A.J. Parameter Estimation Method to Improve the Accuracy of Photovoltaic Electrical Model. *IEEE J. Photovolt.* **2015**, *6*, 278–285. [CrossRef]
5. Wang, G.; Zhao, K.; Shi, J.; Chen, W.; Zhang, H.; Yang, X.; Zhao, Y. An iterative approach for modeling photovoltaic modules without implicit equations. *Appl. Energy* **2017**, *202*, 189–198. [CrossRef]
6. Orioli, A. An accurate one-diode model suited to represent the current-voltage characteristics of crystalline and thin-film photovoltaic modules. *Renew. Energy* **2020**, *145*, 725–743. [CrossRef]
7. Batzelis, E. Non-Iterative Methods for the Extraction of the Single-Diode Model Parameters of Photovoltaic Modules: A Review and Comparative Assessment. *Energies* **2019**, *12*, 358. [CrossRef]
8. Wei, T.; Yu, F.; Huang, G.; Xu, C. A Particle-Swarm-Optimization-Based Parameter Extraction Routine for Three-Diode Lumped Parameter Model of Organic Solar Cells. *IEEE Electron. Device Lett.* **2019**, *40*, 1511–1514. [CrossRef]
9. Zhang, Y.; Jin, Z.; Zhao, X.; Yang, Q. Backtracking search algorithm with hevy flight for estimating parameters of photovoltaic models. *Energy Convers. Manag.* **2020**, *208*, 112615. [CrossRef]
10. Jiao, S.; Chong, G.; Huang, C.; Hu, H.; Wang, M.; Heidari, A.A.; Chen, H.; Zhao, X. Orthogonally adapted Harris hawks optimization for parameter estimation of photovoltaic models. *Energy* **2020**, *203*, 117804. [CrossRef]
11. Mirjalili, S.; Mirjalili, S.M.; Lewis, A. Grey wolf optimizer. *Adv. Eng. Softw.* **2014**, *69*, 46–61. [CrossRef]
12. Kouzou, A.L.; Bentarzi, H.; Mohammedi, R.D.; Laoumer, M. Optimal Placement of Phasor Measurement Unit in Power System using Meta-Heuristic Algorithms. *Electroteh. Electron. Autom. (EEA)* **2019**, *67*, 98–113.
13. Muro, C.; Escobedo, R.; Spector, L.; Coppinger, R. Wolf-pack (Canis lupus) hunting strategies emerge from simple rules in computational simulations. *Behav. Process.* **2011**, *88*, 192–197. [CrossRef]
14. Habes, A.; Amara, A. Design and Implementation of PV Panel Characterization Platform. Master Thesis, University M'hamed Bougara Boumerdes, Boumerdes, Algeria, 2021.

Proceeding Paper

Comparative Study of Optimization Techniques Based PID Tuning for Automatic Voltage Regulator System [†]

Mohamed Cherif Rais [1,*], Fatma Zohra Dekhandji [1], Abdelmadjid Recioui [1], Mohamed Sadek Rechid [2] and Lahcen Djedi [2]

1. Signals and systems Laboratory, Institute of Electrical and Electronic Engineering, University M'Hamed Bougara of Boumerdes, Boumerdes 35000, Algeria; fzdekhandji@univ-boumerdes.dz (F.Z.D.); a.recioui@univ-boumerdes.dz (A.R.)
2. Institute of Electrical and Electronic Engineering, University M'Hamed Bougara of Boumerdes, Boumerdes 35000, Algeria; medsadek072@gmail.com (M.S.R.); lahcendjedi6298@gmail.com (L.D.)
* Correspondence: m.rais@univ-boumerdes.dz
† Presented at the 1st International Conference on Computational Engineering and Intelligent Systems, Online, 10–12 December 2021.

Abstract: A comparative study is performed to design an optimal PID controller for an automatic voltage regulator system using different optimization techniques. The presented approaches are referred to as particle swarm optimization (PSO) algorithm, cuckoo search optimization (CSO) algorithm, moth flame optimization (MFO) algorithm, water cycle optimization (WCO) algorithm, teaching–learning-based optimization (TLBO) algorithm, and hill climbing optimization (HCO) algorithm. Transient response parameters, which are rise time Tr, settling time Ts, and percentage overshoot Mp, are used as comparison criteria. The integral time absolute error ITAE is the used performance index. All the proposed optimization techniques improved the transient response of the AVR system in a different way and gave good preliminary results.

Keywords: optimization techniques; AVR system; PID tuning

1. Introduction

In an electrical power system, the AVR is used to maintain the terminal voltage magnitude of a generator [1]. Controlling the generator excitation keeps the magnitude of this voltage at a specific level. In general, traditional tuning methods such as Ziegler–Nichols (ZN) and gain-phase margin make it difficult to find optimal controller parameters [2]. As a result, several optimization techniques for tuning controller parameters have been proposed. Some of these optimization techniques which used as tuning methods to improve the performance of the (PID) controller are particle swarm optimization (PSO) [3,4], cuckoo search optimization (CSO) algorithm [5,6], moth flame optimization (MFO) algorithm [7,8], water cycle optimization (WCO) algorithm [9,10], teaching–learning-based optimization (TLBO) [11–13]. Hill climbing optimization (HCO) algorithm [14] is tested for the first time in the AVR system in this work. Fractional order PID (FOPID) [15], PID-acceleration (PIDA) [16], gray PID (GPID) [17], and fuzzy logic PID (FLPID) [18] are some of the other controller types used to improve the dynamic response of AVR systems in the literature.

The rest of this paper is organized as follows. Section 2 describes the AVR system and its block diagram model with the used values. Section 3 describes the implementation of the proposed optimizations techniques and provides comparison of the results of the numerical simulations. Section 4 concludes the paper with a summary of the research's main findings.

2. AVR System

The primary consumer demand in the power system is the quality of electrical energy. In addition, the majority of equipment is designed to operate at predetermined voltage and frequency levels, since the interaction between voltage control and frequency control in a power generation system is usually weak enough that they can be analyzed separately. Moreover, a small variation in voltage can result in a significantly large variation in reactive power flow, which can result in massive power loss and, as a result, economic loss. To avoid this, the automatic voltage regulator (AVR) system is used in power generation sites to ensure voltage stability at the generator terminal via the excitation system. An AVR system and its model are shown in Figure 1.

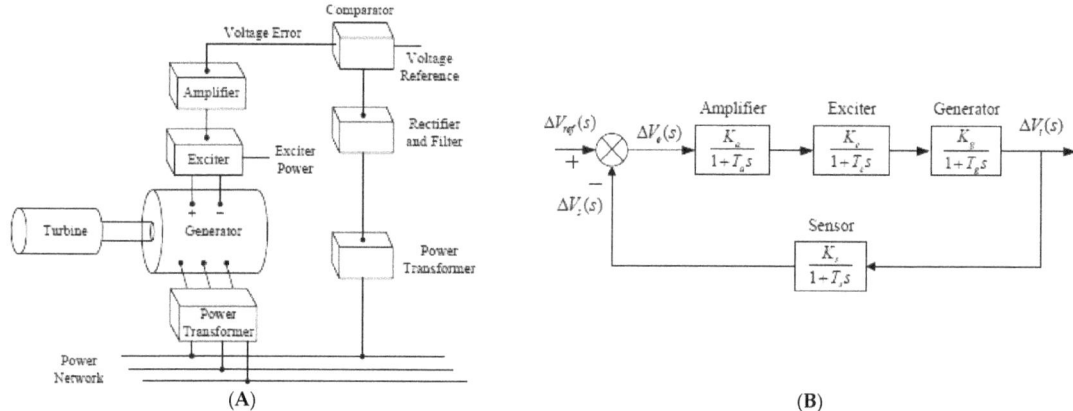

Figure 1. (A) AVR system. (B) Block diagram of the AVR system.

$\Delta V_{ref}(s)$, $\Delta V_s(s)$, $\Delta V_e(s)$, and $\Delta V_t(s)$ are the reference input voltage, sensor output voltage, error voltage, and generator terminal voltage, respectively. Table 1 shows the boundary values of AVR system components as well as the values used in the AVR system.

Table 1. Boundary values of the AVR system.

Model	Parameter Ranges	Used Values in AVR System
Amplifier	$10 \leq Ka \leq 40$ $0.02 \leq Ta \leq 0.1$	KA = 10 TA = 0:1
Exciter	$1 \leq Ke \leq 2$ $0.4 \leq Te \leq 1$	Ke = 1 Te = 0:4
Generator	$1 \leq Kg \leq 2$ $1 \leq Tg \leq 2$	Kg = 1 TG = 1
Sensor	Kr = 1 $0.001 \leq Tr \leq 0.006$	KR = 1 TR = 0:01

The uncontrolled system transfer function is:

$$G(s) = \frac{0.1s + 10}{0.0004s^4 + 0.0454s^3 + 0.555s^2 + 1.5s + 11} \quad (1)$$

Although stable, the AVR system's step response is extremely oscillatory without a controller, as illustrated in Figure 2.

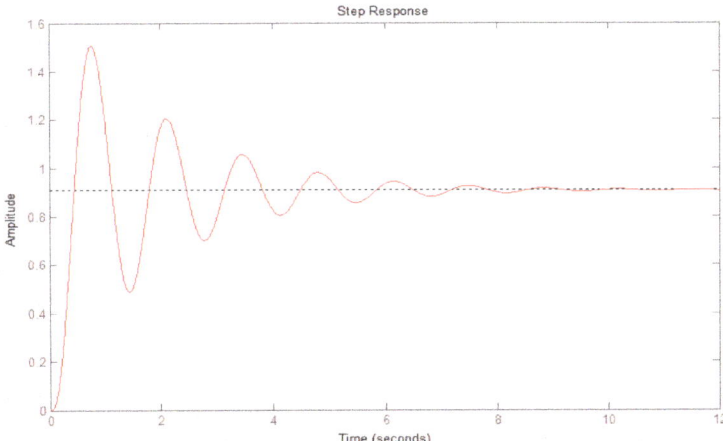

Figure 2. Step response of AVR system in the absence of a controller.

Table 2 summarizes the transient response parameters of the AVR system in the absence of the controller.

Table 2. Transient performance of the AVR system without controller.

Rise Time (s) Tr	Settling Time 2% (s) Ts	Overshoot Mp (%)	Steday State Error Ess
0.261	6.99	65.7	0.091

These results show that by utilizing a PID controller, the transient response of the AVR system can be improved and the steady state error can be removed.

3. Implementation of Proposed Optimization Techniques

The primary goal of this work is to design and construct a high-performance PID controller for AVR systems in synchronous generators. The design challenge is stated as an optimization control problem, and the proposed optimization algorithms are used to find optimal controller parameters. Particle swarm optimization (PSO), cuckoo search optimization (CSO), moth flame optimization (MFO), water cycle optimization (WCO), teaching–learning-based optimization (TLBO), and hill climbing (HCO) have been tested, and a comparison has been carried out. The integral time absolute error (ITAE) is the performance index used in this work to examine and build the suggested OA-PID controller, which is given as

$$\text{Integral time absolute error } ITAE = \int_0^T t|e(t)|dt \qquad (2)$$

The block diagram of the AVR system with the proposed OA-PID controller is shown in Figure 3.

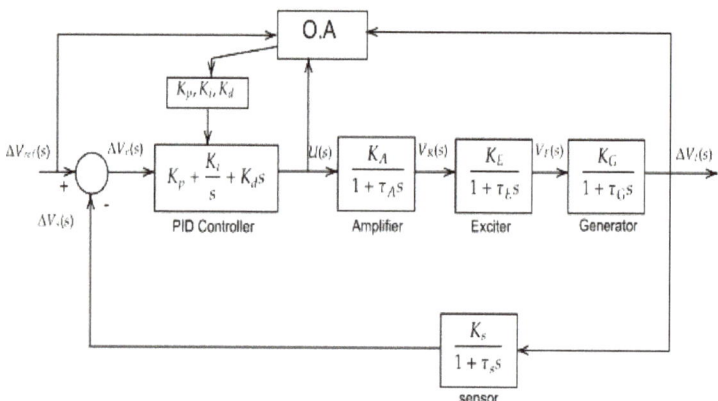

Figure 3. AVR system with proposed OA-PID Controller.

Table 3 shows the adjusted and optimal PID controller settings acquired by proposed optimization techniques and the transient response analysis results after the simulation procedure.

Table 3. Optimized PID parameters and transient response analysis results.

Optimization Technique	Controller Parameters Kp–Ki–Kd	Tr: 0.1→0.9	Ts + 2%	Mp (%)
PSO-ITAE	0.7027–0.5471–0.37852	0.1969	1.3466	1.718
CSO-ITAE	0.6999–0.54672–0.37904	0.1967	1.3498	1.7266
MFO-ITAE	1.5643–1.0713–0.5132	0.1319	0.7518	22.7511
WCO-ITAE	1.4802–1.0153–0.4809	0.1386	0.7769	21.2312
TLBO-ITAE	1.2298–1.8472–0.3944	0.1623	0.8533	16.3603
HCO-ITAE	0.5900–0.4200–0.2000	0.3272	0.5131	0

The comparative simulation results obtained for the terminal voltage step response of the AVR system with the different optimization techniques are shown in Figure 4.

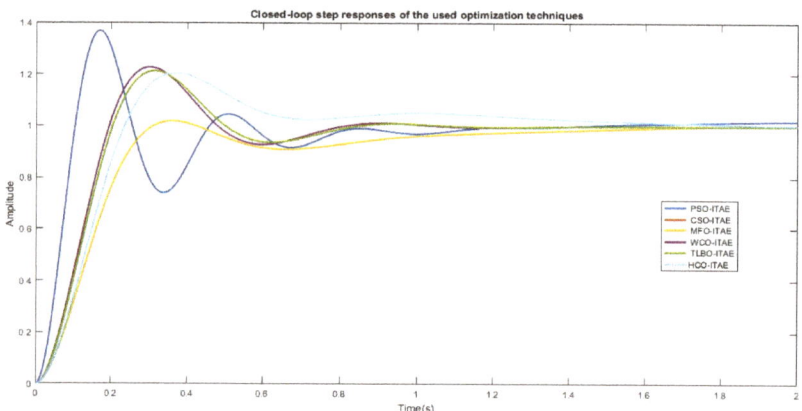

Figure 4. Terminal voltage response curves of the AVR system with various optimization techniques.

It is evident from Figure 4 and Table 3 that the MFO, WCO, and TLBO techniques delivered a response with a high percentage overshoot and quicker rise time than the PSO, HCO, and CSO methods. On the other hand, the HCO technique yielded a system with no oscillation and rapid settling time compared to the other optimization techniques. Furthermore, the PSO and CSO performances are almost the same, producing a response with little overshoot and long settling time. The HCO tuned PID controller with the ITAE fitness function generates a superior control performance in terms of improved overshoot and settling time.

4. Conclusions

The main goal of this study is to design an optimal PID controller parameter for the AVR system using different optimization techniques. A comparison based on integral time absolute error ITAE performance index and transient response parameters was carried out. The most obvious finding to emerge from this study is that all optimization techniques have improved the system performance compared to the uncontrolled case. The second major finding was that each optimization algorithm improves some parameters and, at the same time, deteriorates another one. However, it is worth noting that the hill climbing (HCL) technique yields generally better results in terms of percentage overshoot and settling time. Finally, the current study has only examined one performance index and focused on transient analysis. A natural progression of this work is to analyze the system performance based on other objective functions and other stability criteria and consider a hybridization between best optimization techniques.

Author Contributions: Conceptualization, M.C.R.; methodology, F.Z.D.; software, M.S.R. and L.D.; validation, F.Z.D.; formal analysis, M.C.R.; investigation, M.C.R.; resources, M.S.R. and L.D.; data curation, M.C.R.; writing—original draft preparation, M.C.R.; writing—review and editing, F.Z.D., A.R.; visualization, M.C.R.; supervision, F.Z.D. All authors have read and agreed to the published version of the manuscript.

Funding: This research received no external funding.

Institutional Review Board Statement: Not applicable.

Informed Consent Statement: Not applicable.

Conflicts of Interest: The authors declare no conflict of interest.

References

1. Saadat, H. *Power System Analysis*; McGraw-Hill: New York, NY, USA, 1999.
2. Ogata, K. *Modern Control Engineering*, 4th ed.; Prentice-Hall: Upper Saddle River, NJ, USA, 2002.
3. Gaing, Z.-L. A particle swarm optimization approach for optimum design of pid controller in avr system. *IEEE Trans. Energy Convers.* **2004**, *19*, 384–391. [CrossRef]
4. Rahimian, M.; Raahemifar, K. Optimal pid controller design for avr system using particle swarm optimization algorithm. In Proceedings of the 2011 24th Canadian Conference on Electrical and Computer Engineering (CCECE), Niagara Falls, ON, Canada, 8–11 May 2011; pp. 337–340.
5. Yang, X.-S.; Deb, S. Cuckoo search via lévy flights. In Proceedings of the 2009 World Congress on Nature Biologically Inspired Computing (NaBIC), Coimbatore, India, 9–11 December 2009; pp. 210–214.
6. Bingul, Z.; Karahan, O. A novel performance criterion approach to optimum design of PID controller using cuckoo search algorithm for avr system. *J. Frankl. Inst.* **2018**, *355*, 5534–5559. [CrossRef]
7. Mirjalili, S. Moth-flame optimization algorithm: A novel nature-inspired heuristic paradigm. *Knowl.-Based Syst.* **2015**, *89*, 228–249. [CrossRef]
8. Dixit, A.; Lokhande, M.; Joshi, N. Optimization of automatic voltage regulator using moth flame optimization algorithm. *Int. J. Eng. Dev. Res.* **2016**, *4*, 367–371.
9. Eskandar, H.; Sadollah, A.; Bahreininejad, A.; Hamdi, M. Water cycle algorithm—A novel metaheuristic optimization method for solving constrained engineering optimization problems. *Comput. Struct.* **2012**, *110–111*, 151–166. [CrossRef]
10. Pachauri, N. Water cycle algorithm-based pid controller for AVR. *COMPEL Int. J. Comput. Maths. Electr. Electron. Eng.* **2020**, *39*, 551–567. [CrossRef]
11. Chatterjee, S.; Mukherjee, V. Pid controller for automatic voltage regulator using teaching–learning based optimization technique. *Int. J. Electr. Power Energy Syst.* **2016**, *77*, 418–429. [CrossRef]

12. Abdelmadjid, R.; Khaled, D. Design of Standalone Micro-Grid Systems Using Teaching Learning Based Optimization. *Alger. J. Signals Syst.* **2017**, *2*, 75–85.
13. Bouaraki, M.; Abdelmadjid, R. Optimal placement of power factor correction capacitors in power systems using Teaching Learning Based Optimization. *Alger. J. Signals Syst.* **2017**, *2*, 102–109. [CrossRef]
14. Hill Climbing Algorithm in Artificial Intelligence. Available online: https://www.javatpoint.com/hill-climbingalgorithm-in-ai (accessed on 1 December 2021).
15. Lahcene, R.; Abdeldjalil, S.; Aissa, K. Optimal tuning of fractional order pid controller for avr system using simulated annealing optimization algorithm. In Proceedings of the 2017 5th International Conference on Electrical Engineering Boumerdes (ICEE-B), Boumerdes, Algeria, 29–31 October 2017; pp. 1–6.
16. Sambariya, D.K.; Paliwal, D. Design of PIDA controller using bat algorithm for AVR power system. *Adv. Energy Power* **2016**, *6*, 1–6. [CrossRef]
17. Tang, Y.; Zhao, L.; Han, Z.; Bi, X.; Guan, X. Optimal gray PID controller design for automatic voltage regulator system via imperialist competitive algorithm. *Int. J. Mach. Learn. Cyber.* **2016**, *7*, 229–240. [CrossRef]
18. Al Gizi, A.J.H.; Mustafa, M.W.; Al-Geelani, N.A.; Alsaedi, M.A. Sugeno fuzzy PID tuning, by genetic-neutral for AVR in electrical power generation. *J. Appl. Soft. Comput.* **2015**, *28*, 226–236. [CrossRef]

Proceeding Paper

Frequency Control System Effectiveness in a Combined Cycle Gas Turbine Plant [†]

Djamila Talah * and Hamid Bentarzi

Laboratory Signals and Systems (LSS), IGEE, University M'hamed Bougara Boumerdes (UMBB), Boumerdes 35000, Algeria; h.bentarzi@univ-boumerdes.dz
* Correspondence: d.talah@univ-boumerdes.dz
† Presented at the 1st International Conference on Computational Engineering and Intelligent Systems, Online, 10–12 December 2021.

Abstract: Combined cycle gas turbines (CCGTs) have considerable merits and are mainly the most frequently researched topics in power generation, due to their attractive performance characteristics and low-emission combustion system. A change in power demands throughout a power system is reflected by a change in the frequency in the network. Therefore, a significant loss in a power system without a suitable control system can cause an extreme frequency disturbance in the network. However, it has been observed that many research studies have focused on control issues and voltage stability, contrary to frequency control, which receives less interest in this field. Considering these remarks, our contribution deals with the frequency control system. This study focuses on the effectiveness of the frequency control system in a combined cycle gas turbine plant. Thus, a dynamic model for a CCGT plant has been developed in MATLAB/Simulink, and the power system responses are examined following the frequency deviation.

Keywords: combined cycle; power generation; frequency control; speed governor

Citation: Talah, D.; Bentarzi, H. Frequency Control System Effectiveness in a Combined Cycle Gas Turbine Plant. *Eng. Proc.* **2022**, *14*, 1. https://doi.org/10.3390/engproc2022014001

Academic Editors: Abdelmadjid Recioui and Fatma Zohra Dekhandji

Published: 24 January 2022

Publisher's Note: MDPI stays neutral with regard to jurisdictional claims in published maps and institutional affiliations.

Copyright: © 2022 by the authors. Licensee MDPI, Basel, Switzerland. This article is an open access article distributed under the terms and conditions of the Creative Commons Attribution (CC BY) license (https://creativecommons.org/licenses/by/4.0/).

1. Introduction

Combined cycle gas turbines (CCGTs) are widely used because they can reach a higher efficiency by producing a great amount of electrical power with low carbon dioxide emissions, compared with conventional plants [1,2]. Nowadays, there is an increasing interest in combined cycle gas turbines, especially in countries endowed with huge natural gas resources [3].

Operating power systems have become more complex than traditional systems, due to the great interconnection and presence of new technical equipment. Thus, in a generation power plant, there is more than one generating unit providing power into the system. Generator speed is significant for power generation plant performance, as it is widely dependent on the performance of the fuel system, the feed water, the combustion system, and the air flow system [4]. For satisfactory operation of this system, the frequency should be kept practically constant.

Depending on the frequency deviation, the frequency control system provides local and automatic frequency control by adjusting the speed governor within a few seconds after a disturbance, in order to maintain the stability of the power system [5]. The speed variation and frequency transient have a direct effect on the air flow and fuel flow supply, since the air compressor and the fuel system are both attached to the shaft of the unit (CIGRE, 2003) [6–8]. Therefore, it is necessary to involve a suitable frequency control system, in such power plant.

This study is based on the dynamic model of a CCGT, proposed by Kakimoto and Baba (2003) [5], which was inspired by Rowen (1983) [9]. Our contribution focuses on the governing control system. The simulation model of the system was developed in

MATLAB/Simulink, and the impact of the load variation and the damping change on the CCGT plant was examined.

2. Combined Cycle Process

In a CCGT, the gas turbine provides two-thirds of the total unit power output and the steam turbine provides the other third. Practically, the overall thermal efficiency of the power plant, in a combined cycle system, increases from 37% to 57–61% [3,8]. In a CCGT, air is compressed isentropically in the compressor before being fed into a combustion chamber, where fuel is added and burned. The energy of the expanding air is then converted into mechanical work in a turbine [10]. The gases exhausted from the gas turbine are used to drive a steam turbine, by transmitting these gases through the heat recovery steam generator (HRSG). This process is the basis of a combined cycle gas turbine plant. The mechanical power produced by the steam turbine is converted into electrical power by the generator.

3. Mathematical Modeling of the Combined Cycle Gas Turbine

The thermodynamic process of the gas and steam turbine is modeled using algebraic equations (Spalding and Cole, 1973), consistent with adiabatic compression and expansion, as well as with the heat exchange in the HRSG [6,8]. It is assumed that the mixture of air and gas is almost equal to the air flow. The ratio of the input–output temperatures for the isentropic compression is given as follows [6,8]:

$$x = (P_{r0} \, W)^{\frac{\gamma-1}{\gamma}} \tag{1}$$

where

γ: The ratio of specific heat;
P_r: The actual compressor ratio (for nominal airflow ($W = 1$ pu), $P_r = P_{r0}$).

However, the compressor discharge temperature (t_d) and the gas turbine exhaust temperature (t_e) can be written, respectively, as:

$$t_d = t_i \left(1 + \frac{x-1}{\eta_c}\right) \tag{2}$$

$$t_e = t_f \left[1 - \left(1 - \frac{1}{x}\right)\eta_t\right] \tag{3}$$

where

t_i: The ambient temperature;
t_f: The gas turbine inlet temperature.
η_c and η_t are, respectively, the compressor and turbine efficiency.

The mechanical output power produced by the gas turbine is given by:

$$E_g = K_0 \left[(t_f - t_e) - (t_d - t_i)\right] W \tag{4}$$

The mechanical output power produced by the steam turbine is given by:

$$E_s = K_1 \, t_e \, W \tag{5}$$

In a steady state and for initialization purposes, the generation output power of the plant is given by:

$$P = E_g + E_s \tag{6}$$

The inlet temperature (T_f) and exhaust temperature (T_e) (note that for normalized conditions $T_f = T_e = 1$ (pu)) are:

$$T_f = \frac{t_f - 273}{t_{f0}} \tag{7}$$

$$T_e = \frac{t_e - 273}{t_{e0}} \quad (8)$$

4. Frequency Falls Effect on the CCGT

It is known that various power grid blackouts are caused by the imbalance in frequency control requirements [7,11]. The falling system frequency has several effects on the CCGT plant. One of them is expressed in the inertia response. This response, alongside with the load response, is important to the power system in damping the initial frequency fall [3]. Another effect of droop frequency is a fall in the compressor speed, which leads to a drop in the pressure and a reduction in the airflow, which means an increase in fuel consumption and a rise in temperature [7,12]. At this time, the temperature controller will actually reduce the fuel demand; consequently, the output power of the gas turbine decreases.

5. Power System Frequency Control

Since the frequency network is proportional to the generator speed, frequency control may be achieved by regulating the rotor speed of the generator. This is assumed by the speed governing control system which is installed in order to adjust the output power and regulate the speed and the frequency deviation [13]. Depending on the sign of the frequency deviation, the frequency control action is expected to start automatically and immediately provide power support by increasing or decreasing the active power output [11].

5.1. Load Response to the Frequency Deviation

The generator speed variations lead to a change in the power output and incite a frequency imbalance [4]. The dependency of the speed (frequency) on the load may be expressed as:

$$\Delta P_e = \Delta P_L + D\,\Delta w_r \quad (9)$$

where

ΔP_L: load change;
Δw_r: speed deviation;
D: load damping constant.

The damping constant is expressed as a percent change in load for one percent change in frequency [4]. When more than one generator is operating in parallel, the output power of each unit can only be varied by adjusting its load reference, which directly affects the speed variation. The loads are lumped into an equivalent single damping constant, 'D', and the equivalent generator has an equivalent inertia constant of M_{eq} [4]. The equivalent generator speed represents the frequency, and in per unit (pu), the two are equal ($\Delta w_r = \Delta f$) (Figure 1).

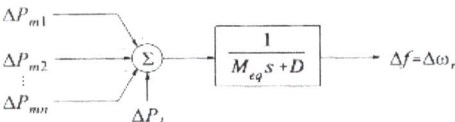

Figure 1. Generating units' power output.

5.2. Turbine Governing Systems Response

It is assumed that the frequency is the same at all times and at all points in the network. Regardless of the location of the load change, all producing units for speed governance will contribute to the global change in generation [4]. Therefore, we consider only a single inertia value, which gathers all the inertia of the individual units. This is done by summing the individual kinetic energies into a single generation kinetic energy value [4]. The speed governing process developed by Kundur [4], shown in Figure 2 is applied in this study.

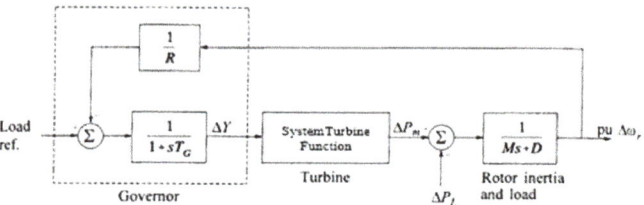

Figure 2. Simplified block diagram of the governing system.

6. Simulation Model of CCGT

The dynamic model of the combined cycle gas turbine plant consists of power generation units and their control system. In this study, the combined cycle system is constituted by two turbines (gas turbine and steam turbine) and one generator unit. The model is based on the simplified transfer function of gas and steam turbines and eventually the control system, which is planned as follows:

The first loop consists of the speed governor (load frequency control), which is necessary for the stability of the system. It detects frequency anomalies and regulates the fuel request signal.

The fuel control is directly related to the rotor speed. The rotor speed and frequency have a direct influence on air and fuel consumption [3].

The temperature control loop has a significant role in the operating system of the power plant, as it adjusts the fuel flow (W_f) and airflow (W) based on measurements of the exhaust temperature, by adjusting the fuel demand when the frequency falls and the output power decreases [2].

The selection of the control loops (frequency or overheat) is achieved using the low-value-select (LVS) by switching the lower value (T_c or F_d).

The simulation model is shown in Figure 3, and the parameters are cited in Appendix A.

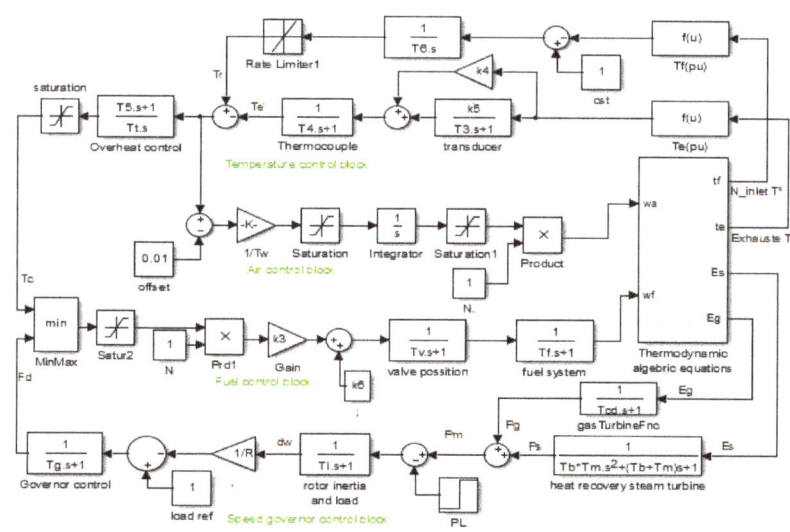

Figure 3. The simulation model used in this study.

7. Simulation Results and Discussion

The effect of the damping constant on the system dynamic is shown in Figure 4. In the transient state, it can be seen that the frequency drop decreases with the increase in damping constant "D". In the steady state, the output power and frequency remain at their nominal values. It is noted that a value of $D = 2$ means that a 1% change in frequency would cause a 2% change in load [4].

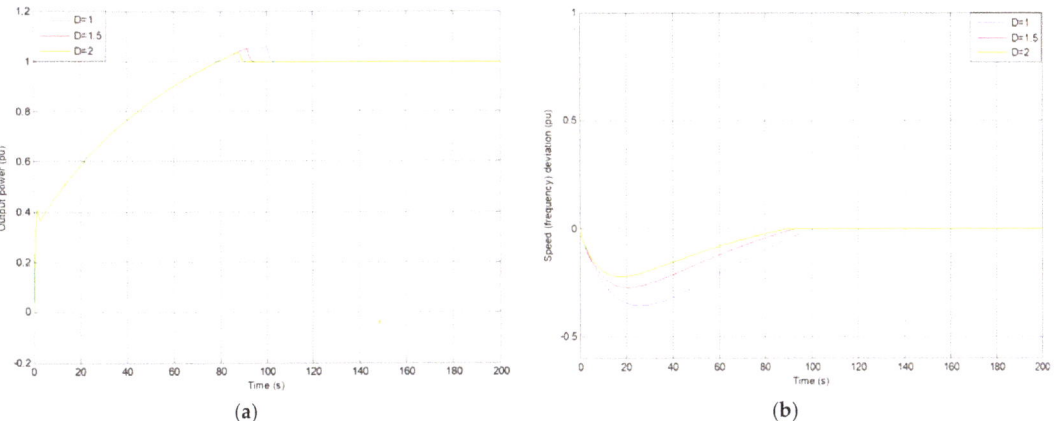

Figure 4. The effect of the damping constant "D" on the system dynamic: (**a**) mechanical output power; (**b**) frequency deviation.

In Figure 5, it can be seen that the output power and frequency deviation decrease as the load change is lower, which means that the system control adjusts the output power generation according to the load change. When the frequency deviation is slight ($\Delta f = -0.09$ Hz), the frequency takes less time to return to its nominal value compared to the case of an overload change, where the frequency drop is about $\Delta f = -0.51$ Hz. It can be noted that the steady state depends on this change. In this phase, for lower load changes, the output power is less than its nominal value and the frequency deviation is very slight, but in a positive sense ($\Delta f = +0.005$ to $\Delta f = +0.01$ Hz). For the overload change, the output power is greater than its nominal value and the frequency deviation still falls ($\Delta f = -0.13$ Hz).

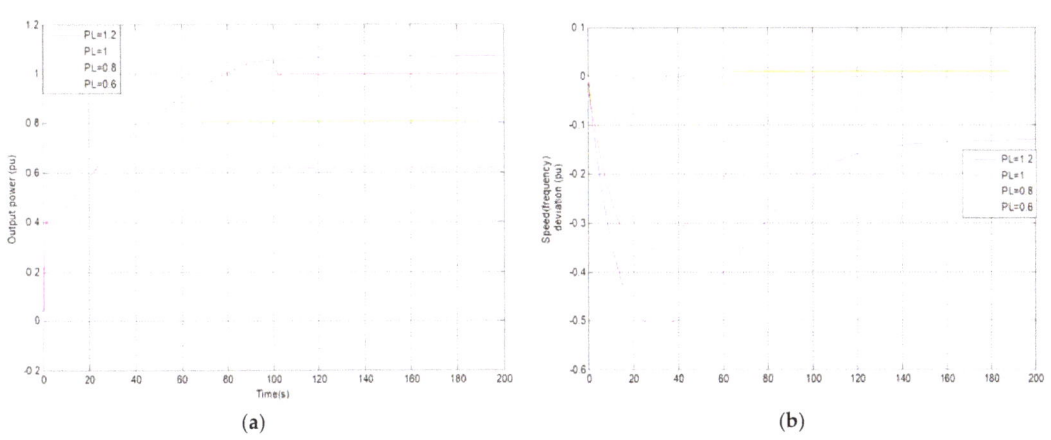

Figure 5. Load change effect on the system: (**a**) mechanical output power; (**b**) frequency deviation.

Figure 6 illustrates that, for a step change in load at $t = 0$ s, the frequency drops in the transient time and then remains at its nominal value (no frequency deviation, $\Delta f = 0$ Hz).

At time $t = 50$ s, a step load is applied to the system. When there is no load, the frequency deviation reaches $\Delta f = +0.2$ Hz; at $t = 50$ s it falls to $\Delta f = -0.03$ Hz. After that, the frequency returns to its nominal value, as does the output power, during the steady state.

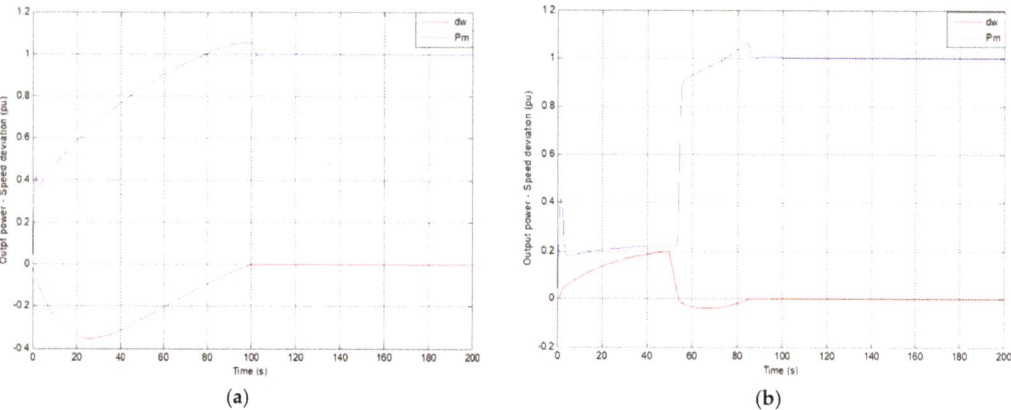

Figure 6. Output power and frequency deviation for $P_L = 1$: (**a**) step time = 0; (**b**) step time = 50 s.

8. Conclusions

The dynamic responses to load and damping changes, which are expressed by a change in frequency, are presented in this paper. Depending on the speed deviation characteristics and the frequency sensitivity to the load change, the action of the speed governor control results in a steady-state frequency deviation. The output power of the CCGT remains at more or less its rated value, until the frequency of the system returns to its nominal value. As the frequency depends on the output power, the frequency should remain nearly constant in order to maintain the speed generator at its rated value. Consequently, the reliability and effectiveness of the frequency control system is necessary for the stability of power system generation.

Author Contributions: Conceptualization, writing—review and editing, D.T.; visualization and supervision, H.B. All authors have read and agreed to the published version of the manuscript.

Funding: This research received no external funding.

Conflicts of Interest: The authors declare no conflict of interest.

Appendix A

Table A1. Simulation parameters used in this study [8].

Symbol	Description	Value
t_i	Compressor inlet temperature	30 °C
t_{d0}	Compressor discharge temperature	390 °C
t_{f0}	Gas turbine inlet temperature	1085 °C
t_{e0}	Gas turbine exhaust temperature	535 °C
P_{r0}	Compressor pressure ratio	11.5
γ	Ratio of specific heat	1.4
η_c	Compressor efficiency	0.85
η_t	Turbine efficiency	0.85
R	Speed Regulation	0.04
T_t	Temperature control integration rate	0.469

Table A1. Cont.

Symbol	Description	Value
$T_{c\ max}$	Temperature control upper limit	1.1
$T_{c\ min}$	Temperature control lower limit	0
$F_{d\ max}$	Fuel control upper limit	1.5
$F_{d\ min}$	Fuel control lower limit	0
T_v	Valve positioner time constant	0.05
T_{fu}	Fuel system time constant	0.4
T_w	Air control time constant	0.4669
T_{cd}	Compressor volume time con-stant	0.2
K_0	Gas turbine output coefficient	0.0033
K_1	Steam turbine output coefficient	0.00043
T_g	Governor time constant	0.05
K_4	Gain of radiation shield (instantaneous)	0.8
K_5	Gain of radiation shield	0.2
T_3	Radiation shield time constant	15
T_4	Thermocouple time constant	2.5
T_5	Temperature control time constant	3.3
K_3	Ratio of fuel adjustment	0.77
K_6	Fuel valve lower limit	0.23
T_m	Time constant heat capacitance of waste heat recovery boiler	5
T_b	Boiler storage time constant	20
T_i	Turbine rotor time constant	18.5

References

1. Raja, A.J.; Christober Asir, R.B.D.; Thiagarajan, C.C.Y. Frequency Excursion and Temperature control of Combined Cycle Gas Plant Including SMES. *Int. J. Comput. Electr. Eng.* **2010**, *2*, 1793–8163. [CrossRef]
2. Talah, D.; Bentarzi, H. Ambient Temperature Effect on the Performance of Gas Turbine in the Combined Cycle Power Plant. *Algerian J. Env. Sci. Technol.* **2021**. Available online: https://www.aljest.net/index.php/aljest/article/view/513 (accessed on 17 January 2022).
3. Spath, P.L.; Mann, M.K. *Life Cycle Assessment of a Natural Gas Combined Cycle Power Generation System*; National Renewable Energy Lab.: Golden, CO, USA, 2000.
4. Kundur, P. *Control of Active Power and Reactive Power. Power System Stability and Control*; McGraw-Hill: New York, NY, USA, 1994; pp. 581–601.
5. Kakimoto, N.; Baba, K. Performance of Gas Turbine-Based Plants During Frequency Drops. *IEEE Trans. Power Syst.* **2003**, *18*, 1110–1115. [CrossRef]
6. Mantzaris, J.; Vournas, C. Modelling and Stability of a Single-Shaft Combined Cycle Power Plant. *Int. J. Thermodyn.* **2007**, *10*, 71–78.
7. Lalor, G.; O'Malley, M. Frequency Control on an Island Power System with Increasing Proportions Combined Cycle Gas Turbines. In Proceedings of the IEEE Bologna Power Tech Conference, Bologna, Italy, 23–26 June 2003.
8. Rai, J.N.; Naimul Hasan, A.B.B.; Garai, R.; Rahul Kapoor, I. Performance Analysis of CCGT Power Plant using MATLAB/Simulink Based Simulation. *Int. J. Adv. Res. Technol.* **2013**, *2*, 285–290.
9. Rowen, W.I. Simplified Mathematical Representation of Heavy Duty Gas Turbines. *J. Power* **1983**, *105*, 865–869. [CrossRef]
10. Lindsley, D. *Power Plant Control and Instrumentation*; The Institution of Electrical Engineers: London, UK, 2005; pp. 10, 25–46.
11. Gezer, D.; Taşcıoğlu, Y.; Çelebioğlu, K. Frequency Containment Control of Hydropower Plants Using Different Adaptive Methods. *Energies* **2021**, *14*, 2082. [CrossRef]
12. Lalor, G.; Ritchie, J.; Flynn, D.; O'Malley, M. The Impact of Combined Cycle Gas Turbine Short-Term Dynamics on Frequency Control. *IEEE Trans. Power Syst.* **2005**, *20*, 1456–1464. [CrossRef]
13. Bevrani, H. *Robust Power System Frequency Control*, 2nd ed.; Springer: Cham, Switzerland, 2014; pp. 23–26.

Proceeding Paper

Optimizing MAG Welding Input Variables to Maximize Penetration Depth Using Particle Swarm Optimization Algorithm [†]

Mohamed Mezaache [1,*], Omar Fethi Benaouda [1], Saad Chaouch [1], Badreddine Babes [2] and Rachid Amraoui [1]

1. Research Center in Industrial Technologies CRTI, P.O. Box 64, Cheraga 16014, Algeria; o.benaouda@crti.dz (O.F.B.); s.chaouch@crti.dz (S.C.); r.amraoui@crti.dz (R.A.)
2. Thin Films Development and Applications Unit UDCMA-CRTI, Industrial Zone 15 A, Setif 19000, Algeria; b.babes@crti.dz
* Correspondence: mohamedmezaache@gmail.com
† Presented at the 1st International Conference on Computational Engineering and Intelligent Systems, Online, 10–12 December 2021.

Abstract: Systems based on artificial intelligence, such as particle swarm optimization and genetic algorithm have received increased attention in many research areas. One of the main objectives in the gas metal arc welding (GMAW) process is to achieve maximum depth of penetration (DP) as a characteristic of quality and stiffness. This article has examined the application of particle swarm optimization algorithm to obtain a better DP in a GMAW and compare the results obtained with the technique of genetic algorithms. The effect of four main welding variables in GMAW process which are the welding voltage, the welding speed, the wire feed speed and the nozzle-to-plate distance on the DP have been studied. For the implementation of optimization, a source code has been developed in MATLAB 8.3. The results showed that, in order to obtain the upper penetration depth, it is necessary that: the welding voltage, the welding speed and the nozzle-to-plate distance must be at their lowest levels; the wire feed speed at its highest level.

Keywords: artificial intelligence; particle swarm optimization; genetic algorithm; GMAW; penetration depth; optimization; MATLAB

1. Introduction

M.I.G. (Metal Inert Gas) and M.A.G. (Metal Active Gas) or G.M.A.W. (Gas Metal Arc Welding) is one of the most commonly used processes for joining metal. The basis behind heat production in this process is Joule's law of heating, where an applied electric current produces heat due to resistance across an electric arc, which heats the filler metal and base metal to form a weld pool. This molten metal is protected from oxidation of the surrounding atmosphere by inert shielding gas coverage [1].

Weld quality plays an important role as it improves the material strength, toughness and hardness of the product. The quality of a welded product is evaluated by various parameters like deposition rate, weld bead geometry and hardness. These characteristics are controlled by a number of welding parameters like welding speed, welding current and welding voltage. Therefore, to obtain good quality, it is important to define the appropriate welding process parameters [2].

To solve an optimization problem, metaheuristics (artificial intelligences) were used to find the optimal solution. The main advantage of metaheuristics lies in their efficiency and applicability. A wide variety of metaheuristics exists as well as several approaches used to classify them. One approach characterizes the type of search strategy, for example, one type of search strategy is to improve simple local search algorithms, and the other type of search strategy contains a learning component in research [3].

One of the approaches of artificial intelligence such as Particle Swarm Optimization (abbreviated as PSO) has received a lot of attention in combinatorial optimization. PSO is a part of the swarm intelligence family [4], it is based on swarm behavior in nature, like fish and bird schooling. In actuality, PSO has become one of the most widely used algorithms due to its flexibility and simplicity [5].

PSO is based on the principle that each possible solution can be represented as a particle in a swarm. Each particle has a position, which is updated at each step of iteration, by adding the current position of the particle to its velocity term [6].

The objective of the optimization phase was to maximize the depth of penetration through the use of a specially developed PSO. In our work, five levels and four input process parameters are selected. These input parameters chosen are welding voltage (V), welding speed (S), wire feed speed (W) and nozzle-to-plate distance (N). The output parameter was depth of penetration (DP).

The penetration of weld bead is illustrated in Figure 1, with the lightest gray representing the base metal, and the darkest gray being the weld metal.

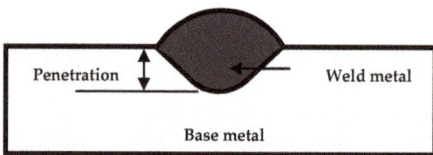

Figure 1. Depth of penetration of weld bead.

2. Experimental Procedure

The experimental procedure used for this work is briefly explained below.

2.1. Description

The experiments were performed by means of a GMAW machine using a direct current electrode positive. Test pieces of dimensions (200 mm × 100 mm × 6 mm) were cut from steel plates. Filler wire (class ER70S-6) in the form of a coil of 0.8 mm diameter was used to deposit the weld beads. The experimental setup consisted of three parts: wire feed unit, welding power source and welding manipulator, where the welding gun was held in a frame mounted directly above the work table, and it was provided with an attachment on the manipulator for both up and down movement to adjust the required nozzle-to-plate distance. The bead-on-plate technique was adopted for welding the test pieces. The spray transfer mode has been used in this process. The composition of the shielding gas was argon (75%) and carbon dioxide (25%). The gas flow rate used was 14 liters/min.

The chemical composition of the base metal and the filler metal are given in Tables 1 and 2, respectively [7].

Table 1. Chemical composition of base metal (ST37 steel).

Elements	Mn	C	Cr	Si	S	P	Ti	Fe
Weight %	0.417	0.113	0.031	0.024	0.01	0.007	0.002	Bal.

Table 2. Standard chemical composition of filler metal (Typical).

Elements	Mn	Si	Cu	C	S	P	Fe
Weight %	1.65	0.95	0.35	0.09	0.018	0.012	Bal.

2.2. Identification of Input Process Parameters

The limits of input process parameters with their notations and units are presented in Table 3.

Table 3. Selected input process parameters and their limits values.

Input Process Parameters	Notation and Units	Limits				
Welding voltage	V (volts)	26	28	30	32	34
Welding speed	S (m/min)	0.20	0.23	0.27	0.30	0.34
Wire feed speed	W (m/min)	8	9	10	11	12
Nozzle-to-plate distance	N (mm)	12	14	16	18	20

2.3. Recording the Response Variables

Depth of penetration was measured according to the following steps: cutting the test piece, mechanical polishing, revealing the structure by a chemical attack and finally macro-graphic observation.

For this study, the observed experimental input and output values are shown in Table 4.

Table 4. Optimal experimental input and output values obtained.

No.	V (volts)	S (m/min)	W (m/min)	N (mm)	DP (mm)
1	30	0.27	10	16	1.232
2	30	0.27	8	16	0.852
3	30	0.34	10	16	0.982
4	30	0.27	10	20	1.034
5	28	0.23	9	14	1.095
6	28	0.23	9	18	1.042
7	32	0.23	9	18	1.056
9	32	0.23	11	14	1.355
9	28	0.23	11	14	1.428
10	32	0.30	11	18	0.857

2.4. Obtaining the Mathematical Models

The regression procedure was used to develop a mathematical model to predict penetration depth. The response function representing any depth of penetration dimensions can be expressed using the equation DP = f (V, S, W, N), where DP is the output parameter and V, S, W, N are the input variables.

The second-order polynomial representing the response surface for four factors is given by [8,9]:

$$Y = b_0 + \sum_{i=1}^{4} b_i X_i + \sum_{i=1}^{4} b_{ii} X_i^2 + \sum_{i,j=1 \text{ and } i \neq j}^{4} b_{ij} X_i X_j \tag{1}$$

where Y (DP) is the dependent variable; X_i (V, S, W, N) are four independent variables; the coefficient b_0 is the free term of the regression equation; the coefficients b_i (b_1, b_2, b_3 and b_4) are linear terms; the coefficients b_{ii} (b_{11}, b_{22}, b_{33} and b_{44}) are quadratic terms; and the coefficients b_{ij} (b_{12}, b_{13}, b_{14}, b_{23}, b_{24} and b_{34}) are interaction terms.

The final mathematical model, being a second-degree response surface, is expressed as follows:

$$\begin{aligned} DP = &\ b_0 + b_1 V + b_2 S + b_3 W + b_4 N + b_{11} V^2 + b_{22} S^2 + b_{33} W^2 + b_{44} N^2 \\ &+ b_{12} VS + b_{13} VW + b_{14} VN + b_{23} SW + b_{24} SN + b_{34} WN \end{aligned} \tag{2}$$

3. Overview of the Proposed Algorithm (PSO)

Particle Swarm Optimization (PSO) is an optimization metaheuristic, invented by Russel Eberhart and James Kennedy in 1995 [10], as an alternative to Genetic Algorithm (GA) [11].

PSO is inspired by the observation of the social behavior of bird flocks. It initializes the population with random potential solutions of the problem. Individuals in the population are called particles; everyone has their own position and velocity [12].

Using the last two parameters, the fitness function of the particle has been calculated, and each particle in the problem space would have its best solution. That personal best experience of each particle is called "Pbest". When a particle completes its population, the best value of all particles is global best experience "Gbest". After finding the two best values, the particle updates its velocity "$V_i(t+1)$" and position "$X_i(t+1)$" according to the following equations [13]:

$$V_i(t+1) = W V_i(t) + C_1 R_1 (Pbest_i(t) - X_i(t)) + C_2 R_2 (Gbest(t) - X_i(t)) \quad (3)$$

$$X_i(t+1) = X_i(t) + V_i(t+1) \quad (4)$$

where i-th is the particle, N is the number of particles in the swarm, so $i = 1, 2, \ldots, N$ particles; the index t denotes the iteration counter; $V_i(t+1)$, and $X_i(t+1)$ are, respectively, the particle's velocity and position at the new iteration $(t+1)$; $V_i(t)$, and $X_i(t)$ represent the velocity value and position at the current iteration (t), respectively; W is the inertia weight; C_1 and C_2 are positive constants, referred to as cognitive and social parameters respectively; R_1 and R_2 are two separate random numbers distributed in the range [0, 1]; $Pbest_i$ (t) is the personal best position of the ith particle at the t_{th} iteration; Gbest (t) is the global best position of particles at t iteration [14–16].

Figure 2 illustrates the position and velocity update of PSO:

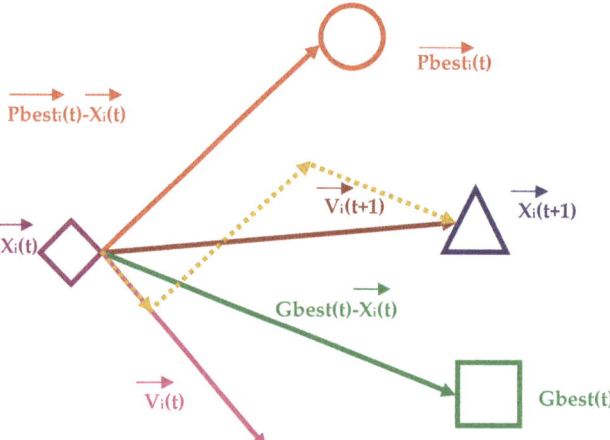

Figure 2. PSO position and velocity update.

The flow chart of the basic optimization process of particles is shown in Figure 3.

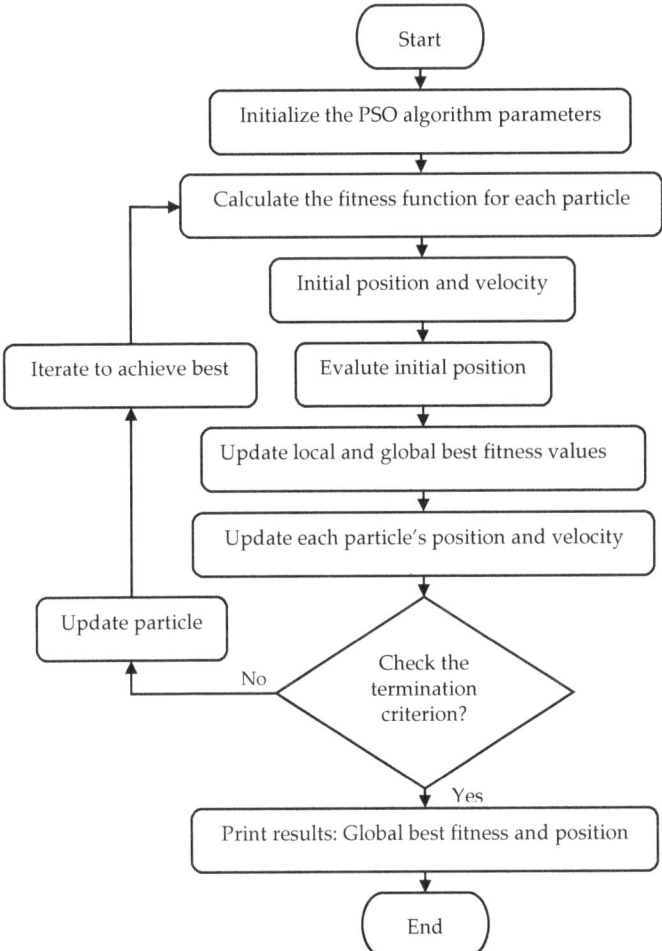

Figure 3. Flow chart of PSO algorithm.

4. Results Validation

4.1. Confirmation Test

After collecting data, and applying the least squares method, the regression equation of Depth of Penetration "DP" was obtained as below:

$$DP = \begin{aligned}&-5.0731\,V + 10.2058\,W + 3.3435\,N + 0.2694\,V^2 - 0.0449\,W^2 - 0.0035\,N^2 \\ &-0.1190\,VS - 0.6198\,VW - 0.3044\,VN + 0.5866\,WN\end{aligned} \quad (5)$$

After that, the regression equation was maximized by the PSO and GA methods. In PSO algorithm, number of populations, learning factors ($C_1 = C_2$), inertia weight (W) and maximum iteration were 35, 2, 0.7, 300, respectively. The operators of GA are: number of populations was 50, type of selection was a tournament, the crossover type was heuristic, the type of mutation was uniform, probability of crossover was 0.85, probability of mutation was 0.02, and maximum iteration was 300.

In order to show the effectiveness of the proposed methods, programs developed in a MATLAB are used. The optimal values of the process variables obtained from PSO and GA are presented in Table 5.

Table 5. Confirmation test results of maximization.

Variables	V(volts)	S(m/min)	W(m/min)	N(mm)	DP(mm)
Optimal solution with PSO	26	0.2	12	12	4.6096
Optimal solution with GA	26.001	0.201	11.999	12.001	4.5952

It should be noted that the value "4.6096 mm" obtained with the PSO technique for penetration depth is better than the value obtained with GA "4.5952 mm". The results show that the two optimization algorithms proposed to make it possible to effectively maximize the objective function.

4.2. Effect of Inputs on Depth of Penetration

Getting deeper penetration or at least adequate penetration is very important in welding. Many variables affect penetration, some more than others, but in general we always want good penetration. It is important to know how each variable affects the deposited weld metal. The optimized direct effects of the four input parameters on the depth of penetration are shown in Figures 4–7.

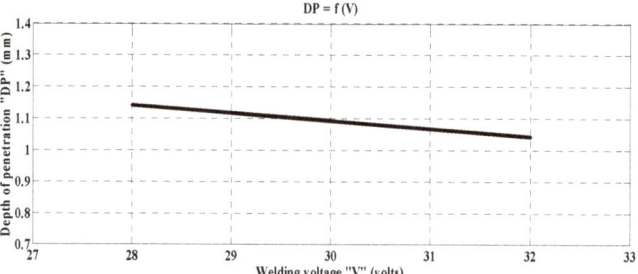

Figure 4. Direct effect of welding voltage "V" on depth of penetration "DP".

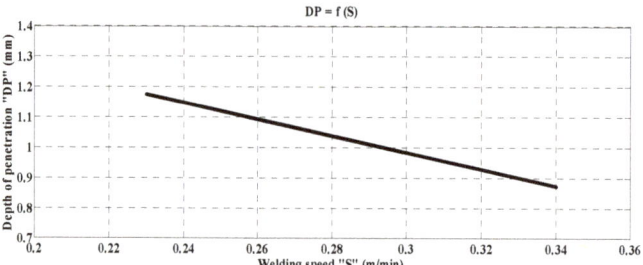

Figure 5. Direct effect of welding speed "S" on depth of penetration "DP".

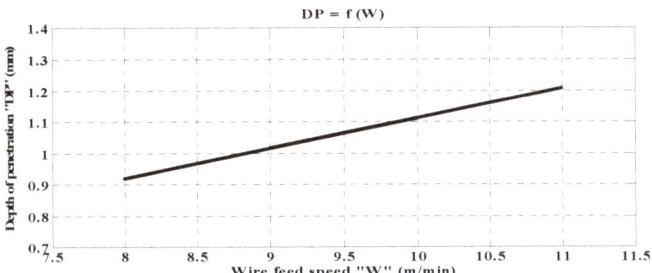

Figure 6. Direct effect of wire feed speed "W" on depth of penetration "DP".

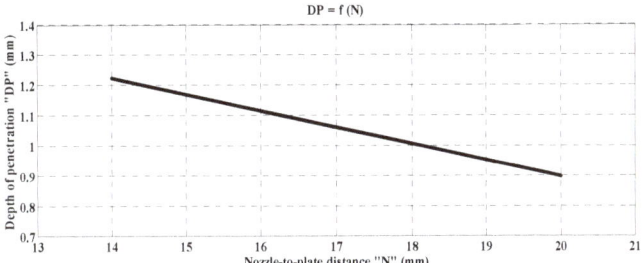

Figure 7. Direct effect of nozzle-to-plate distance "N" on depth of penetration "DP".

From Figure 4, increasing the arc welding voltage resulted in a slow decrease in penetration depth. If the welding voltage was increased from 28 V to 32 V the depth of penetration decreased from 1.143 mm to 1.044 mm.

Higher voltage spreads the arc out and drops a wider bead. Less energy density is exhibited as the voltage goes up, so penetration drops. If the voltage is too low and you get an erratic arc, you will begin to lose some penetration [17].

If the welding speed was increased from 0.23 m/min to 0.34 m/min the depth of penetration decreased from 1.176 mm to 0.873 mm. Increasing the welding speed results in a gradual decrease in the penetration depth. This can be attributed to a lower heat input at higher speeds per unit length of the weld bead, resulting in a decrease in weld pool and a decrease in penetration depth [18].

In Figure 6, it can be noted that the depth of penetration increases progressively with the wire feed speed. If the wire feed speed was increased from 8 m/min to 11 m/min the depth of penetration increased from 0.919 mm to 1.209 mm.

Wire feed speed controls the amperage as well as the amount of weld penetration. A speed that is too high can lead to burn-through. The voltage needs to be balanced with wire feed speed for an efficient metal transfer. If W/amperage is too high setting the wire feed speed or amperage too high may cause improper starting of the arc, and lead to an excessively large weld bead, burn-through, excessive spatter and poor penetration. If W/amperage is too low a narrow cord, oftentimes convex bead with poor tie-in at the toes of the weld, indicates insufficient amperage [19].

In Figure 7, it should be noted that the depth of penetration decreases gradually with the nozzle-to-plate distance (N). If N was increased from 14 mm to 20 mm the depth of penetration decreased from 1.224 mm to 0.898 mm. As N increases, more resistance to the flow of electricity through the electrode occurs; this increase causes a decrease in current, resulting in a decrease in the level of penetration. Conversely, when N decreases, resistance also decreases. As a result, current increases and thus penetration increases.

5. Conclusions

In this research, an attempt was made to obtain the best set of values for welding voltage (V), welding speed (S), wire feed speed (W) and nozzle-to-plate distance (N) to produce the best quality of weld in terms of penetration depth.

Based on this investigation, it can be concluded that the optimization method (PSO) can be used to find optimum welding conditions for maximum weld bead penetration within the specified limits of the process parameters.

Optimization results indicate that to reach the maximum depth penetration, the three factors V, S and N should be at their minimum values and the factor W must be at its maximum value. There are many other variables that can affect penetration such as gas flow rate and variables include base: like material surface condition (rust, presence of oil . . .), base material thickness, base material type, and electrode diameter [18].

Author Contributions: Conceptualization, M.M; methodology, M.M.; software, M.M.; validation, M.M., O.F.B. and S.C.; formal analysis, M.M., B.B. and R.A.; investigation, M.M. and S.C.; resources, M.M. and B.B.; data curation, M.M. and O.F.B.; writing—original draft preparation, M.M., O.F.B. and S.C.; writing—review and editing, M.M.; visualization, M.M., O.F.B. and S.C.; supervision, M.M.; project administration, M.M.; funding acquisition, M.M. All authors have read and agreed to the published version of the manuscript.

Funding: This research received no external funding.

Institutional Review Board Statement: Not applicable.

Informed Consent Statement: Informed consent was obtained from all subjects involved in the study.

Data Availability Statement: Not applicable.

Conflicts of Interest: The authors declare no conflict of interest.

References

1. Chandrasekaran, R.R. Predication of Bead Geometry in Gas Metal Arc Welding by Statistical Regression Analysis. Master's Thesis, Applied Science in Mechanical and Mechatronics Engineering, University of Waterloo, Waterloo, ON, Canada, 2019.
2. Edwin Raja Dhas, J.; Kumanan, S. Optimization of Parameters of Submerged Arc Weld Using Non Conventional Techniques. *Appl. Soft Comput.* **2011**, *11*, 5198–5204. [CrossRef]
3. Pérez Pozo, L.; Fernando Olivares, Z.; Orlando Durán, A. Optimization of Welding Parameters Using a Genetic Algorithm: A Robotic Arm-Assisted Implementation for Recovery of Pelton Turbine Blades. *Adv. Mech. Eng.* **2015**, *7*, 1–17. [CrossRef]
4. Del Valle, Y.; Venayagamoorthy, G.K.; Mohagheghi, S.; Hernandez, J.C.; Harley, R.G. Particle Swarm Optimization: Basic Concepts, Variants and Applications in Power Systems. *IEEE Trans. Evol. Comput.* **2008**, *12*, 171–195. [CrossRef]
5. Tang, R.L.; Fang, Y.J. Modification of Particle Swarm Optimization with Human Simulated Property. *Neurocomputing* **2015**, *153*, 319–331. [CrossRef]
6. Abdelhafiz, A.; Behjat, L.; Ghannouchi, F.M. Generalized Memory Polynomial Model Dimension Selection Using Particle Swarm Optimization. *IEEE Microw. Wirel. Compon. Lett.* **2018**, *28*, 96–98. [CrossRef]
7. Aghakhani, M.; Jalilian, M.M.; Karami, A.; Jalilian, M.M. Optimization of GMAW Process Using Imperialist Competitive Algorithm. In *Applied Mechanics and Materials*; Fan, W., Ed.; Trans Tech Publications Ltd.: Freienbach, Switzerland, 2012; Volume 110–116, pp. 3575–3579.
8. Sudhakaran, R.; Vel Murugan, V.; Sivasakthivel, P.S.; Balaji, M. Prediction and Optimization of Depth of Penetration for Stainless Steel Gas Tungsten Arc Welded Plates Using Artificial Neural Networks and Simulated Annealing Algorithm. In *Neural Comput & Applic*; Springer: London, UK, 2011.
9. Sudhakaran, R.; Vel Murugan, V.; Sivasakthivel, P.S. Optimization of Process Parameters to Minimize Angular Distortion in Gas Tungsten Arc Welded Stainless Steel 202 Grade Plates Using Particle Swarm Optimization. *J. Eng. Sci. Technol.* **2012**, *7*, 195–208.
10. Li, S.F.; Cheng, C.Y. Particle Swarm Optimization with Fitness Adjustment Parameters. *Comput. Ind. Eng.* **2017**, *113*, 831–841. [CrossRef]
11. Tungadio, D.H.; Numbi, B.P.; Siti, M.W.; Jimoh, A.A. Particle Swarm Optimization for Power System State Estimation. *Neurocomputing* **2015**, *148*, 175–180. [CrossRef]
12. Kong, Z.; Jia, W.; Zhang, G.; Wang, L. Normal Parameter Reduction in Soft Set Based on Particle Swarm Optimization Algorithm. *Appl. Math. Model.* **2015**, *39*, 4808–4820. [CrossRef]
13. Dhal, P.K. Improvement of Stability by Optimal Location with Tuning STATCOM Using Particle Swarm Optimization Algorithm. In *Information Systems Design and Intelligent Applications, Advances in Intelligent Systems and Computing*; Satapathy, S., Mandal, J., Udgata, S., Bhateja, V., Eds.; Springer: New Delhi, India, 2016; Volume 434, pp. 583–593.

14. AlRashidi, M.R.; El-Hawary, M.E. A Survey of Particle Swarm Optimization Applications in Electric Power Systems. *IEEE Trans. Evol. Comput.* **2009**, *13*, 913–918. [CrossRef]
15. Sharaf, A.M.; El-Gammal, A.A.A. Particle Swarm Optimization PSO: A New Search Tool in Power System and Electro Technology. In *Computational Intelligence in Power Engineering, Studies in Computational Intelligence*; Panigrahi, B.K., Abraham, A., Das, S., Eds.; Springer: Berlin/Heidelberg, Germany, 2010; Volume 302, pp. 235–294.
16. Parsopoulos, K.E.; Vrahatis, M.N. Particle Swarm Optimization and Intelligence: Advances and Applications. In *Premier Reference Source*; Information Science Reference: Hershey, NY, USA, 2010; p. 328.
17. Welding Answers. 7 Variables That Affect Weld Penetration. Group of Professionals in the Welding Industry: USA. Available online: http://weldinganswers.com/7-variables-that-affect-weld-penetration/ (accessed on 25 March 2020).
18. Mostafa, N.B.; Khajavi, M.N. Optimization of welding parameters for weld penetration in FCAW. *J. Achiev. Mater. Manuf. Eng.* **2006**, *16*, 132–138.
19. Miller. MIG Welding: Setting the Correct Parameters. Miller Electric Manufacturing Company: Appleton, WI, USA, 2020. Available online: https://www.millerwelds.com/resources/article-library/miggmaw-101-setting-the-correct-parameters (accessed on 29 April 2020).

Proceeding Paper

Sub-Synchronous Torsional Interaction Study and Mitigation Using a Synchro-Phasors Measurement Unit [†]

Mohammed Tsebia * and Hamid Bentarzi

Signals and Systems Laboratory (LSS), Institute of Electrical and Electronic Engineering, University of M'hamed Bougara, Boumerdes 35000, Algeria; h.bentarzi@univ-boumerdes.dz
* Correspondence: m.tsebia@univ-boumerdes.dz
† Presented at the 1st International Conference on Computational Engineering and Intelligent Systems, Online, 10–12 December 2021.

Abstract: In a power plant, sub-synchronous resonance is not encountered very often, but when it occurs, it can cause a very serious problem and severe damage. Many efforts have been investigated to study and hence mitigate a resonance produced between electrical synchronous machines and the electrical grid that may arise for frequencies other than the fundamental one (50 Hz). Natural resonances in the electrical grid incorporating series capacitors can appear for sub-synchronous frequencies and can be both a series and parallel resonance nature. Mitigation techniques are required for a power plant with an extensive turbine-generator string located near a long power transmission line with series capacitors. Due to the severe consequences, power plants that risk sub-synchronous resonance (SSR) may be equipped with appropriate protection. However, if the sub-synchronous resonance frequencies of the network coincide with any of the mechanical frequencies of the turbine-generator shaft, torsional interaction that is called sub-synchronous torsional interaction (SSTI). If the electrical damping for a specific frequency in the network is insufficient or negative in comparison to mechanical damping, it may lead to this sub-synchronous torsional interaction. This phenomenon can be hazardous causing fatigue in the turbine-generator shaft, which results in the failure of the power generation unit. It can also occur due to the interaction between a control system of converters and the turbine generators. In this research paper, a study using different methods of analysis developed by transmission system operators (TSOs) and the manufacturers with one case study is presented. Additionally, different mitigation techniques, such as filtering and damping, are suggested. Furthermore, a demonstration for measuring principles as well as monitoring and protection against SSTI using a synchro-phasors measurement unit has been presented.

Keywords: sub-synchronous resonance; sub-synchronous torsional interaction; synchro-phasors measurement unit; mitigation techniques

1. Introduction

The stability of power systems has a major and continuous concern in the system operation. Under steady state conditions, each of the connected generators may have the same electrical speed in the power system, which is also known as the synchronism of generators. Any disturbance can effect the synchronous operation of the alternators. The stability of a power system, defined as the capability of the system to return to its normal steady state situation after the transients, is detached.

The disturbance can be of two types: (a) a small disturbance and (b) a large disturbance. Small signal analysis, i.e., linear equations are used for the analysis of small signal disturbances. The random or uneven changes in the load or generation are called small disturbances. Faults or the loss of large loads resulting in a voltage dip are called large disturbances and require fast action to clear out the fault. The protection system may take action in this case.

Sub-synchronous resonance is a special type of power system dynamic and stability problem, due to which the turbine-generator shaft experiences torsional oscillations. These oscillations can be hazardous causing fatigue in the turbine-generator shaft, which results in the failure of the power generation unit [1].

A definition for SSR is provided by the IEEE [2]: "Subsynchronous resonance is a condition where the electric network exchanges energy with a turbine generator at one or more of the natural frequencies of the combined system below the synchronous frequency of the system."

Any system operation condition, during which energy is exchanged at a given sub-synchronous frequency, has been included in the same IEEE definition previously mentioned. This also includes the "natural" modes of oscillation that occur because of the inherent system characteristics, as well as the "forced" modes of oscillation that are driven by a particular device or controlling scheme or controller.

Sub-synchronous torsional interaction (SSTI) is an instability phenomenon mainly associated with synchronous machines (SMs) [3]. A torsional resonance in the turbine-generator (T-G) shaft is destabilized through the interaction with the electrical synchronous machine and network dynamics.

2. Sub-Synchronous Interaction

2.1. Sub-Synchronous Resonance (SSR)

Most often in the electrical power system the compensation of line transmission is a series type, the sub-synchronous resonance is the exchange of energy with the turboalternator at one or more natural frequencies lower than the fundamental frequency of 60 or 50 Hz.

There are three types of sub-synchronous resonance.

2.1.1. Torsional Interaction (SSR-TI)

The interaction between the mechanical system and a power supply system compensated in series when small disturbances occur.

2.1.2. Induction Generator Effect (IGE)

This is the self-excitation of a series compensated power supply system. This is independent of the torsion modes of the generator shaft.

2.1.3. Torque Amplification (TA)

The stress amplification of the turbine generator shaft system by transient torques on the generator rotors caused by serious disturbances in a series of compensated power systems.

2.2. Subsynchronous Control Interactions (SSCI)

This is the interaction of the electronic devices (for instance, SVC, STATCOM and HVDC) with the electric power system containing nearby series compensated transmissions.

2.3. Subsynchronous Torsional Interaction (SSTI)

Sub-synchronous torsional interaction (SSTI) occurs when the operation of the electrical system causes mechanical damping to the generator, and which is large enough to exceed the inherent mechanical damping of the shaft at a natural torsional frequency of the system mechanical.

3. Sub-Synchronous Torsional Interaction (SSTI)

Networks containing transmission lines, as Figure 1, with series compensation are the most noted example of a natural mode of sub-synchronous operation. These lines have natural frequencies, ω_n, that are defined by Equation (1) with their series inductance, L, and capacitance, C, combination given as follows.

$$\omega_n = \sqrt{\frac{1}{LC}} = \omega_B \sqrt{\frac{X_c}{X_l}} \tag{1}$$

where ω_n is the natural frequency associated with a particular line LC product, ω_B is the system base frequency and X_l and X_C are the inductive and capacitive reactance, respectively.

The oscillations of the rotating element of the generator at a sub-synchronous frequency, fm, induces voltages in the armature with components of (i) sub-synchronous frequency (fa − fm) and (ii) super-synchronous frequency (fa + fm), where fa is the operating system frequency [4]. This also sets up currents in the armature (and network) whose magnitudes and phase angles are determined by the impedances existing in the network. Both current components (sub- and super-synchronous) set up electromagnetic torques of the same frequency, fm. It can be noted that the positive damping torque appears as a result of the super-synchronous frequency, whereas the negative damping torque appears as a result of the sub-synchronous frequency.

The net torque can result in negative damping if the magnitudes of the sub-synchronous frequency currents are large and in phase with the voltages (of the sub-synchronous frequency). This situation can appear when the electrical network connected to the generator armature resonates around the frequency of (fa − fm).

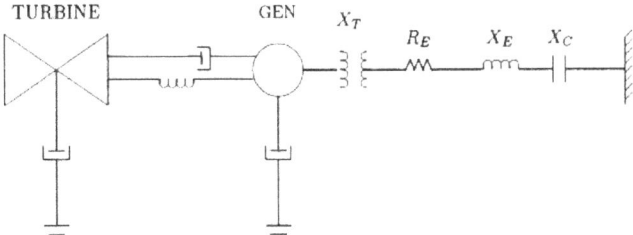

Figure 1. A simple model of the distribution network.

Torsion mode oscillations (frequencies) of the shaft are generally identified and can be obtained from the manufacturer sheet of the generator. The frequencies at which the network oscillates depend on many factors, such as the network switching arrangement at a particular time and the amount of series capacitance in service.

The power system engineer needs a method for examining a large number of feasible operating conditions to determine the possibility of SSR interactions. The eigenvalue program can be used as a tool for SSR analysis. Moreover, the eigenvalue computation tracks the locus of the system eigenvalues as parameters, such as the series capacitance that changed to characterize the equipment outages. If the root locus of a given eigenvalue approaches or crosses the imaginary axis, then a critical situation generally appears that needs the application of one or more SSR countermeasures.

There are many situations in which the system and the generator may interact with sub-synchronous effects. A few interactions are of more concern to a power system engineer, such as the induction generator effect, transient torque effect and torsional interaction effect. In this study, the latter is taken into consideration: when the sub-synchronous torque induced in the generator is close to one of the torsional natural modes of the turbine-generator shaft, torsional interactions are produced. Under this operation condition, the increase in the oscillations in the generator rotor begins, and the armature voltage components at both the sub-synchronous and super-synchronous frequencies are induced due to this motion. The induced sub-synchronous frequency voltage is phased to maintain the sub-synchronous torque. If the inherent mechanical damping torque is equal to or greater than the rotating system torque, the system itself will be excited. This phenomenon is called "torsional interaction."

4. Synchro-Phasors Measurement Unit

A synchro-phasor is defined according the IEEE standard C37.118 as "A phasor calculated from data samples using a standard time signal as the reference for the measurement; however, synchronized phasors from remote sites have a defined common phase relationship" [5]. According to the same standard, a synchronizing source that provides the common timing reference may be local or global. One commonly utilized synchronizing signal is the satellite signal broadcast from the global positioning system (GPS). A PMU is a standalone apparatus that measures 50 (or 60) Hz in AC voltage and current signals, and presents them in phasor form with their frequencies, as Figure 2.

The techniques that are mainly used to measure the steady state frequency are based on the assumption of the fixed frequency model. In wide area monitoring and control application, the dynamic frequency or instantaneous frequency is more useful to explain the behavior of the system. The developed Smart DFT algorithm [6] was used to estimate the instantaneous frequency, and then the estimated phasor amplitude and phase angle were corrected.

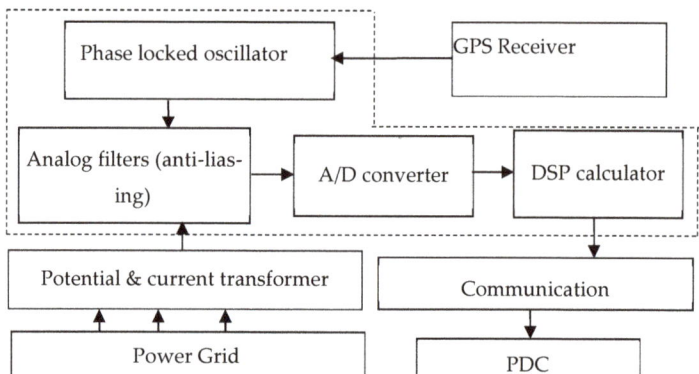

Figure 2. Functional block diagram of the PMU.

During power system disturbances, the sinusoidal frequency f(t) was no longer constant and was a function of time 't'. The sinusoidal signal waveform can be represented by its nominal frequency, f_0, varying with a frequency deviation, $\Delta f(t)$, as follows:

$$x(t) = X_m \cos(2\pi(f_0 + \Delta f) + \varphi_i) \qquad (2)$$

where
X_m: maximum value of the input signal;
f_0: the nominal frequency
Δf: the frequency offset;
φ_i: the initial phase of the input signal.
It is traditionally represented by a phasor:

$$\overline{X} = \frac{X_m}{\sqrt{2}} e^{j(2\pi \Delta f t + \varphi_i)} = X e^{j\phi} = X \cos\phi + jX \sin\phi \qquad (3)$$

Assuming that, the signal x(t) is sampled 'm' times per period of the nominal frequency, f_0 (50 Hz or 60 Hz), to generate the sample set:

$$x_k = X_m \cos\left(\frac{2\pi}{N}k\left(1+\frac{\Delta f}{f_0}\right)+\varphi_i\right) \quad (4)$$

The phasor tracking algorithm (SDFT) may be applied by defining θ as

$$\theta = \frac{2\pi}{f_0}\frac{\Delta f}{N} \quad (5)$$

Assuming that, the sampling rate is 'm' times of the correcting computation frequency, the exact solution of the phasor at the off-nominal frequency can be obtained by the following equations.

Using the sampling set given by Equation (3), the fundamental frequency component of DFT of {x̃(k)} can be obtained:

$$\bar{x}(r) = \frac{\sqrt{2}}{N}\sum_{k=0}^{N-1}\tilde{x}(k+r)je^{-\frac{2\pi}{N}k} \quad (6)$$

The instantaneous frequency can then be calculated from the previous equations and given by the following relation:

$$f(t) = f_0 + \Delta f \quad (7)$$

The local frequency, f, can be defined as a derivative of the angle variation of a phasor (IEEE standard C37.118). Under frequency variations due to sub-synchronous torsional oscillations, the local frequency is the sum of the fixed nominal frequency component, f_0, and the off-nominal frequency variation, Δf (t), due to Δθ sub (t):

$$f(t) = f_0 + \Delta f_{sub}(t) = f_0 + \frac{1}{2\cdot\pi}\frac{d}{dt}\Delta\theta_{sub}(t) \quad (8)$$

Let Δf $_{sub}$ = Δf (t):

$$\Delta f_{sub}(t) = \frac{1}{2\cdot\pi}\frac{d}{dt}\frac{X_{sub}(t)}{|X_{now}(t)|} = f_{\omega,\,sub}\cdot\Delta\theta_{sub}(t) \quad (9)$$

The advantage of this technique is the rapid detection of this phenomenon in real-time and then the mitigation techniques can be applied rapidly.

The synchronized phasor measurement technology is relatively new, and consequently several research groups around the world are actively developing applications using this technology. It seems clear that many of these applications can be conveniently grouped as follows:

- Power System Real Time Monitoring;
- Advanced network protection;
- Advanced control schemes.

5. Case Study

This proposed approach has been implemented in a power network, as Figure 3, in the GNL company situated in Oran, Algeria [7]. The configuration of the system that is based on SPMUs and other equipment is shown in Figure 4. The scenario of the operation can be summarized as follows:

- Two gas turbine generators (GTGs) supply the electricity to the GNL factory;
- A motor of 17 MW starts to operate through the use of VSD;
- Some of the resistive and inductive loads (about 12 MW) are connected.

When the motor speed has attained around 95% of its rated speed using VSD, GTG1 has been disconnected due to the high vibration caused by SSTI. Then, only GTG2 supplies the electricity to the whole power network of the factory. After a few seconds, GTG2 will also have been disconnected due to the same phenomenon (SSTI), before finishing the starting steps investigated by VSD. This leads to the blackout. The spectral of the vibrations that may be measured during this phenomenon is shown in Figure 4. Using the data provided by SPMU and the implemented system may present the results, as shown in Figure 5. It can be noted that the peaks of the angle variation is at the frequencies 12.5 and 25 Hz, as shown in Figure 6.

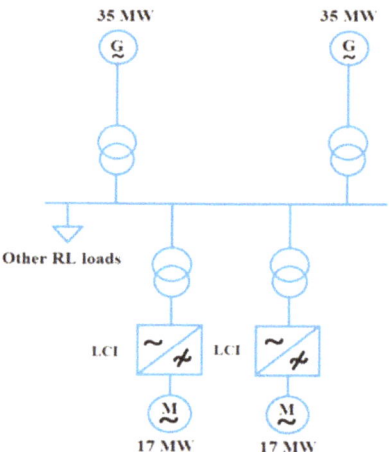

Figure 3. Power network of the GNL factory.

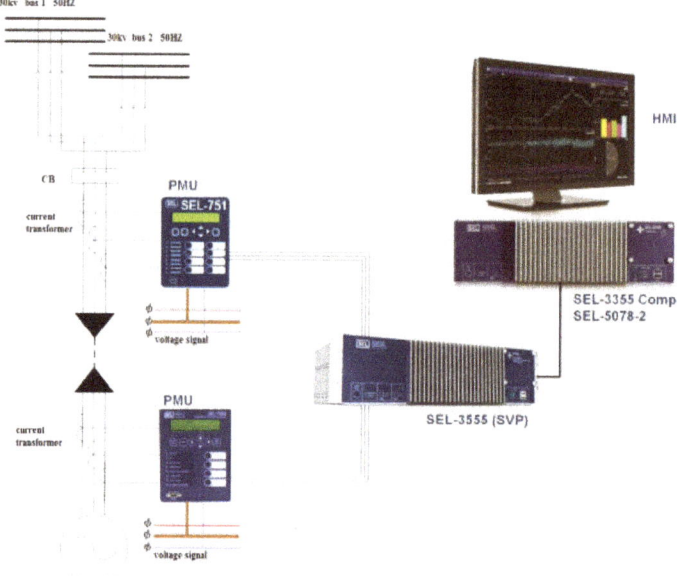

Figure 4. Implemented system configuration with SPMUs and the necessary equipment.

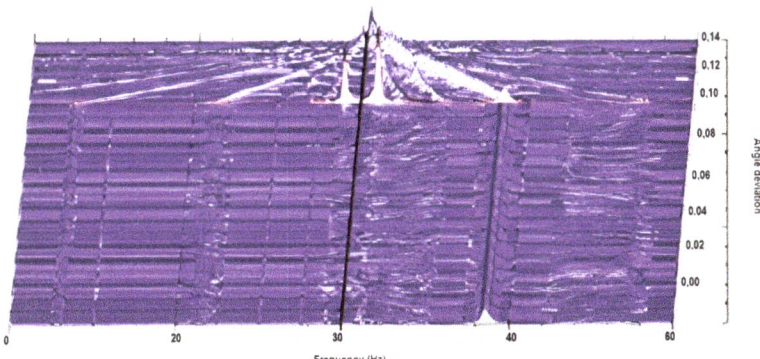

Figure 5. Spectral of vibration.

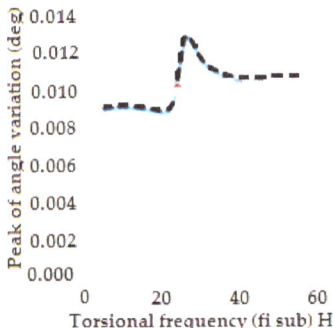

Figure 6. Sub-synchronous variation in the voltage phasor angle at the terminals.

6. Conclusions

This paper investigated the sub-synchronous torsional interaction (SSTI) for two gas turbine generators that were disconnected.

This proposed approach can be rapidly implemented and its cost is low. It can be used to detect the sub-synchronous torsional interaction phenomenon, and as a rapid method for analyzing it. Then, the mitigation technique, such as the active damping technique, can be applied.

Author Contributions: Conceptualization, M.T. and H.B.; methodology M.T. and H.B.; validation, M.T. and H.B.; writing—original draft preparation, M.T.; writing—review and editing, H.B.; supervision, M.T.; project administration, H.B.; funding acquisition, H.B. All authors have read and agreed to the published version of the manuscript.

Funding: This research funded by DGRSDT/MESRS Algeria.

Institutional Review Board Statement: Not applicable.

Informed Consent Statement: Not applicable.

Data Availability Statement: The data presented in this study are available on request from the corresponding author.

Acknowledgments: This work was supported by the Signals and Systems Laboratory (LSS), IGEE, University M'hamed BOUGARA of Boumerdes (UMBB), under the research Phd Project: "Inter-area oscilla-tion minimization in power system" funded by DGRSDT/MESRS Algeria.

Conflicts of Interest: The authors declare no conflict of interest.

References

1. Anderson, P.M.; Agrawal, B.L.; Van Ness, J.E. *Subsynchronous Resonance in Power Systems*; The Institute of Electrical and Electronics Engineers, Inc.: New York, NY, USA, 1989.
2. IEEE SSR Working Group. Terms, Definitions, and Symbols for Subsynchronous Oscillations. *IEEE Trans.* **1985**, *PAS-104*, 1326–1334. [CrossRef]
3. Padiyar, K.R. *Analysis of Subsynchronous Resonance in Power Systems*; Department of Electrical Engineering, Indian Institute of Science: Bangalore, India, 1999; ISBN 978-1-4613-7577-7.
4. Choo, Y.; Agalgaonkar, A.; Muttaqi, K.M.; Perera, S.; Negnevitsky, M. Subsynchronous torsional interaction behaviour of wind turbine-generator unit connected to an HVDC system. In Proceedings of the IECON 2010: 36th Annual Conference of the IEEE Industrial Electronics Society, Glendale, AZ, USA, 7–10 November 2010; pp. 996–1003.
5. IEEE Standard for Synchrophasors for Power Systems. *IEEE Std C37.118.1-2011*, 3rd ed.; Advanced Engineering Thermodynamics; Bejan, A., Ed.; Wiley: New York, NY, USA, 2011. [CrossRef]
6. Yang, J.-Z.; Liu, C.-W. A precise calculation of power system frequency and phasor. *IEEE Trans. Power Del.* **2000**, *15*, 494–499. [CrossRef]
7. *Internal Report*; GNL: Arzew, Algeria, 2017.

Proceeding Paper

Performance Enhancement of Photovoltaic Water Pumping System Based on BLDC Motor under Partial Shading Condition [†]

Abdelkarim Ammar [1,*][iD], Kahina Hamraoui [2], Moufida Belguellaoui [2] and Aissa Kheldoun [1]

1. Signals and Systems Laboratory LSS, Institute of Electrical and Electronic Engineering, University of M'hamed BOUGARA of Boumerdes, Boumerdes 35000, Algeria; aissa73@gmail.com
2. Power and Control Engineering Department, Institute of Electrical and Electronic Engineering, University of M'hamed BOUGARA of Boumerdes, Boumerdes 35000, Algeria; hamraouikahina7@gmail.com (K.H.); beluellaoui.moufida@gmail.com (M.B.)
* Correspondence: a.ammar@univ-boumerdes.dz
† Presented at the 1st International Conference on Computational Engineering and Intelligent Systems, Online, 10–12 December 2021.

Abstract: The use of photovoltaic (PV) energy for water pumping is considered one of the most promising areas of photovoltaic applications. This work aims to improve the power extraction of a battery-less photovoltaic pumping system. The DC–DC converter is used to accomplish the maximum power point tracking (MPPT). In addition, the BLDC motor is used for maximum exploitation of the delivered power by the PV array, and to enhance the reliability of the pumping system. Furthermore, an MPPT strategy, based on the cuckoo swarm optimization technique, has been developed to improve the control performance under partial shading conditions. The effectiveness of the proposed system has been examined through simulation using MATLAB and Simulink software.

Keywords: photovoltaic (PV); solar water pumping system (SWPS); maximum power point tracking (MPPT); brushless direct current (BLDC) motor; partial shading; cuckoo search (CS)

Citation: Ammar, A.; Hamraoui, K.; Belguellaoui, M.; Kheldoun, A. Performance Enhancement of Photovoltaic Water Pumping System Based on BLDC Motor under Partial Shading Condition. *Eng. Proc.* **2022**, *14*, 22. https://doi.org/10.3390/engproc2022014022

Academic Editors: Abdelmadjid Recioui, Hamid Bentarzi and Fatma Zohra Dekhandji

Published: 15 February 2022

Publisher's Note: MDPI stays neutral with regard to jurisdictional claims in published maps and institutional affiliations.

Copyright: © 2022 by the authors. Licensee MDPI, Basel, Switzerland. This article is an open access article distributed under the terms and conditions of the Creative Commons Attribution (CC BY) license (https://creativecommons.org/licenses/by/4.0/).

1. Introduction

Water resources are essential for satisfying human needs, ensuring food production and protecting health, as well as for social and economic development. Worldwide, water pumping is generally dependent on electricity or diesel-generated electricity. Diesel is expensive and scarce in the countryside of many developing countries, and even when it is available, transporting it to remote areas is difficult. This is because there are no roads or supporting infrastructure in most of the remote villages. In rural areas, the installation of a new transmission line and transformers is extremely expensive for irrigation or drinking water [1]. A solar water pumping system (SWPS) is made up of various components that can be classified as mechanical, electrical, or electronic. These components have different construction, operation, and performance characteristics [2].

PV pumping systems based on AC motors, especially induction motors (IM), are often favored because they are more dependable, cost less, and do not need regular maintenance. DC motors are commonly used in low-power solar PV water pumps [3]. However, DC motors with brushes possess low efficiency, and they need frequent maintenance, owing to the sliding brush contacts and the commutator. Three-phase brushless direct-current (BLDC) motors are suitable options, due to their high-efficiency capabilities, compactness, and easy-to-drive qualities [4]. Therefore, this motor has gained considerable attention for water pumping in the recent decade, due to its many advantages, which constitute its desirable characteristics, especially for this application [3].

The use of maximum power point tracking (MPPT) methods is critical to increase the efficiency of photovoltaic (PV) systems. Because of its good balance between complexity, precision, and dependability, the perturb and observe (P&O) approach is the most prevalent algorithm [5]. It does, however, have several disadvantages, such as a delayed response time, steady-state power oscillation around the MPP, and poor tracking under abrupt irradiance changes or shading effects [6]. Particle swarm optimization (PSO) and cuckoo search (CS) are two optimization strategies that have been proposed to increase the performance of MPPT [7]. Cuckoo search (CS) is an evolutionary optimization technique that was inspired by a type of bird, named the cuckoo [8], by Yang and Deb (2009). Cuckoos put their eggs in other birds' or species' nests [9]. They fly from one nest to the next, looking for the best one, the one that offers the greatest possibility of the eggs hatching successfully. Several papers [10,11] have discussed the applicability of CS to MPPT. It is shown that it is more stable, has greater convergence, and is more efficient.

In this paper, we present a method for tracking the maximum power point of solar water pumping systems under partial shading conditions. The proposed system is based on a BLDC motor to improve the reliability and efficiency of the system. Moreover, a cuckoo search algorithm is proposed to overcome the disadvantages of the conventional MPPT algorithm. The proposed system has been investigated using MATLAB/Simulink software.

2. Configuration of the PV Pumping System

Figure 1 depicts the designed solar water pumping system's configuration. The photovoltaic generator (PVG) is a group of solar panels with connections that are selected to meet the power needs of the association's power electronic converters, motor, and centrifugal pump. The DC–DC converter is connected between a PVG and a pump to extract the maximum energy possible throughout the day. The peak power operating point of the PVG is tracked using an MPPT algorithm, under various conditions [12].

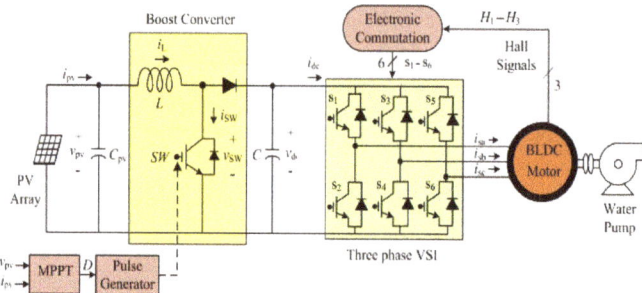

Figure 1. Configuration of the solar PV boost converter BLDC motor-driven water pump.

To control the BLDC motor, a voltage source inverter must be included, which provides three-phase voltages. The boost duty cycle is obtained by the MPPT algorithm, which mainly depends on irradiance.

2.1. Photovoltaic Module

For simplicity and accuracy, the single-diode model is the most studied and used in this work. The single-diode model is shown in Figure 2, and includes a photo current source, a parallel diode, and series and shunt resistors, R_s and R_{sh}, respectively [13].

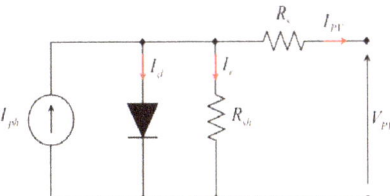

Figure 2. The equivalent circuit of a PV cell.

The model in Figure 2 can be mathematically described by the following equation:

$$I_{PV} = I_{ph} - I_d - I_r = I_{ph} - I_o \left(e^{\frac{V_{PV}+R_s I_{PV}}{nV_t}} - 1 \right) - \frac{V_{PV}+R_s I_{PV}}{R_{sh}} \quad (1)$$

where V_t is the thermal voltage, given by the following:

$$V_t = \frac{kT}{q} \quad (2)$$

k is the Boltzmann constant (1.38×10^{-23} J/K), T is the absolute temperature (k), and q is the electronic charge (1.6×10^{-19} C).

The PV array output current and voltage can be computed according to the parallel- and series-connected modules. The PV module considered in this work is the TSM-250PA05.08 PV module, Trinasolar, China.

2.2. DC–DC Boost Converter

The step-up chopper can be applied to MPPT systems in which the output voltage needs to be greater than the input voltage. The relation between the output and input voltages (V_{out} and V_{in}, respectively) is as follows:

$$\frac{V_{out}}{V_{in}} = \frac{1}{1-D} \quad (3)$$

where D is the duty cycle; the duty cycle always ranges from zero to one.

2.3. Brushless DC Motor

The BLDC motor's mathematical model can be formed in the same way as a three-phase synchronous machine. Similarly, with the BLDC motor, the armature winding model is stated as follows [14]:

$$\begin{cases} V_a = Ri_a + L\frac{di_a}{dt} + e_a \\ V_b = Ri_b + L\frac{di_b}{dt} + e_b \\ V_c = Ri_c + L\frac{di_c}{dt} + e_c \end{cases} \quad (4)$$

2.4. Centrifugal Pump

A centrifugal pump is a mechanical device that uses centrifugal force to transfer mechanical energy into pressure in a fluid. Its efficiency is rather good, and it can pump a huge amount of water [1]. The pump's torque is proportional to the rotor's squared speed, as follows:

$$T_L = K_P \Omega_r^2 \quad (5)$$

where K_P is the proportionality constant, and it is given by the following:

$$K_p = P_{np}/\Omega_{rn}^3 \quad (6)$$

The pump's head and available mechanical power at the rotating impeller determine the pump's water flow and pressure. Affinity laws, which only require the pump ratings and actual input parameters, rotor speed and torque [1], might simplify the estimation of the pump's output characteristics.

$$\begin{cases} H' = (\Omega_r/\Omega_{rn})^2 \cdot H \\ Q' = (\Omega_r/\Omega_{rn}) \cdot Q \\ P' = (\Omega_r/\Omega_{rn})^3 \cdot P \end{cases} \quad (7)$$

where H, Q and P are the rated parameters of the pump at the rated speed, and Ω_{rn}, H', Q' and P' are the parameters of the pump at speed Ω_r, which is different to the rated speed.

3. Solar Water Pumping System Control

3.1. Maximum Power Point Tracking

The perturb and observe (P&O) method is a basic iterative approach. It perturbs the operational point of the system, causing the PV array terminal voltage to oscillate about the MPP voltage, even though the solar irradiation and the cell temperature are constant. Figure 3 depicts the P&O algorithm flowchart [15].

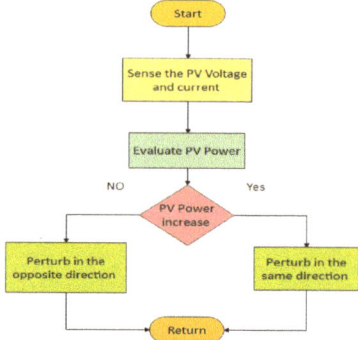

Figure 3. Flowchart of P&O algorithm.

3.2. Commutation and BLDC Drive

In the BLDC motor, Hall effect sensors are required. The signal is generated by the motor's Hall effect sensor, and must be decoded in order to determine the right phase-switching sequence [4]. Figure 4 shows the control scheme of the BLDC motor; the reference current I_{ref} is delivered by an outer PI speed controller. Then, the current is controlled using hysteresis controllers.

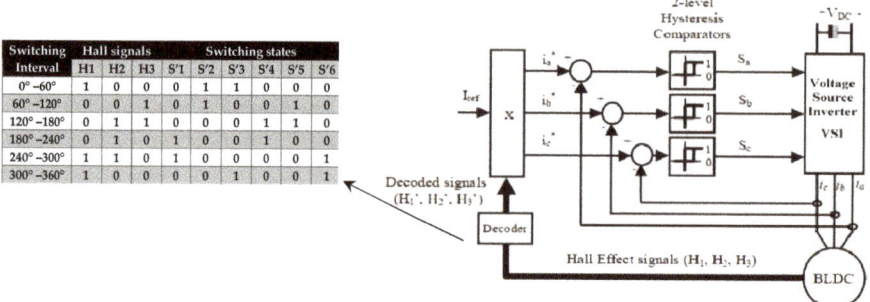

Figure 4. Structure of current control drive for BLDC motor.

4. Partial Shading Effect

Shading in a PV module reduces power, but also creates current mismatch inside a PV series, and string and voltage mismatch between parallel strings. In order to reduce the power damage to the panel, a bypass diode is connected in parallel with the PV module to provide an alternate current channel. A module's cells, on the other hand, no longer carry the same current. As a result, there are numerous maxima on the power–voltage curve. Unfortunately, most standard MPPT algorithms cannot tell the difference between local and global maxima. To investigate the performance of the SWPS under partial shade conditions, the PV modules were adjusted to varied irradiance values (400, 800, and 1000). The P–V characteristic exhibits different maxima, due to the influence of bypass diodes (Figure 5).

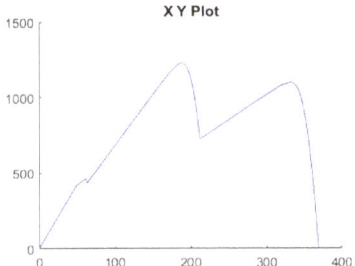

Figure 5. P–V characteristic curves under partial shading.

5. Cuckoo Search Algorithm

5.1. Cuckoo Search Methodology

Firstly, each cuckoo lays one egg at a time and dumps its egg into a randomly chosen nest. Then, the best nest, with high-quality eggs, will carry over to the next generation. The number of available hosts' nests is fixed, and the egg laid by a cuckoo is discovered by the host bird with a probability Pa, such that $0 \leq Pa \leq 1$. In this case, the host bird can either throw the egg away or abandon the nest and build a completely new nest. For simplicity, this last assumption can be approximated by the fraction, Pa, of nests, n, that are replaced by new nests [9].

5.2. Lévy Flight

Lévy flight is a random walk, where step sizes are extracted from Lévy distribution according to the power law $y = l^{-\lambda}$ [10], where l is the flight length and λ is the variance. Since $1 < \lambda < 3$, y has infinite variance. In CS, the nest searching steps of the cuckoo are characterized by Lévy flight. Figure 6 depicts an example of Lévy flight in a 2D plane.

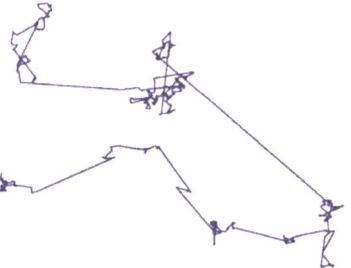

Figure 6. Lévy flight in a 2-dimensional plane.

To generate a new solution, xt + 1, for a cuckoo, Lévy flight is performed, as dictated by the following expression [10]:

$$x_i^{(t+1)} = x_i^{(t)} + \alpha \oplus Lévy(\lambda) \tag{8}$$

where:

$\oplus$: Entry wise multiplication

λ is the Levy exponent, $x_i^{(t+1)}$ is the new solution, and $x_i^{(t)}$ is the current location (samples/eggs).

$$Lévy(\lambda) \approx u = l^{-\lambda}, (1 < \lambda < 3) \tag{9}$$

Based on the constraints imposed by the optimization problem, it is important to tune the value of α to obtain the desired step size. In most cases, α is used as follows:

$$\alpha = \alpha_0 \left(x_j^{(t)} - x_i^{(t)} \right) \tag{10}$$

where α_0 is the initial step change.

5.3. MPPT for PV Using CS

To use CS for designing MPPT, appropriate variables have to be selected for the search. Firstly, the samples are used, which are the PV voltages in our case, i.e., $V_i(i = 1, 2, \ldots, n)$. The total number of samples is defined as n. Then, the step size is denoted by the fitness function J, which is the value of PV power at the MPP. Since J is dependent on the PV voltage, $J = f(V)$. Initially, the generated samples are applied to the PV modules and the power is set as the initial fitness value. The maximum power provided by its corresponding voltage is considered as the current best sample. Thereafter, Lévy flight is performed; consequently, new voltage samples are generated, as follows:

$$V_i^{(t+1)} = V_i^{(t)} + \alpha \oplus Lévy(\lambda) \tag{11}$$

where $\alpha = \alpha_0(V_{best} - V_i)$. A simplified scheme of the Lévy distribution is presented as follows:

$$S = \alpha_0(V_{best} - V_i) \oplus Lévy(\lambda) \approx K \times \left(\frac{u}{(|v|)^{\frac{1}{\beta}}} \right) (V_{best} - V_i) \tag{12}$$

where k is the Lévy multiplying coefficient. In the following equation, u and v are determined from the normal distribution curves:

$$u = N\left(0, \sigma_u^2\right), v = N\left(0, \sigma_v^2\right) \tag{13}$$

If Γ denotes the integral gamma function, then the variables σ_u and σ_v are defined as follows:

$$\sigma_u = \left(\frac{\Gamma(1+\beta) \times sin(\pi \times \beta/2)}{\Gamma\left(\frac{1+\beta}{2}\right) \times \beta \times (2)^{\left(\frac{\beta-1}{2}\right)}} \right)^{\frac{1}{\beta}}, \sigma_v = 1 \tag{14}$$

The greatest power provided by the voltage is chosen as the new best sample by comparing the power values. Aside from this best sample, the rest are destroyed at random, with a probability of Pa. This procedure mimics the behavior of the host bird finding and then destroying the cuckoo's eggs. Then, to replace the destroyed samples, new random samples are created. As a result, all the sample powers are measured again, and the current best is chosen by assessing J. The process is repeated until all of the samples have arrived at the MPP.

6. Simulation Results

The proposed SWPS is simulated using MATLAB/Simulink 2018a. A PV array with four solar modules, connected 2 × 2 in series and in parallel, is considered. In normal conditions, the PV array would be expected to produce 2500 W, with an MPPT voltage and current of 310 V and 8.5 A, respectively, at 1000 W/m² solar irradiance and 25 °C.

The simulation results of the PV side in SWPS, under shaded conditions, using P&O and CS MPPT algorithms, give the resulting waveforms shown in Figures 7 and 8, where "a–b" indicate P&O and "c–d" indicate CS.

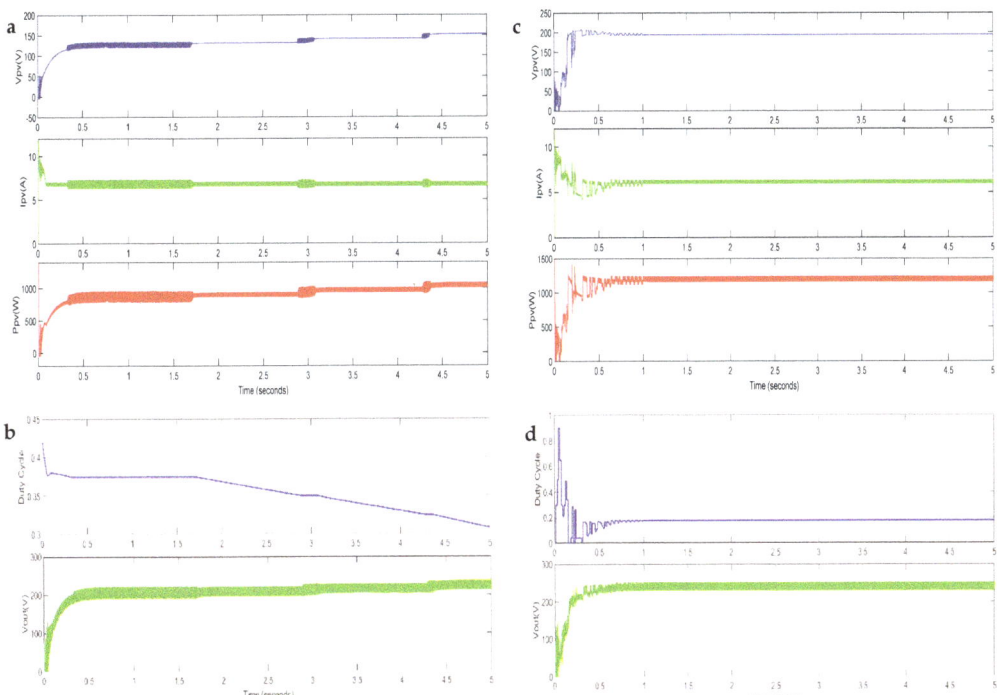

Figure 7. Dynamic performance of the PV generator under shaded conditions using P&O (**a**,**b**) and CS (**c**,**d**).

As can be observed from the results, the P&O algorithm failed to track the global MPP (Figure 7a,b); it converged to the third peak in Figure 5. The output power from the PV array is reduced. Under partial shading conditions, the output power from the PV array is reduced. On the other hand, the CS method (Figure 7c,d) captured the global peak effectively, avoiding the local maximums, under partial shading conditions, which indicates maximum extraction of the PV power. Compared to P&O, which tracked a local peak, the CS exhibits a faster convergence speed, less oscillation around the MPP under steady-state conditions, and no divergence from the MPP during varying weather conditions. Figure 8 shows the dynamic performance of the BLDC motor under shaded conditions, using P&O and cuckoo search. The BLDC motor shows better performance (i.e., torque and speed) when using the CS algorithm, since it runs on the maximum possible power, as the CS tracks the MPP of the PV array. Table 1 presents the comparison between the two MPPT algorithms, in regards to the power delivered to the pump and the rotor speed.

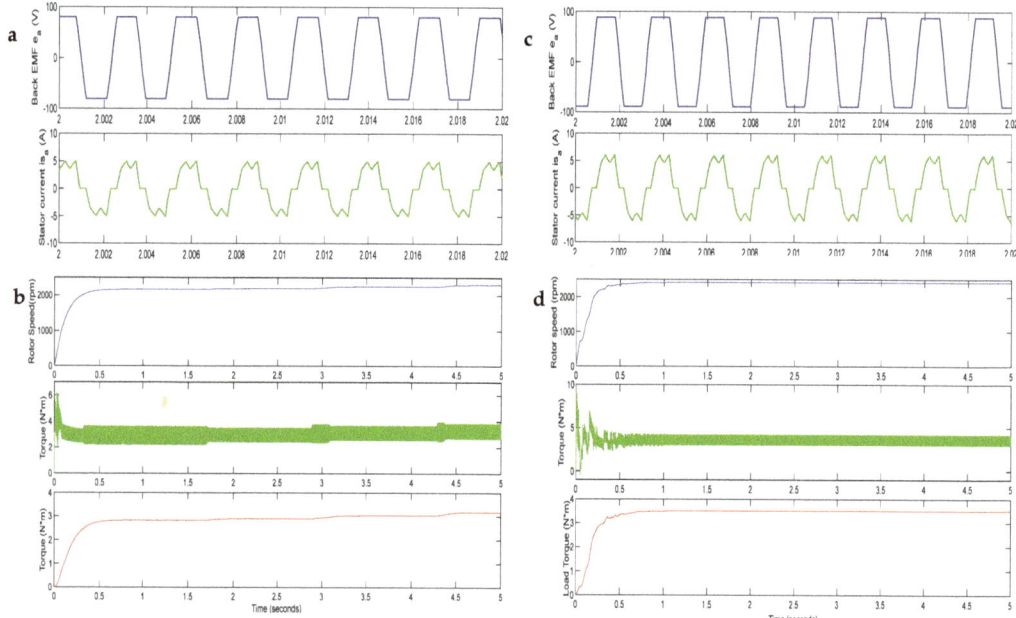

Figure 8. Dynamic performance of the BLDC motor under shaded conditions using P&O (**a**,**b**) and CS (**c**,**d**).

Table 1. The power and speed values of both MPPT algorithms.

MPPT	Power (W)	Speed (rpm)
P&O	800	2100
Cuckoo Search	1250	2500

7. Conclusions

In this work, a BLDC motor-driven water pumping system, based on PV generation, was designed. The power generated from such systems does not only depend on the climatic conditions, but also highly depends on the applied control technique. MPPT control techniques were used in order to improve the total system efficiency and extract the maximum PV energy under different operating conditions.

The proposed system was simulated and tested using P&O and cuckoo MPPT techniques in MATLAB/Simulink. The performance of the two algorithms was compared under partial shading conditions, where P&O failed to track the global MPP, while the cuckoo search did successfully. Moreover, the results show the improvement in performance of the BLDC motor under non-uniform irradiance conditions.

The parameters of the BLDC motor are as follows:

Rated torque 4.2 N·m, power 1.5 kW, speed 2889 rpm, number of poles 10, phase resistance 0.7 Ω, phase inductance 4 mH, torque constant $K_t = 0.7$ N·m/A, and moment of inertia 0.0028 kg/m^3.

The parameters of the DC–DC converter are as follows:

$C = 2.34 \times 10^{-5}$ F and $L = 0.023$ H.

Author Contributions: K.H. and M.B. were the major contributors in this work, especially and performing simulation results. A.A. handle writing the manuscript and contributed also in simulation work. A.K. have substantively revised the paper. All authors have read and agreed to the published version of the manuscript.

Institutional Review Board Statement: Not applicable.

Informed Consent Statement: Not applicable.

Data Availability Statement: Not applicable.

Conflicts of Interest: The authors declare no conflict of interest.

Nomenclature

I_{PV} is the cell/module output current (A); I_{ph} is the cell photocurrent (A); I_d is the diode current (A); I_r is the derived current by the shunt resistance (A); I_o is the reverse saturation current of the diode (A); V_{PV} is the cell/module output voltage (V); R and L are BLDC phase resistance and self-inductance; V_a, V_b and V_c are the BLDC terminal phase voltages; i_a, i_b and i_c are the BLDC input currents; e_a, e_b and e_c are the motor back EMF; i is the sample number; t is the number of iterations; β = 1.5.

References

1. Djeriou, S.; Kheldoun, A.; Mellit, A. Efficiency Improvement in Induction Motor-Driven Solar Water Pumping System Using Golden Section Search Algorithm. *Arab. J. Sci. Eng.* **2018**, *43*, 3199–3211. [CrossRef]
2. Sontake, V.C.; Kalamkar, V.R. Solar photovoltaic water pumping system—A comprehensive review. *Renew. Sustain. Energy Rev.* **2016**, *59*, 1038–1067. [CrossRef]
3. Kumar, R.; Singh, B. Single Stage Solar PV Fed Brushless DC Motor Driven Water Pump. *IEEE J. Emerg. Sel. Top. Power Electron.* **2017**, *5*, 1377–1385. [CrossRef]
4. Kumar, R.; Singh, B. BLDC Motor-Driven Solar PV Array-Fed Water Pumping System Employing Zeta Converter. *IEEE Trans. Ind. Appl.* **2016**, *52*, 2315–2322. [CrossRef]
5. Talbi, B.; Krim, F.; Rekioua, T.; Laib, A.; Feroura, H. Design and hardware validation of modified P&O algorithm by fuzzy logic approach based on model predictive control for MPPT of PV systems. *J. Renew. Sustain. Energy* **2017**, *9*, 043503. [CrossRef]
6. Mohapatra, A.; Nayak, B.; Das, P.; Mohanty, K.B. A review on MPPT techniques of PV system under partial shading condition. *Renew. Sustain. Energy Rev.* **2017**, *80*, 854–867. [CrossRef]
7. Alshareef, M.; Lin, Z.; Ma, M.; Cao, W. Accelerated particle swarm optimization for photovoltaic maximum power point tracking under partial shading conditions. *Energies* **2019**, *12*, 623. [CrossRef]
8. Yang, X. Suash Deb Cuckoo Search via Lévy flights. In Proceedings of the 2009 World Congress on Nature & Biologically Inspired Computing (NaBIC), Coimbatore, India, 9–11 December 2009; pp. 210–214.
9. Mohamad, A.B.; Zain, A.M.; Nazira Bazin, N.E. Cuckoo Search Algorithm for Optimization Problems—A Literature Review and its Applications. *Appl. Artif. Intell.* **2014**, *28*, 419–448. [CrossRef]
10. Ahmed, J.; Salam, Z. A Maximum Power Point Tracking (MPPT) for PV system using Cuckoo Search with partial shading capability. *Appl. Energy* **2014**, *119*, 118–130. [CrossRef]
11. Eltamaly, A.M. An improved cuckoo search algorithm for maximum power point tracking of photovoltaic systems under partial shading conditions. *Energies* **2021**, *14*, 953. [CrossRef]
12. Malla, S.G.; Bhende, C.N.; Mishra, S. Photovoltaic based water pumping system. In Proceedings of the 2011 International Conference on Energy, Automation and Signal, Bhubaneswar, India, 28–30 December 2011; pp. 1–4.
13. Xiao, W.; Dunford, W.G.; Capel, A. A novel modeling method for photovoltaic cells. In Proceedings of the 2004 IEEE 35th Annual Power Electronics Specialists Conference (IEEE Cat. No.04CH37551), Aachen, Germany, 20–25 June 2004; Volume 3, pp. 1950–1956.
14. Sashidhar, S.; Guru Prasad Reddy, V.; Fernandes, B.G. A Single-Stage Sensorless Control of a PV-Based Bore-Well Submersible BLDC Motor. *IEEE J. Emerg. Sel. Top. Power Electron.* **2019**, *7*, 1173–1180. [CrossRef]
15. Kamran, M.; Mudassar, M.; Fazal, M.R.; Asghar, M.U.; Bilal, M.; Asghar, R. Implementation of improved Perturb & Observe MPPT technique with confined search space for standalone photovoltaic system. *J. King Saud Univ. Eng. Sci.* **2020**, *32*, 432–441. [CrossRef]

Proceeding Paper

Online Adaptation of a Compensatory Neuro-Fuzzy Controller Parameters Using the Extended Kalman Filter: Application on an Inverted Pendulum [†]

Hocine Khati *, Hand Talem, Mohand Achour Touat, Rabah Mellah and Said Guermah

Design and Drive of Production Systems Laboratory, Department of Automation, Faculty of Electrical and Computing Engineering, University Mouloud Mammeri of Tizi-Ouzou, Tizi-Ouzou 15000, Algeria; talemhand2015@gmail.com (H.T.); mohand_touat@yahoo.fr (M.A.T.); mellah.rab@gmail.com (R.M.); saidguermah@yahoo.fr (S.G.)
* Correspondence: hoc.khati@gmail.com or hocine_khati@yahoo.fr; Tel.: +213 556-83-24-73
† Presented at the 1st International Conference on Computational Engineering and Intelligent Systems, Online, 10–12 December 2021.

Abstract: This paper presents the implementation of a Compensatory Adaptive Neuro-Fuzzy Inference System (CANFIS) controller to control an inverted pendulum. This controller is developed in order to readjust the parameters relating to the membership functions and the fuzzy rules used as well as to optimize the dynamics of the latter, using a learning algorithm based on the extended Kalman filter. The CANFIS controller is developed on the Simulink environment of the MATLAB software and is implemented on a Raspberry Pi 3 board, with a view to analyzing its real behavior, and testing its speed as well as its robustness through the use of the "Processor-In-the-Loop" (PIL) technique. The results obtained through PIL tests showed the effectiveness of the neuro-fuzzy controller equipped with a compensator.

Keywords: CANFIS; extended Kalman filter; Raspberry Pi 3

1. Introduction

The control of non-linear systems is always a rather complex task in the field of automation, because several control techniques require a perfect knowledge of the behavior of the system in order to be able to achieve good performance. The description of a system equipped with its actuators and sensors and the various physical phenomena that appear during operation show the high complexity due to numerous non-linearities as well as the difficulty in perfectly modeling the dynamics of the mechanical sensors-actuators-system. Controlling the system for performing tasks requiring good performance becomes difficult, as knowledge of the system is incomplete and imperfect.

Adaptive control using artificial intelligence techniques has been the subject of several research works in the control of nonlinear systems [1–4]. The combination of fuzzy logic with neural networks has been recognized as a promising solution to compensate for the non-structural uncertainties of nonlinear systems. Therefore, combining fuzzy logic with neural networks in the form of a single network structure allows building more efficient neuro-fuzzy controllers, and this by taking advantage of the inference capacity of fuzzy reasoning and computational parallelism of neural networks. Among the most efficient adaptive neuro-fuzzy systems, we cite the CANFIS (Compensatory Adaptive Neuro-Fuzzy Inference System) structure, which consists of using a fuzzy compensator which compensates for the bad choice of membership functions, and which uses techniques which allow us to adjust the dynamics of fuzzy rules, so as to adapt to the environment [5]. However, the use of such an adaptive structure requires a high computation time and its implementation in practice then requires powerful control boards in order to minimize the computational time of the algorithm in order to converge on the desired performance.

Due to the computational complexity of these algorithms, several processes are generally necessary so that the controllers are suitable for implementations, because on the one hand, many development boards do not support the double-precision floating-point data type on the MATLAB-Simulink software, and on the other hand, designs based on this floating-point data type consume a significant number of hardware resources compared to designs based on the fixed-point data type [6]. However, in this design methodology, the adaptation of the controller is limited by the fixed point encoding. Several research works have been carried out in this area [7–10]. In this article, we will use MATLAB-Simulink software to implement the CANFIS controller on a Raspberry Pi 3 board to control an inverted pendulum. These control boards are known by their powerful processors, namely the ARM Cortex processors, and support both fixed and floating point data types. The MATLAB software therefore allows us to considerably reduce the design time of the algorithm, and to implement it on the Raspberry board. The use of the Processor-In-the-Loop (PIL) technique makes it possible to test the behavior of the CANFIS controller on the hardware, while the rest of the control loop is on the Simulink.

This document is organized as follows: in the second part, we present the structure of the fuzzy neuro network with a fuzzy compensator as well as the mathematical formalism, then, we study the learning algorithm. In the third part, we present the control scheme based on the Raspberry Pi 3 board, suitable for dynamic control of the inverted pendulum using the CANFIS controller. In the fourth part, we present the results of the PIL tests obtained by applying this synthesized strategy to the command in tracking of a reference trajectory of the inverted pendulum. Finally, we end our work with a general conclusion and some perspectives.

2. Description of the Adaptive Neuro-Fuzzy Network with a Compensator

CANFIS is a fuzzy inference system based on a multi-layered adaptive network, where the learning algorithm not only adjusts the membership functions, but also optimizes the dynamics of fuzzy reasoning by adjusting the degree of compensation. In this section, we develop an ANFIS controller equipped with a fuzzy compensator, where the adaptation of its parameters is ensured by a learning algorithm based on the extended Kalman filter. To simplify understanding and without loss of generality, we consider a system with two inputs x_1, x_2 and one output u (Figure 1), modeled by a fuzzy system of the Takagi–Sugeno type, composed of the following four fuzzy rules:

$$\text{Rule 1}: \text{ if } x_1 \text{ is } A_1 \text{ and } x_2 \text{ is } B_1 \text{ then } u_1 = f_1(x_1, x_2) = a_1 x_1 + b_1 x_2 + c_1 \quad (1)$$

$$\text{Rule 2}: \text{ if } x_1 \text{ is } A_1 \text{ and } x_2 \text{ is } B_2 \text{ then } u_2 = f_2(x_1, x_2) = a_2 x_1 + b_2 x_2 + c_2 \quad (2)$$

$$\text{Rule 3}: \text{ if } x_1 \text{ is } A_2 \text{ and } x_2 \text{ is } B_1 \text{ then } u_3 = f_3(x_1, x_2) = a_3 x_1 + b_3 x_2 + c_3 \quad (3)$$

$$\text{Rule 4}: \text{ if } x_1 \text{ is } A_2 \text{ and } x_2 \text{ is } B_2 \text{ then } u_4 = f_4(x_1, x_2) = a_4 x_1 + b_4 x_2 + c_4 \quad (4)$$

The degree of activation of a rule is defined by w_i.

We consider the pessimistic and optimistic operations, given respectively as follows:

$$z_i = w_i \quad (5)$$

$$m_i = (w_i)^{\frac{1}{2}}. \quad (6)$$

The fuzzy compensator expressed by this relation:

$$C_i(z_i, m_i, \gamma_i) = (z_i)^{1-\gamma_i}(m_i)^{\gamma_i}, \quad (7)$$

where $\gamma_i \in [0, 1]$ is the compensatory degree. Therefore, the net value of the fuzzy neural-network equipped with a fuzzy compensator is given as follows:

$$u = \frac{\sum_{i=1}^{4}(a_i e + b_i \Delta e + c_i)(w_i)^{\alpha_i}}{\sum_{i=1}^{4}(w_i)^{\alpha_i}} \tag{8}$$

$$\alpha_i = 1 - \frac{\gamma_i}{2} \tag{9}$$

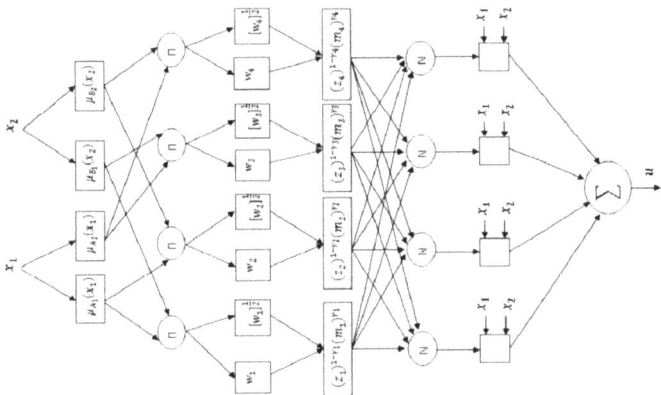

Figure 1. Structure of the Adaptive Neuro-Fuzzy Inference System Controller with compensator.

Consider that x_1 and x_2 are the position error e and its derivative Δe. We associate two fuzzy sets for each of the inputs, namely N (Negative) and P(Positive). μ_N et μ_P represent the appropriate membership degrees of the variables x_i with respect to fuzzy subsets A_i and B_i, defined by the following member functions:

$$\mu_N(x_1) = \exp\left(-\left(\frac{x_1 - \rho_1}{\sigma_1}\right)^2\right) \tag{10}$$

$$\mu_P(x_1) = \exp\left(-\left(\frac{x_1 - \rho_2}{\sigma_2}\right)^2\right) \tag{11}$$

$$\mu_N(x_2) = \exp\left(-\left(\frac{x_2 - \beta_1}{\delta_1}\right)^2\right) \tag{12}$$

$$\mu_P(x_2) = \exp\left(-\left(\frac{x_2 - \beta_2}{\delta_2}\right)^2\right), \tag{13}$$

with: (ρ_i, σ_i) and (β_i, δ_i) being the (mean, variance) of the fuzzy set of the membership functions respectively of x_1 and x_2.

Learning Algorithm

The controller is characterized by a vector of parameters Φ. Our objective is to find the values of the vector $\hat{\Phi}$ by minimizing the following criterion [11]:

$$J(k) = \frac{1}{2}(y_d(k) - y(k))^2 = \frac{1}{2}(e(k))^2, \tag{14}$$

where: $y(k)$ is the real output of the system and $y_d(k)$ is its desired output. The extended Kalman filter approach consists of linearizing the output regulator u_d at each step k around the estimated vector $\Phi_d(k)$. This is equivalent to writing:

$$u_d(k) = u(k) + \Psi(k)(\Phi_d(k) - \Phi(k)). \tag{15}$$

With:

$$\Psi(k) = \frac{\partial u(k)}{\partial \Phi(k)} = \left[\frac{\partial u(k)}{\partial \Phi_1(k)}, \ldots, \frac{\partial u(k)}{\partial \Phi_n(k)}\right], \tag{16}$$

where n is the dimension of the vector Ψ^T. Consequently, the parameters are adjusted according to the following relation [12]:

$$\Phi(k+1) = \Phi(k) + K'(k)\Psi^T(k)e_u \tag{17}$$

$$K'(k) = \frac{P(k)}{\Psi(k)P(k)\Psi^T(k) + B(k)} \tag{18}$$

$$P(k+1) = P(k) - K(k)\Psi(k)P(k) \tag{19}$$

$$K(k) = K'(k)\Psi^T(k), \tag{20}$$

where $\Psi(k)$ is the Jacobian matrix (the observation matrix of the system), $P(k)$ is the estimation matrix of the error covariance and $B(k)$ is the measurement covariance matrix. In order to approximate the variation e_u, we linearize the inverse model of the system around $y(k)$ according to the following relation:

$$u = \frac{\partial u(k)}{\partial y(k)}(y - y(k)) + u(k), \tag{21}$$

where $y(k)$ is the system output and $u(k)$ its input. For this linearized model, the value $u_d(k)$ can be expressed as follows:

$$u_d(k) = \frac{\partial u(k)}{\partial y(k)}(y_d(k) - y(k)) + u(k). \tag{22}$$

Therefore, we have:

$$u_d(k) - u(k) = \frac{\partial u(k)}{\partial y(k)}(y_d(k) - y(k)). \tag{23}$$

Then:

$$e_u(k) = \frac{\partial u(k)}{\partial y(k)}e(k). \tag{24}$$

We also have: $\partial e(k) = \partial y_d(k) - \partial y(k)$. We assume that $y_d(k)$ is constant in the neighborhood of $y(k)$. Then:

$$\partial e(k) = -\partial y(k). \tag{25}$$

Therefore:

$$e_u(k) = \frac{-\partial(k)}{\partial e(k)}e(k). \tag{26}$$

The relation (17) can be written as follows:

$$\Phi(k+1) = \Phi(k)K'(k)\Psi^T(k)\frac{\partial u(k)}{\partial e(k)}e(k). \tag{27}$$

In order to eliminate the constraint $\gamma_i \in [\;0\;\;1\;]$ defined in Equation (7), we define:

$$\gamma_i = \frac{p_i^2}{p_i^2 + q_i^2}. \tag{28}$$

Consequently, the parameters vector to be readjusted is given by:

$$\Phi_i^T(k) = [a_1, b_1, c_1, p_1, q_1, \ldots, a_4, b_4, c_4, p_4, q_4] \tag{29}$$

$$\Psi(k) = \left[\frac{\partial u(k)}{\partial a_1}, \frac{\partial u(k)}{\partial b_1}, \frac{\partial u(k)}{\partial c_1}, \frac{\partial u(k)}{\partial p_1}, \frac{\partial u(k)}{\partial q_1}, \ldots, \frac{\partial u(k)}{\partial a_4}, \frac{\partial u(k)}{\partial b_4}, \frac{\partial u(k)}{\partial c_4}, \frac{\partial u(k)}{\partial p_4}, \frac{\partial u(k)}{\partial q_4}\right] \tag{30}$$

With:

$$\frac{\partial u}{\partial a_i} = \frac{e[w_i]^{\alpha_i}}{\sum_{i=1}^{4}[w_i]^{\alpha_i}} \tag{31}$$

$$\frac{\partial u}{\partial b_i} = \frac{\Delta e[w_i]^{\alpha_i}}{\sum_{i=1}^{4}[w_i]^{\alpha_i}} \tag{32}$$

$$\frac{\partial u}{\partial c_i} = \frac{[w_i]^{\alpha_i}}{\sum_{i=1}^{4}[w_i]^{\alpha_i}} \tag{33}$$

$$\frac{\partial u}{\partial \gamma_i} = -\frac{1}{2}\left[\sum_{i=1}^{4} a_i e + b_i \Delta e + c_i\right] \frac{z_i \ln(w_i)}{\sum_{i=1}^{4} z_i} \tag{34}$$

$$\frac{\partial u}{\partial p_i} = -\left[\frac{2p_i(q_i)^2}{(p_i)^2 + (q_i)^2}\right] \frac{\partial u}{\partial \gamma_i} \tag{35}$$

$$\frac{\partial u}{\partial q_i} = \left[\frac{2q_i(p_i)^2}{(p_i)^2 + (q_i)^2}\right] \frac{\partial u}{\partial \gamma_i}. \tag{36}$$

We have:

$$u = \frac{\sum_{i=1}^{4}(a_i e + b_i \Delta e + c_i)(w_i)^{\alpha_i}}{\sum_{i=1}^{4}(w_i)^{\alpha_i}} = \frac{h}{g}. \tag{37}$$

Then:

$$\frac{\partial u}{\partial e} = \frac{\frac{\partial h}{\partial e} \cdot g - \frac{\partial g}{\partial e} \cdot h}{g^2}. \tag{38}$$

With:

$$\frac{\partial h}{\partial e} = \sum_{i=1}^{4}\left([a - 2(e - \rho_j)(a_i e + b_i \Delta e + c_i)]w_i^{\alpha_i}\right) \tag{39}$$

$$\frac{\partial g}{\partial e} = -2\sum_{i=1}^{4}\left((e - \rho_j)w_i^{\alpha_i}\right), \tag{40}$$

where j is the integer part of $(i-1)/2$.

3. Implementation of the CANFIS Controller Equipped with a Compensator on the Raspberry Pi 3 Board: Application on the Inverted Pendulum

In this section, we use the "Processor-In-the-Loop" technique in MATLAB-Simulink, which allows us to test the behavior of the CANFIS controller on the Raspberry Pi 3 board [13]. In this mode of execution, the CANFIS controller runs in the hardware while the rest of the closed loop runs on the Simulink environment. In order to test the performances of the controller, we considered the stabilization problem of an inverted pendulum on a cart. The dynamic equations of the nonlinear system are given by [14]:

$$\dot{x}_1 = x_2 \tag{41}$$

$$\dot{x}_2 = \frac{g \sin x_1 - \cos x_1 (\frac{ml}{m_c+m} x_2^2 \sin x_1 - \frac{1}{m_c+m} \tau(t))}{\frac{4}{3}l - \frac{ml}{m_c+m} \cos^2 x_1}, \tag{42}$$

where x_1 is the position of the vertical rod (in radian), x_2 is the angular velocity and $\tau(t)$ the torque applied to the rod. Its parameters are given in the Table 1.

Table 1. Inverted pendulum parameters.

g	Gravity constant	9.8 m/s^2
m_c	Carriage mass	1 kg
m	Pendulum mass	0.1 kg
l	Rod length	0.5 m

The implementation of the CANFIS controller was done with a frequency of 10 KHz. The execution diagram of the regulation chain (CANIFIS controller, System and disturbance) in PIL mode under the MATLAB Simulink environment is presented in Figure 2.

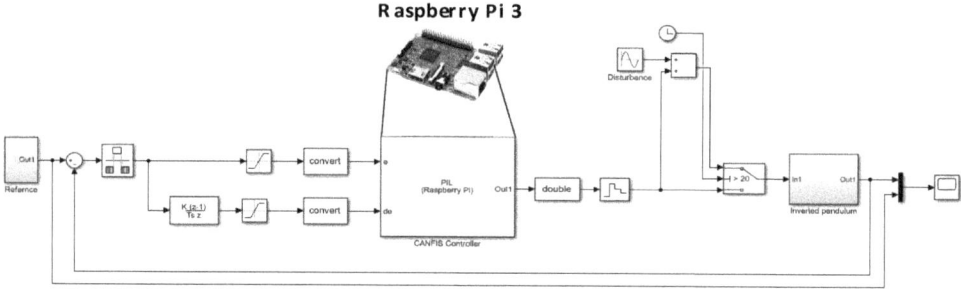

Figure 2. Execution diagram in PIL mode under Simulink.

4. Results of the PIL Tests

In this section, we present the simulation results of the PIL mode. In order to test the robustness of the two proposed controllers, we added a disturbance on the input of the system at the instant $t = 20$ s, given as follows:

$$D(t) = 150 \sin(t). \tag{43}$$

Figure 3a,b, Figure 4a,b and Figure 5a,b represent the results of the position tracking, the position tracking errors as well as the control signals delivered by the CANFIS controller. From these figures, we can see that the proposed controller has good performance (tracking, response time and robustness) with a low precision error, in both test cases (with and without disturbances). This is due to the use of a compensator which compensates for errors in the choice of membership functions, even readjusting the dynamics of fuzzy rules, using a learning algorithm based on the extended Kalman filter. The implementation of the proposed controller allowed us to obtain good performances thanks to the sampling frequency of the Raspberry Pi 3 board.

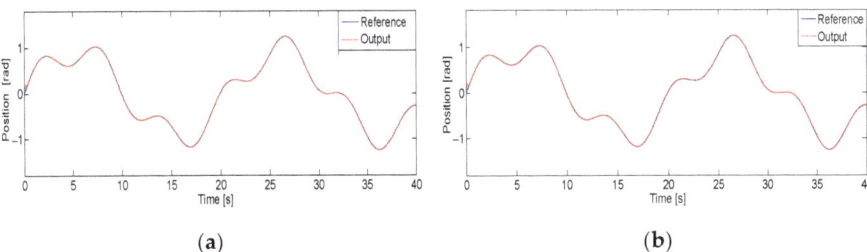

Figure 3. Position tracking: (**a**) Without disturbances; (**b**) With disturbances.

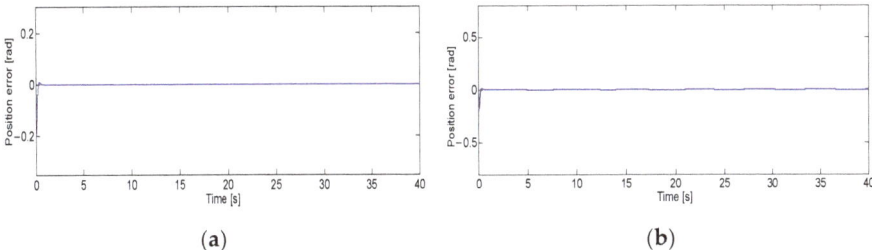

Figure 4. Position error: (**a**) Without disturbances; (**b**) With disturbances.

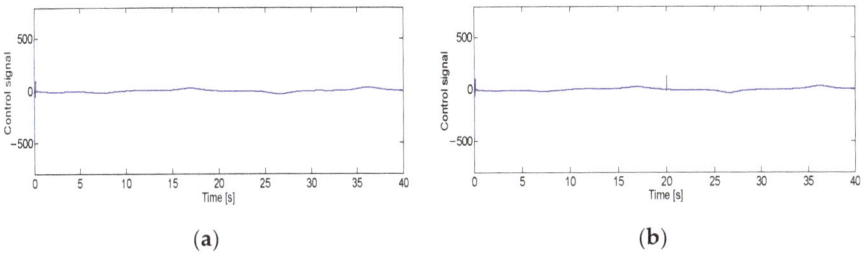

Figure 5. Control signal: (**a**) Without disturbances; (**b**) With disturbances.

5. Conclusions

In this article, we have proposed the implementation on a Raspberry Pi 3 board of a neuro-fuzzy controller CANFIS, in order to control an inverted pendulum. The CANFIS controller presents good results because it uses a learning algorithm based on the extended Kalman filter, which converges very quickly, and which readjusts the membership functions and optimizes at the same time the dynamics of fuzzy reasoning by adjusting the degree of compensation. The development and implementation of the controller was done through MATLAB's Simulink environment, which simplified the study and implementation of the code on the Raspberry Pi 3 board.

In conclusion, we have tried through this article to show the efficiency of the CANFIS controller on real hardware (Raspberry Pi 3) in the control of non-linear systems. The implementation of such a controller using the PIL technique has demonstrated its speed and robustness to disturbance rejection.

Author Contributions: Conceptualization, H.K. and H.T.; methodology, H.K., H.T. and R.M.; software, H.K. and H.T.; validation, H.K., H.T. and R.M.; formal analysis, H.K., H.T., M.A.T. and R.M.; investigation, M.A.T. and R.M.; resources, M.A.T.; data curation, H.K. and H.T.; writing—original draft preparation, H.K., H.T., R.M. and S.G.; writing—review and editing, H.K., H.T. and S.G.;

visualization, H.K. and H.T.; supervision, H.K. and H.T.; project administration, H.K.; funding acquisition, H.K., H.T., M.A.T. and R.M. All authors have read and agreed to the published version of the manuscript.

Funding: This research received no external funding.

Institutional Review Board Statement: No Institutional Review Board.

Informed Consent Statement: Patient consent was waived.

Data Availability Statement: Study did not report any data.

Conflicts of Interest: The authors declare no conflict of interest.

References

1. Gil, P.; Oliveira, T.; Palma, L. Adaptive neuro–fuzzy control for discrete-time nonaffine nonlinear system. *IEEE Trans. Fuzzy Syst.* **2019**, *27*, 1602–1615. [CrossRef]
2. Sarhadi, P.; Rezaie, B.; Rahmani, Z. Adaptive predictive control based on adaptive neuro fuzzy inference system for a class of nonlinear industrial processes. *J. Taiwan Inst. Chem. Eng.* **2016**, *61*, 132–137. [CrossRef]
3. Song, S.; Zhang, B.; Song, X.; Zhang, Z. Adaptive neuro fuzzy backstepping dynamic surface control for uncertain fractional-order nonlinear systems. *Neurocomputing* **2019**, *360*, 172–184. [CrossRef]
4. Song, S.; Park, J.H.; Zhang, B.; Song, X.; Zhang, Z. Adaptive command filtered neuro-fuzzy control design for fractional-order nonlinear systems with unknown control directions and input quantization. *IEEE Trans. Syst. Man Cybern. Syst.* **2020**, *51*, 7238–7249. [CrossRef]
5. Mellah, R.; Khati, H.; Talem, H.; Guermah, S. Compensatory of adaptive neural fuzzy inference system. In *Fuzzy Systems*; IntechOpen: London, UK, 2021.
6. Finnerty, A.; Ratigner, H. *Reduce Power and Cost by Converting from Floating Point to Fixed Point*; Xilinx All Programmable, v. 1.0; Xilinx, Inc.: San Jose, CA, USA, 2017; pp. 1–14.
7. Karakuzu, C.; Karakaya, F.; Çavuşlu, M.A. FPGA implementation of neuro-fuzzy system with improved PSO learning. *Neural Netw.* **2016**, *79*, 128–140. [CrossRef] [PubMed]
8. Khati, H.; Mellah, R.; Talem, H. Neuro-fuzzy control of a position-position Teleoperation system using FPGA. In Proceedings of the 24th International Conference on Methods and Models in Automation and Robotics, Miedzyzdroje, Poland, 26–29 August 2019; pp. 64–69.
9. Khati, H.; Talem, H.; Mellah, R.; Bilek, A. Neuro-fuzzy control of bilateral teleoperation system using FPGA. *Iran. J. Fuzzy Syst.* **2019**, *16*, 17–32.
10. Dorzhigulov, A.; Bissengaliuly, B.; Spencer, B.F.; Kim, J. ANFIS based quadrotor drone altitude control implementation on Raspberry Pi platform. *Civ. Environ. Eng.* **2018**, *95*, 335–345. [CrossRef]
11. Mellah, R.; Guermah, S.; Toumi, R. Adaptive control of bilateral teleoperation system with compensatory neural-fuzzy controllers. *Int. J. Control Autom. Syst.* **2017**, *15*, 1–11. [CrossRef]
12. Hayki, S. *Kalman Filtering and Neural Networks*; John Wiley and Sons Inc.: Hoboken, NJ, USA, 2001.
13. Simulink Support Package for Raspberry Pi Hardware. *User's Guide*; MathWorks, MATLAB and SIMULINK, r2021a; The MathWorks Inc.: Natikc, MA, USA, 2021.
14. Yoo, B.; Ham, W. Adaptive fuzzy sliding mode control of nonlinear system. *IEEE Trans. Fuzzy Syst.* **1998**, *6*, 315–321.

Proceeding Paper

Backstepping Control of Drone [†]

Ali Saibi [1], Razika Boushaki [2] and Hadjira Belaidi [1,*]

1. Signals and Systems Laboratory, Institute of Electrical and Electronic Engineering, University M'hamed Bougara of Boumerdes, Boumerdes 35000, Algeria; a.saibi@univ-boumerdes.dz
2. Laboratoire d'Automatique Appliquée, Institute of Electrical and Electronic Engineering, University M'hamed Bougara of Boumerdes, Boumerdes 35000, Algeria; r.boushaki@univ-boumerdes.dz
* Correspondence: ha.belaidi@univ-boumerdes.dz or hadjira983@yahoo.fr
† Presented at the 1st International Conference on Computational Engineering and Intelligent Systems, Online, 10–12 December 2021.

Abstract: This work derives the models which can be used to design and implement control laws for six degrees-of-freedom (DOF) quadrotor stability. The first part of this paper deals with the presentation of the background of quadrotor modeling; the second part describes the direct control of the drone using the backstepping control principal. This principal is based on the division of the system into several sub-systems in a cascade, which makes the control laws generated on each subsystem, in a decreasing manner, until a global control law for the whole system is generated. The simulation results for the sm controller are generated on the MATLAB/Simulink platform; the results show a good performance in both the transient and steady-state operations.

Keywords: quadrotor; dynamic model; backstepping

Citation: Saibi, A.; Boushaki, R.; Belaidi, H. Backstepping Control of Drone. *Eng. Proc.* **2022**, *14*, 4. https://doi.org/10.3390/engproc2022014004

Academic Editors: Abdelmadjid Recioui, Hamid Bentarzi and Fatma Zohra Dekhandji

Published: 24 January 2022

Publisher's Note: MDPI stays neutral with regard to jurisdictional claims in published maps and institutional affiliations.

Copyright: © 2022 by the authors. Licensee MDPI, Basel, Switzerland. This article is an open access article distributed under the terms and conditions of the Creative Commons Attribution (CC BY) license (https://creativecommons.org/licenses/by/4.0/).

1. Introduction

Drones are used as a means of monitoring and following important events such as forest fires and political demonstrations; they can also be used to rescue people in earthquakes in the civilian field. Additionally, they can be used as tools for supervision and fault diagnostic in smart grid systems. Drones can also act as aerial base stations (BSs) to deliver communication services (both uplink and downlink) for the subscribers on the ground [1]. In the military field, drones reduce human losses and material; they are able to closely monitor the enemy and reveal their location without exposing individuals to danger, and can direct precise strikes, like helicopters and aircrafts.

Many control approaches were developed for unmanned aerial vehicles (UAVS) in the literature. Hence, a detailed drone description model is described in [2–4]. The sliding mode control strategy based on backstepping control is widely used as it can produce high performances and a faster response for drone systems in general [5–9] and in indoor micro-quadrotors in particular [10]. Modeling- and backstepping-based nonlinear control for a six-DOF quadrotor helicopter is proposed by [11], in addition to the proposition of an adaptive sliding mode control for a quadrotor helicopter in [12].

Quadrotor mathematical modeling is very complicated [13]. It presents non-linearity due to having six degrees of freedom (translational and rotational motion) with only four control inputs. To preserve the equilibrium or the desired attitude of the drone, a traditional PID controller is commonly used; however, it does not ensure the robustness of the quadrotor, whatever the controlling target Euler angle or angular rate is. Hence, new approaches have proposed the use of a cascade PID algorithm to provide better performance and motion stabilization [14,15]. However, the implemented system still needs to tackle the drone system's non-linearity.

Hence, to control such a system, a backstepping method is the best choice [16,17]. Backstepping control is based on the Lyapunov stability principle of dynamic systems, and it is robust to parametric variation; thus, it ensures the stability of the system and gives good performances results.

This work describes the direct control of the drone using the backstepping control principal, where the quadrotor is supposed to track the desired trajectories with an acceptable dynamic. This paper is treated in three mean parts, organized as follows: first, the mathematical model of the quadrotor is developed; in the second step, the algorithm of backstepping control is presented; in the last section, the simulation results and their interpretations are presented. Finally, the conclusion and possible future developments of the work are presented.

2. Quadrotor Dynamic Modeling

The quadrotor consists of four rotors in a cross-configuration, as shown in Figure 1. The four-rotor design allows the quadrotor to be relatively simple in design yet highly reliable and maneuverable. The dynamic equation of movement of the attitude could be deduced from the Euler equation. The quadrotor mathematical and state-space models are explained in the following subsections.

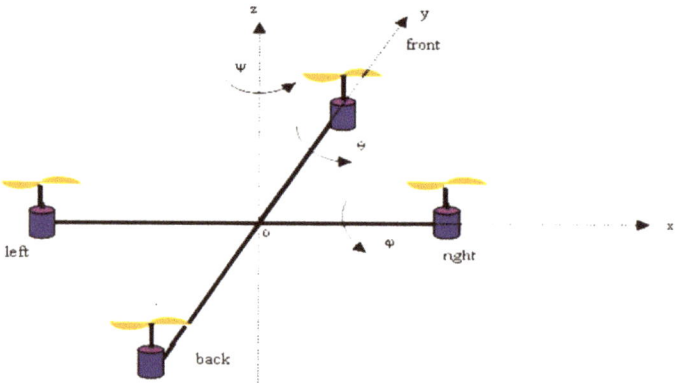

Figure 1. Quadrotor configuration.

2.1. Drone Dynamic Model

The dynamic model of the quadrotor can be defined in terms of the position vector and force expressions as given in Equations (1)–(3).

$$\begin{cases} x'' = -\frac{T}{m}[\sin(\varphi)\sin(\psi) + \cos(\varphi)\cos(\theta)\cos(\psi)] \\ y'' = -\frac{T}{m}[\cos(\varphi)\sin(\theta)\sin(\psi) - \sin(\psi)\cos(\theta)] \\ z'' = g - \frac{T}{m}[\cos(\varphi)\cos(\theta)] \end{cases} \quad (1)$$

Such that (x'', y'', z'') represents the second derivative of position vector, T is the torque, and m denotes the mass of the drone.

The moment equations can be expressed in terms of the orientation angles (φ, θ, ψ) —roll, pitch, and yaw, respectively—as given in Equations (2) and (3).

$$\begin{cases} p' = \frac{I_z - I_y}{I_x} qr - \frac{J_r}{I_x}\Omega q + \frac{1}{I_x}\tau_\varphi \\ q' = \frac{I_z - I_x}{I_y} pr - \frac{J_r}{I_y}\Omega p + \frac{1}{I_y}\tau_\theta \\ r' = \frac{I_y - I_x}{I_z} pq + \frac{1}{I_z}\tau_\psi \end{cases} \quad (2)$$

$$\begin{cases} \varphi' = p + q\sin(\varphi)tg(\theta) + r\cos(\varphi)tg(\theta) \\ \theta' = q\cos(\varphi) - r\sin(\varphi) \\ \psi' = q\frac{\sin(\varphi)}{\cos(\theta)} + r\frac{\cos(\varphi)}{\cos(\theta)} \end{cases} \quad (3)$$

τ_φ, τ_θ, and τ_ψ represent the total rolling, pitching, and yawing torques, while p, q, and r represent the angular velocities in the body frame.

2.2. State-Space Model

A state-space representation is a mathematical model of a physical system as a set of inputs, outputs, and state variables related by first-order differential equations. "State space" refers to the space whose axes are the state variables. The state of the system can be represented as a vector within that space.

In this work, the state-space model of the quadrotor in the inertial frame is developed. Thus, the dynamic model of the quadrotor in the inertial frame can be expressed by the system referred to as Equation (4):

$$\begin{cases} x'_1 = x_2 \\ x'_2 = a_1 x_4 x_6 + a_3 \Omega x_4 + b_1 U_2 \\ x'_3 = x_4 \\ x'_4 = a_4 x_2 x_6 + a_6 \Omega x_2 + b_2 U_3 \\ x'_5 = x_6 \\ x'_6 = a_7 x_2 x_4 + b_3 U_4 \\ x'_7 = x_8 \\ x'_8 = \frac{\cos(x_1)\cos(x_2)}{m} U_1 - g \\ x'_9 = x_{10} \\ x'_{10} = U_y \frac{U_1}{m} \\ x'_{11} = x_{12} \\ x'_{12} = U_x \frac{U_1}{m} \end{cases} \quad (4)$$

The parameters a_1, a_4, a_7, b_1, b_2, and b_3 can be calculated as follows:

$$a_1 = \frac{I_y - I_z}{I_x},\ a_3 = \frac{J_r}{I_x},\ a_4 = \frac{I_z - I_x}{I_y},\ a_6 = \frac{J_r}{I_y},\ a_7 = \frac{I_x - I_y}{I_z},$$
$$b_1 = \frac{d}{I_x},\ b_2 = \frac{d}{I_y},\ b_3 = \frac{d}{I_z}$$

I_x, I_y, and I_z denote the inertias of the x-, y-, and z-axis of the quadrotor, respectively; J_r denotes the z-axis inertia of the propellers' rotors.

whereas $U_x = \cos(x_1)\cos(x_3)\cos(x_5) + \sin(x_1)\sin(x_5)$
$U_y = \cos(x_1)\sin(x_3)\sin(x_5) - \sin(x_1)\cos(x_5)$

To solve the given system, a backstepping control scheme is used as detailed in the following section.

3. Backstepping Control of Drone

The principle of backstepping is to divide the system into several sub-systems in a cascade. The control laws are then made for each subsystem, in a decreasing manner, until a global control law for the whole system is generated.

3.1. Control of the Angle φ

Considering the first subsystem mentioned below:

$$\begin{cases} x'_1 = x_2 \\ x'_2 = x_4 x_6 a_1 - x_4 \Omega a_2 + b_1 U_2 \end{cases} \quad (5)$$

step1

The error ε_1 between the desired and actual roll angle is expressed as follows: $\varepsilon_1 = x_1^d - x_1$. Consider the Lyapunov function $V_1 = \frac{1}{2}\varepsilon_1^2$, where the derivate of V_1 along x_1 trajectory, V', is computed as follows:

$$V'_1 = \varepsilon_1 \varepsilon'_1 \text{ with}: \varepsilon'_1 = x_1^{d'} - x'_1 = x_1^{d'} - x_2$$

Choosing $\varepsilon'_1 = -K_1\varepsilon_1$ (knowing that: $K_1\varepsilon_1$ is positive definite function). Thus, the desired x_2^d is extracted as: $x_2^d = x_1^{d'} + K_1\varepsilon_1$

step2

Denoting ε_2 the error between desired and actual roll angle rate, so that: $\varepsilon_2 = x_2^d - x_2$. Using $V_2 = V_1 + \frac{1}{2}\varepsilon_2^2$ as a candidate Lyapunov function, we obtain:

$$V'_2 = V'_1 + \varepsilon_2\varepsilon'_2 = \varepsilon_1\varepsilon'_1 + \varepsilon_2\varepsilon'_2 = \varepsilon_2\left(x_1^{d'} - x_2\right) + \varepsilon_2(x_2^d - x'_2)$$
$$= \varepsilon_1(x_1^d - (x_2^{d'} - \varepsilon_2)) + \varepsilon_2(x_2^d - (x_4x_6a_1 - x_4\Omega a_2 + b_1U))$$
$$= \varepsilon_1(x_1^d - x_2^{d'}) + \varepsilon_1\varepsilon_2 + \varepsilon_2(x_2^{d'} - (x_4x_6a_1 - x_4\Omega a_2 + b_1U))$$
$$= -K_1\varepsilon_1^2 + \varepsilon_2(\varepsilon_1 + x_2^d - x_4x_6a_1 + x_4\Omega a_2 - b_1U)$$
$$\varepsilon_1 + x_2^{d'} - x_4x_6a_1 + x_4\Omega a_2 - b_1U = -K_2\varepsilon_2$$

where K_2 is a positive constant and $x_2^{d'} = \alpha'_1 = \left[K_1\left(x_1^d - x_1\right) + x_1^{d'}\right] = -K_1(x_2)$.

Thus, the control law is expressed by: $U_2 = \frac{1}{b}[\varepsilon_1 - K_1x_2 - x_4x_6a_1 + x_4\Omega a_2 + K_2\varepsilon_2]$

3.2. Control of the Angle θ

Considering the second subsystem mentioned below:

$$\begin{cases} x'_3 = x_4 \\ x'_4 = x_2x_6a_4 + x_2\Omega a_6 + b_2U_3 \end{cases} \quad (6)$$

step1

Considering ε_3 is the error between the desired and actual angle θ and can be found by:

$$\varepsilon_3 = x_3^d - x_3 \Rightarrow \varepsilon'_3 = x_3^{d'} - x'_3$$

using Lyapunov stability by choosing: $V(\varepsilon_3) = \frac{1}{2}\varepsilon_3^2$. Therefore, if V' is negative, then the system trajectory is ensured to verify this condition:

$$v'(\varepsilon) = \varepsilon_3\varepsilon'_3 = \varepsilon_3(x_3^{d'} - x_4) < 0, \text{ then}: x_3^{d'} - x_4 = -K_3\varepsilon_3 \Rightarrow x_4^d = x_3^{d'} + K_3\varepsilon_3$$

step2

The error $\varepsilon_4 = x_4^d - x_4 \Rightarrow x_4 = x_4^d - \varepsilon_4 \Rightarrow \varepsilon'_4 = x_4^{d'} - x'_4$

$$V_4 = V_3 + \frac{1}{2}\varepsilon_4^2 \Rightarrow V'_4 = \varepsilon_3\varepsilon'_3 + \varepsilon_4\varepsilon'_4$$
$$\varepsilon'_3 = x_3^{d'} - x_4^d + \varepsilon_4 \Rightarrow \varepsilon_3\varepsilon'_3 = \varepsilon_3(x_3^{d'} - x_4^d + \varepsilon_4) + \varepsilon_4\left(\varepsilon'_4\right)$$
$$\varepsilon_3\varepsilon'_3 = \varepsilon_3\left(x_3^{d'} - x_4^d\right) + \varepsilon_3\varepsilon_4 + \varepsilon_4\left(\varepsilon'_4\right) = \varepsilon_4(\varepsilon_3 + x_4^{d'} - (a_3x_2x_6 + a_4\Omega x_2 + b_2U_3))$$
$$\varepsilon_3 + x_4^{d'} - a_3x_2x_6 - a_4\Omega x_2 - b_2U_3 = -K_4\varepsilon_4$$
$$b_2U_3 = \varepsilon_3 + x_4^{d'} - a_3x_2x_6 - a_4\Omega x_2 + K_4\varepsilon_4$$
$$U_3 = \frac{1}{b_2}[\varepsilon_3 - a_3x_2x_6 - a_4\Omega x_2 + K_4\varepsilon_4 - K_3x_4]$$

3.3. Control of the Angle ψ

Now, consider the third subsystem mentioned below:

$$\begin{cases} x'_5 = x_6 \\ x'_6 = a_7x_2x_4 + b_3U_4 \end{cases} \quad (7)$$

step1

Let us name ε_5 the error between the desired and actual angle ψ. Thus:

$$\varepsilon_5 = x_5^d - x_5 \Rightarrow \varepsilon'_5 = x_5^{d'} - x'_5$$

With Lyapunov function being $V(\varepsilon_5) = \frac{1}{2}\varepsilon_5^2$, such that $v'(\varepsilon) = \varepsilon_5\varepsilon'_5 = \varepsilon_5(x_5^{d'} - x_5) < 0$

Thus, $x_5^{d'} - x_5' = -K_5\varepsilon_5 \Rightarrow x_6^d = x_5^{d'} + K_5\varepsilon_5$
The error $\varepsilon_6 = x_6^d - x_6 \Rightarrow x_6 = x_6^d - \varepsilon_6 \Rightarrow \varepsilon_6' = x_6^{d'} - x_6'$

$$V_6 = V_5 + \tfrac{1}{2}\varepsilon_6^2 \Rightarrow V_6' = \varepsilon_5\varepsilon_5' + \varepsilon_6\varepsilon_6'$$
$$\varepsilon_5' = x_5^{d'} - x_6^d + \varepsilon_6 \Rightarrow V_6' = \varepsilon_5(x_5^{d'} - x_6^d + \varepsilon_6) + \varepsilon_6(\varepsilon_6')$$
$$= \varepsilon_5\left(x_5^{d'} - x_6^d\right) + \varepsilon_5\varepsilon_6 + \varepsilon_6(\varepsilon_6')$$

$\Rightarrow \varepsilon_5 + x_6^{d'} - a_5x_2x_4 - b_3U_4 = -K_6\varepsilon_6$
$= \varepsilon_6(\varepsilon_5 + x_6^{d'} - (a_5x_2x_4 + b_3U_4))$
$b_3U_4 = \varepsilon_5 + x_6^{d'} - a_5x_2x_4 + K_6\varepsilon_6 \Rightarrow U_4 = \tfrac{1}{b_3}[\varepsilon_5 - a_5x_2x_4 - K_6\varepsilon_6 - K_5x_6]$

3.4. Control of the Position z

Equation (8) represents the fourth subsystem:

$$\begin{cases} x_7' = x_8 \\ x_8' = \dfrac{\cos(x_1)\cos(x_2)}{m}U_1 - g \end{cases} \quad (8)$$

step1
ε_7 is the error between the desired and actual position z, such that:

$$\varepsilon_7 = x_7^d - x_7 \text{ ; thus,}$$

The Lyapunov function is $V(\varepsilon_7) = \tfrac{1}{2}\varepsilon_7^2 \Rightarrow v'(\varepsilon) = \varepsilon_7\varepsilon_7' = \varepsilon_7(x_7^{d'} - x_8) < 0$ Then,
$x_7^{d'} - x_8 = -K_7\varepsilon_7 \Rightarrow x_8^d = x_7^{d'} + K_7\varepsilon_7$
step2
The error $\varepsilon_8 = x_8^d - x_8 \Rightarrow x_8 = x_8^d - \varepsilon_8$ thus, $\varepsilon_8' = x_8^{d'} - x_8'$

$$V_8 = V_7 + \tfrac{1}{2}\varepsilon_8^2 \Rightarrow V_8' = \varepsilon_7\varepsilon_7' + \varepsilon_8\varepsilon_8'$$
$$\varepsilon_7' = x_7^{d'} - x_8^d + \varepsilon_8 \Rightarrow \varepsilon_7\varepsilon_7' = \varepsilon_7(x_7^{d'} - x_8^d + \varepsilon_8) + \varepsilon_8(\varepsilon_8')$$
$$\varepsilon_7\varepsilon_7' = \varepsilon_7\left(x_7^{d'} - x_8^d\right) + \varepsilon_7\varepsilon_8 + \varepsilon_8(\varepsilon_8') = \varepsilon_8(\varepsilon_7 + x_8^{d'} - (g - \tfrac{U_1}{m}\cos(x_1)\cos(x_3)))$$
$$\varepsilon_7 + x_8^{d'} - g + \tfrac{U_1}{m}\cos(x_1)\cos(x_3) = -K_8\varepsilon_8$$
$$\tfrac{U_1}{m}\cos(x_1)\cos(x_3) = -\varepsilon_7 - x_8^{d'} + g - K_8\varepsilon_8$$
$$U_1 = \tfrac{m}{\cos(x_1)\cos(x_3)}[-\varepsilon_7 + g - K_8\varepsilon_8 - K_7x_8]$$

3.5. Control of the Position y

Equation (9) represents the fifth subsystem:

$$\begin{cases} x_9' = x_{10} \\ x_{10}' = U_y \dfrac{U_1}{m} \end{cases} \quad (9)$$

step1
Name ε_9 the error between the desired and actual position y

$$\varepsilon_9 = x_9^d - x_9 \Rightarrow \varepsilon_9' = x_9^{d'} - x_9'$$

The Lyapunov function is $V(\varepsilon_9) = \tfrac{1}{2}\varepsilon_9^2 \Rightarrow V'(\varepsilon) = \varepsilon_9\varepsilon_9' = \varepsilon_9\left(x_9^{d'} - x_{10}\right) < 0$ Then,
$x_9^{d'} - x_{10} = -K_9\varepsilon_9 \Rightarrow x_{10}^d = x_9^{d'} + K_9\varepsilon_9$
step2
The error will be: $\varepsilon_{10} = x_{10}^d - x_{10} \Rightarrow x_{10} = x_{10}^d - \varepsilon_{10} \Rightarrow \varepsilon_{10}' = x_{10}^{d'} - x_{10}'$

$$V_{10} = V_9 + \tfrac{1}{2}\varepsilon_{10}^2 \Rightarrow V' = \varepsilon_9\varepsilon_9' + \varepsilon_{10}\varepsilon_{10}'$$
$$\varepsilon_9' = x_9^{d'} - x_{10}^d + \varepsilon_{10} \Rightarrow \varepsilon_9\varepsilon_9' = \varepsilon_9(x_9^{d'} - x_{10}^d + \varepsilon_{10}) + \varepsilon_{10}(\varepsilon_{10}')$$

$$= \varepsilon_9\left(x_9^{d'}-x_{10}^d\right)+\varepsilon_9\varepsilon_{10}+\varepsilon_{10}\left(\varepsilon_{10}'\right)=\varepsilon_{10}\left(\varepsilon_9+x_{10}^{d'}-\left(-\frac{U_1}{m}U_y\right)\right)$$
$$\varepsilon_9+x_{10}^{d'}+\frac{U_1}{m}U_y=-K_{10}\varepsilon_{10} \Rightarrow \frac{U_1}{m}U_y=-\varepsilon_9-x_{10}^{d'}-K_{10}\varepsilon_{10}$$

$$U_y=\frac{m}{U_1}[-\varepsilon_9-K_{10}\varepsilon_{10}-K_9 x_{10}]$$

3.6. Control of the Position x

The last subsystem is represented by Equation (10) below:

$$\begin{cases} x_{11}' = x_{12} \\ x_{12}' = U_x \frac{U_1}{m} \end{cases} \quad (10)$$

step1
Name ε_{11} the error between the desired and actual position x, such that

$$\varepsilon_{11}=x_{11}^d-x_{11} \Rightarrow \varepsilon_{11}'=x_{11}^{d'}-x_{11}' \quad (11)$$

The Lyapunov function is $V(\varepsilon_{11})=\frac{1}{2}\varepsilon_{11}^2 \Rightarrow v'(\varepsilon)=\varepsilon_{11}\varepsilon_{11}'=\varepsilon_{11}\left(x_{11}^{d'}-x_{12}\right)<0$
Thus, $x_{11}^{d'}-x_{12}=-K_{11}\varepsilon_{11} \Rightarrow x_{12}^d=x_{11}^{d'}+K_{11}\varepsilon_{11}$
step2
The error is defined by: $\varepsilon_{12}=x_{12}^d-x_{12} \Rightarrow x_{12}=x_{12}^d-\varepsilon_{12}$ its derivative is $\varepsilon_{12}'=x_{12}^{d'}-x_{12}'$

$$V_{12}=V_{11}+\frac{1}{2}\varepsilon_{12}^2 \Rightarrow V'=\varepsilon_{11}'+\varepsilon_{12}\varepsilon_{12}'$$
$$\varepsilon_{11}'=x_{11}^{d'}-x_{12}^d+\varepsilon_{12} \Rightarrow \varepsilon_{11}\varepsilon_{11}'=\varepsilon_{11}\left(x_{11}^{d'}-x_{12}^d+\varepsilon_{12}\right)+\varepsilon_{12}\varepsilon_{12}'$$
$$\varepsilon_{11}+x_{12}^{d'}+\frac{U_1}{m}U_x=-K_{12}\varepsilon_{12}$$
$$\frac{U_1}{m}U_x=-\varepsilon_{11}-x_{11}^{d'}-K_{12}\varepsilon_{12}$$
$$U_x=\frac{m}{U_1}[-\varepsilon_{11}-K_{12}\varepsilon_{12}-K_{11}x_{12}]$$

All the previous steps of the backstepping control, used to generate a global control law for the whole system, are summarized in the block diagram shown in Figure 2.

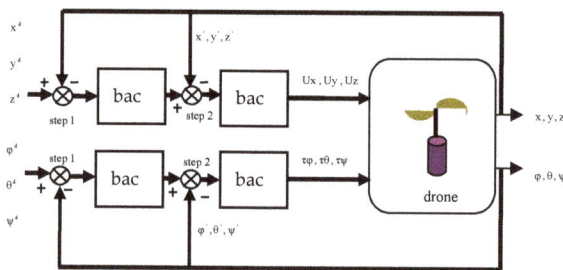

Figure 2. System block diagram.

4. Results and Discussions

In order to validate our proposed control solution, the model is simulated under Matlab Simulink software. For that purpose, the results are obtained based on the application of the real parameters summarized on Table 1 [2].

Table 1. Quadrotor parameter used in our simulation [2].

Gravitational Acceleration	g	9.8 m/s^2
Mass of quadrotor	m	0.4794 Kg
Length of wings	l	0.225 m
Rotational inertia	J_x J_y J_z	0.0086 Kg m^2 0.0086 Kg m^2 0.0172 Kg m^2
Residual inertia	J_r	3.740 × 10^{-5} Kg m^2

In this scenario, it is desired to follow a circular trajectory on the XY plane, centered in the origin. The height z increases uniformly from zero to 15 m (as shown in Figure 3b), where the drone stabilizes.

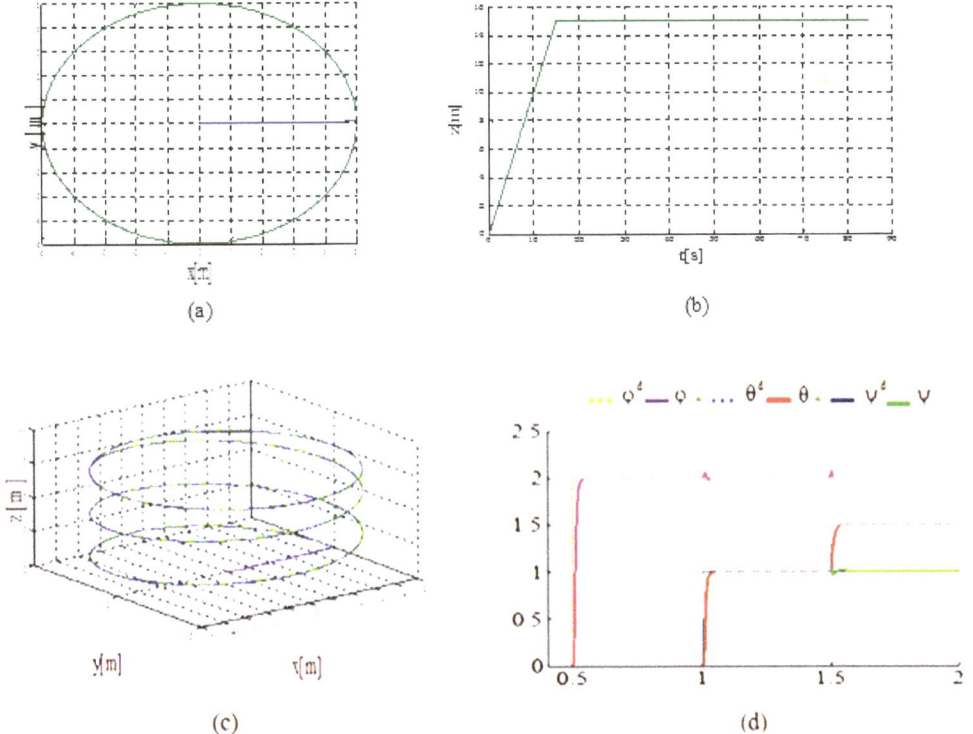

Figure 3. Simulation results. (a) *xy* drone control. (b) Uniform increase in z height from zero to 15 m. (c) Real and the desired positions exactly meet each other. (d) Orientation angles' response.

Figure 3a shows the response of the drone controller to the xy desired value; where we see that the estimated value follows the set-point perfectly. Figure 3c illustrates that the real and the desired positions exactly meet each other in three-dimensional space.

Figure 3d illustrates the response of orientation angles (roll, pitch, and yaw), where the dotted lines denote the desired values and continues-lines shows the estimated values. It is clearly demonstrated that the estimated values track the desired trajectories with an acceptable dynamic.

5. Conclusions

In this paper, a backstepping control is used to provide the dynamic control of the quadrotor. The models derived in this paper are used to design and implement control laws for six-DOF quadrotor stability. For this purpose, firstly, the mathematical model of the quadrotor was developed. Secondly, the backstepping control strategy was devised to control the position and orientation of the quadrotor subsystem. Several scenarios were performed to examine the performance of the backstepping strategy, and we noticed that the simulation results showed the effectiveness of the proposed control. For further work, this approach will be implemented on a quadrotor that will be applied for monitoring and fault diagnostic on a multi-agent-based smart grid [18].

Author Contributions: Conceptualization, A.S. and H.B.; methodology, H.B. and A.S.; software, A.S.; validation, A.S., H.B. and R.B.; formal analysis, A.S.; investigation, A.S.; resources, A.S.; data curation, A.S.; writing—original draft preparation, A.S.; writing—review and editing, A.S., R.B. and H.B.; visualization, A.S.; supervision, R.B.; project administration, H.B.; funding acquisition, A.S. All authors have read and agreed to the published version of the manuscript.

Funding: This research received no external funding.

Institutional Review Board Statement: Not applicable.

Informed Consent Statement: Not applicable.

Data Availability Statement: Not applicable.

Acknowledgments: The authors would like to thank the "la Direction Générale de la Recherche Scientifique et du Développement Technologique (DGRSDT)" for its financial support.

Conflicts of Interest: The authors declare no conflict of interest.

References

1. Alsamhi, S.H.; Ma, O.; Ansari, M.S.; Almalki, F.A. Survey on Collaborative Smart Drones and Internet of Things for Improving Smartness of Smart Cities. *IEEE Access* **2019**, *7*, 128125–128152. [CrossRef]
2. Shahid, F.; Kadri, B.; Jumani, N.A.; Pirwani, Z. Dynamical Modeling and Control of quadrotor. *Trans. Mach. Des.* **2016**, *4*, 50–63.
3. Tuan, L.L.; Won, S. PID based sliding mode controller design for the micro quadrotor. In Proceedings of the 2013 13th International Conference on Control, Automation and Systems (ICCAS 2013), Gwangju, Korea, 20–23 October 2013; pp. 1860–1865. [CrossRef]
4. Erginer, B.; Altug, E. Modeling and PD Control of a Quadrotor VTOL Vehicle. In Proceedings of the 2007 IEEE Intelligent Vehicles Symposium, Istanbul, Turkey, 13–15 June 2007; pp. 894–899. [CrossRef]
5. Bouadi, H.; Bouchoucha, M.; Tadjine, M. Sliding Mode Control based on Backstepping Approach for an UAV Type-Quadrotor. *World Acad. Sci. Eng. Technol. Int. J. Mech. Mechatron. Eng.* **2007**, *1*, 2. [CrossRef]
6. Zahran, S.; Moussa, A.; El-Sheimy, N. Enhanced Drone Navigation in GNSS Denied Environment Using VDM and Hall Effect Sensor. *Int. J. Geo Inf.* **2019**, *8*, 169. [CrossRef]
7. Labbadi, M.; Cherkaoui, M.; Houm, Y.E.; Guisser, M. Modeling and Robust Integral Sliding Mode Control for a Quadrotor Unmanned Aerial Vehicle. In Proceedings of the 2018 6th International Renewable and Sustainable Energy Conference (IRSEC), Rabat, Morocco, 5–8 December 2018; pp. 1–6. [CrossRef]
8. Mohamed, H.A.F.; Yang, S.S.; Moghavvemi, M. Sliding mode controller design for a flying quadrotor with simplified action planner. In Proceedings of the 2009 ICCAS-SICE, Fukuoka, Japan, 18–21 August 2009; pp. 1279–1283.
9. Bouadi, H.; Cunha, S.S.; Drouin, A.; Mora-Camino, F. Adaptive sliding mode control for quadrotor attitude stabilization and altitude tracking. In Proceedings of the 2011 IEEE 12th International Symposium on Computational Intelligence and Informatics (CINTI), Budapest, Hungary, 21–22 November 2011; pp. 449–455. [CrossRef]
10. Bouabdallah, S.; Siegwart, R. Backstepping and Sliding-mode Techniques Applied to an Indoor Micro Quadrotor. In Proceedings of the 2005 IEEE International Conference on Robotics and Automation, Barcelona, Spain, 18–22 April 2005; pp. 2247–2252. [CrossRef]
11. Mian, A.; Daobo, W. Modeling and backstepping-based nonlinear control strategy for a 6 dof quadrotor helicopter. *Chin. J. Aeronaut.* **2008**, *21*, 261–268. [CrossRef]
12. Lee, D.; Kim, H.J.; Sastry, S. Feedback linearization vs. adaptive sliding mode control for a quadrotor helicopter. *Int. J. Control. Autom. Syst.* **2009**, *7*, 419–428. [CrossRef]
13. McKerrow, P. Modelling the Draganflyer four-rotor helicopter. In Proceedings of the IEEE International Conference on Robotics and Automation, 2004 Proceedings. ICRA '04. 2004, New Orleans, LA, USA, 26 April–1 May 2004; Volume 4, pp. 3596–3601. [CrossRef]

14. Hanani, N.; Syazwanadira, F.; Fakharulrazi, N.A.; Yakub, F.; Rasid, Z.A.; Sarip, S. Full Control of Quadrotor Unmanned Aerial Vehicle using Multivariable Proportional Integral Derivative Controller. In Proceedings of the 2019 IEEE 9th International Conference on System Engineering and Technology (ICSET), Shah Alam, Malaysia, 7 October 2019; pp. 447–452. [CrossRef]
15. Wang, P.; Man, Z.; Cao, Z.; Zheng, J.; Zhao, Y. Dynamics modelling and linear control of quadcopter. In Proceedings of the 2016 International Conference on Advanced Mechatronic Systems (ICAMechS), Melbourne, VIC, Australia, 30 November–3 December 2016; pp. 498–503. [CrossRef]
16. Glida, H.E.; Abdou, L.; Chelihi, A.; Sentouh, C.; Hasseni, S.-E.-I. Optimal model-free backstepping control for a quadrotor helicopter. *Nonlinear Dyn.* **2020**, *100*, 3449–3468. [CrossRef]
17. Basri, M.A.M.; Noordin, A. Optimal backstepping control of quadrotor UAV using gravitational search optimization algorithm. *Bull. Electr. Eng. Inform.* **2020**, *9*, 1819–1826. [CrossRef]
18. Hadjira, B.; Rabiai, Z. Decentralized Energy Management System Enhancement for Smart Grid. In *Optimizing and Measuring Smart Grid Operation and Control*; Recioui, A., Bentarzi, H., Eds.; IGI Global: Hershey, PA, USA, 2021; pp. 156–169. [CrossRef]

Proceeding Paper

Fuzzy-PI Controller Tuned with HBBO for 2 DOF Robot Trajectory Control †

Achouri Mourad [1] and Youcef Zennir [2,*]

[1] LRPCSI Laboratory Skikda, Université 20 Aout 1955 Skikda, 21000 Skikda, Algeria; m.achouri@univ-Skikda.dz
[2] Automatic Laboratory of Skikda, Université 20 Aout 1955 Skikda, 21000 Skikda, Algeria
* Correspondence: y.zennir@univ-Skikda.dz
† Presented at the 1st International Conference on Computational Engineering and Intelligent Systems, Online, 10–12 December 2021.

Abstract: The main aim of our study is to control a 2 DOF robot manipulator with Fuzzy-PI and adjust its parameters with human behavior-based optimization. The fuzzy system that we have introduced is based on Takagi–Sugeno-type: it adequately handles uncertainties, ambiguities and it is able to tune the PID parameters in non-linearity situations. The HBBO was dedicated to find the best scaling factor of fuzzy logic as well as the PI's parameter. The results of our study show the effectiveness of the proposed algorithm to optimize the controller's parameter; therefore, the dynamics of robot follows perfectly a desired trajectories.

Keywords: Fuzzy-PI controller; HBBO; robot manipulator trajectory control

1. Introduction

The PID controller has gathered a lot of concern regarding its application in several industrial fields; nevertheless, it is difficult to design its parameters for a complex nonlinear system. Therefore, several techniques have been introduced such as Fuzzy logic and meta-heuristic optimization schema to fix this problem [1–6].

Among all methods that can address the abovementioned problem, there exists so-called fuzzy logic. Fuzzy logic was introduced by Lotfi Zeddah in 1965. It uses a set of mathematical principles expressed by a linguistic variable (spoken or non-numeric) rather than crisp membership of classical logic (0–1) [7], hence it can operate in an environment where the information is not well known. FLC has gained a lot of interest in recent years and has many applications in several industrial fields because of its simplicity and capability to reflect system uncertainties, as well as non-linearity situations. However, despite its success in many applications, it was a target of criticism for its mathematical rigor, requiring knowledge of expert and systematic design [8].

Other effective methods that can solve the aforementioned issue is meta-heuristic optimization schema. Meta-heuristic is an approach that seeks the minimum value for a minimization problem or maximum value for a maximization problem in a stochastic way. Many techniques have been introduced in this field in order to improve solutions and find the best optimum value and, regarding their behaviors, these methods might be divided into four principle groups, which are evolutionary algorithms (Genetic algorithm), physics-based methods (Gravitational Local Search), swarm-based technique (particle swam optimization) and population-based meta-heuristic optimization (teaching–learning-based optimization) [9].

Human behavior-based optimization HBBO is a relatively new meta-heuristic algorithm, which belongs to the fourth category and may be used to find the best optimum value in a wide range of search space. HBBO is able to solve several types of meta-heuristic problems such as unimodel function and bypassing local minima; furthermore, it provides height accuracy and fast convergence.

In order to extract the best parameters from the Fuzzy and PID controllers, the control objective can be formulated as an optimization problem. Optimization problems can be solved using meta-heuristic optimization methods or other methods such as neural networks. In [10], particle swarm optimization-based fuzzy neural networks (FNN) were successfully employed in real life situations, especially for the navigation of a mobile robot and the motion control of a redundant manipulator. They proposed PSO to train FNNs, which can accurately output the crisp control signals for robot systems. The authors of [11] introduced a Takagi–Sugeno (TS)-type neuro-fuzzy system (NFS) trained by PSO, which provides a proper position, velocity and control strategy for the robot manipulators. In [12] Fuzzy-PI was used to control a 2 DOF robot manipulator and the parameters of this were later tuned with GWO. In [13], they test the performances of GWO, WOA and TLBO to tune the parameters of Fuzzy-PI controller to force a 2 DOF robot manipulator to follow a given trajectory. In [6], they used PSO to adjust the parameters of FLC and PID to force the dynamics of the manipulator robot to follow a given trajectory. The authors of [14] proposed ALO and ACO to control the trajectory of a mobile robot with HMI interface. In [15] they investigate the performance of HHO and WOA to the trajectory of a mobile robot with HMI interface.

Motivated by the above discussion, our study aims to control a 2 DOF robot manipulation with Fuzzy-PI in the presence of fractional force and to use HBBO in order to find the optimal parameters of this, later.

2. Dynamic Model of the Planar Robot

Robot dynamic analysis studies a relationship between torques/forces carried out by actuators on the position, speed and acceleration of the robot manipulator. The dynamic equations of the robot are mainly expressed by:

$$\tau = D(q)\ddot{q} + C(q,\dot{q}) + G(q), \qquad (1)$$

where $D(q)$ is the inertia matrix, $C(q,\dot{q})$ is the Coriolis/centripetal matrix, $G(q)$ is the gravity vector and τ is the torque. The variable q is a vector of the angles for the robot manipulator. The dynamics of the robot with 2 degrees of freedom can be calculated by:

$$\begin{pmatrix} \tau_1 \\ \tau_2 \end{pmatrix} = \begin{pmatrix} (m_1+m_2)l_1^2 + m_2 l_2^2 + 2m_2 l_1 l_2 \cos\theta_2 & m_2 l_2^2 + 2m_2 l_1 l_2 \cos\theta_2 \\ m_2 l_2^2 + m_2 l_1 l_2 \cos\theta_2 & m_2 l_2^2 \end{pmatrix} \begin{pmatrix} \ddot{\theta}_1 \\ \ddot{\theta}_2 \end{pmatrix} + \begin{pmatrix} -m_2 l_1 l_2 \left(2\dot{\theta}_1 \dot{\theta}_2 + \dot{\theta}_2^2\right) \sin\theta_2 \\ m_2 l_1 l_2 \dot{\theta}_1^2 \sin\theta_2 \end{pmatrix} + \begin{pmatrix} (m_1+m_2)gl_1 \cos\theta_1 + m_2 g l_2 \cos(\theta_1+\theta_2) \\ m_2 g l_2 \cos(\theta_1+\theta_2) \end{pmatrix}, \qquad (2)$$

where m_i is the mass of the link, l_i is the length of the link, g is the gravity and θ, $\dot{\theta}$ and $\ddot{\theta}$, respectively, are the positions, speeds and accelerations of the robot.

3. Human Behavior-Based Optimization HBBO

HBBO is a new meta-heuristic optimization proposed by Seyed-Alireza Ahmadi. In spite of the biological, animal and societal inspiration, this newly developed optimization algorithm describes the behavior mechanism of humans in the way of getting success. Humans in society seek to obtain success based on their different personal purposes. A successful person is evaluated based on the achievement of their purposes. Since humans do not share the same objectives and viewpoints, every individual looks for success in different fields and opts to achieve it in a different manner; therefore, they are studying and working in different fields. After finding their own objectives and targets, people move toward experts in order to learn and enhance their ability.

Furthermore, each person may have other passions, such as music, painting, etc., regardless of their own professional field. Due to life's conditions, every person may experience many undesired problems in their professional life or meet some people who can change their mind; hence, an individual's conviction and viewpoints may not remain the same throughout their entire life. Just for the sake of achieving a better position and improving their self, every individual in some societies may change their field by consulting advisors.

In order to model this aforementioned mechanism, HBBO uses five main phases which are Initialization, Education, Consultation, Field Changing probability and Finalization [16].

3.1. Initialization

As with all metaheuristic optimization algorithms, HBBO starts with initialization. In this step, HBBO engages and evaluates the initial people and divides them through different fields as depicted in Figure 1, in an optimization problem with $Nvar$ variables, where people is expressed by:

$$\text{people} = [x_1, x_2, x_3, \ldots, x_{Nvar}], \quad (3)$$

The algorithm employs N_{pop} of initial people and aleatory divides them through N_{field} of initial fields. The number of initial people in every domain is computed by:

$$N.Indi = round\left\{\frac{N_{pop}}{N_{field}}\right\}, \quad (4)$$

where $N.Indi$ is the number of initial people in i-th field. After the initialization, the fitness values of each people can be evaluated by [16]:

$$\text{fitness value} = f(x_1, x_2, x_3, \ldots, x_{Nvar}), \quad (5)$$

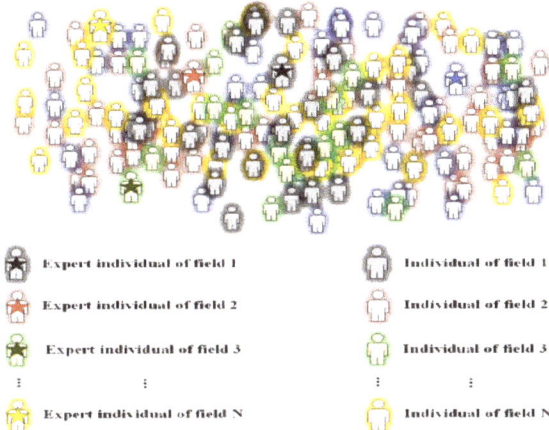

Figure 1. Engaging and dividing peoples through initial fields.

3.2. Education

This process describes the fact that individuals move toward the person with the lowest fitness value (if it is a minimization problem) or highest score (if it is a maximization problem) of their professional domain (field). For the sake of investigating this step, a coordinate system is implemented where the best person (expert) is the origin. The convergence of people toward the best person is highlighted in Figure 2, and the positions will be updated according to the spherical coordinates system. The position of every individual is restricted by a sphere around the best person of their field.

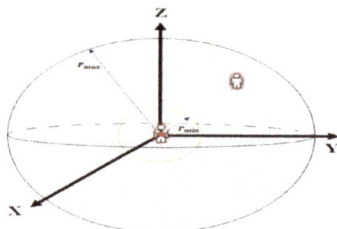

Figure 2. Education moving around the expert individual.

In meta-heuristic schema with more than three decision variables, by performing the coordinates of a spherical system with more than three dimensions of Euclidean space [17], the proposed technique will determine a random radial coordinate (r) between $r_{min} = k_1 d$ and $r_{max} = k_2 d$, where d is the Euclidian distance between the expert and people, and ki is a constant that will be set by a designer. Furthermore, the proposed meta-heuristic will determine $N - 1$ random angular coordinates ($\theta_1, \theta_2 ... \theta_{N-1}$), where θ_{N-1} will be determined between 0 and 2π radians and the other angles will be found between 0 and π radians [16].

3.3. Consultation

As we have already mentioned, each person can randomly find within society an adviser who can change their way of perceiving things. This consultation can be effective if the fitness score in a minimization problem is a smallest score or in a maximization problem is a bigger score; therefore, an advisor will change some of the individual variables in a way that is shown in Figure 3—otherwise, nothing will be changed, meaning the consultation was not effective. The number of random decisions variables which will be replaced is found by:

$$N_c = round(\sigma . N_{var}), \quad (6)$$

where σ is the consultation constant that will select the number of random variables, N_c, which might be replaced in this step [16].

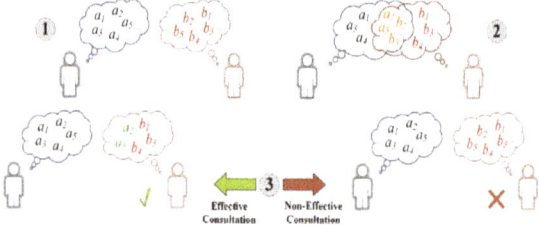

Figure 3. Consultation mechanism.

3.4. Field Changging Probability

According to the above discussion, an individual in a field may change their field. This step is devoted to calculating the changing probability of each field by using the rank probability. In order to compute this probability, we first sort each field based on the fitness score of its best person through this method:

$$sort\ fields = [field_1,\ field_2,\ field_3,\ \ldots,\ field_N], \quad (7)$$

where the best person of $field_1$ and $field_N$ possess the minimum and the maximum fitness score of the remaining fields, respectively. Then, the ranking probability for every domain (field) can be obtained by:

$$p_i = \frac{O_i}{N_{field} + 1},\qquad(8)$$

where p_i and O_i are ranking probability and the index of the i-th sorted field, respectively. By performing this technique, the field whose best person possesses a lower fitness score has less of a chance, and the field whose best person possesses an upper fitness score has a higher chance to make this process occur. Secondly, we provide a random number between 0 and 1, and by checking the equation below we will determine if the field change for one of the people in this field will occur:

$$if\ rand\ \leq p_i \rightarrow field\ changing\ occurs,\qquad(9)$$

In this step, from the fitness score, a selection probability for every person is computed by:

$$P.S_j = \left|\frac{f(individual_j)}{\sum_{k=1}^{Nind} f(individual_k)}\right|,\qquad(10)$$

where $P.S_j$ is the selection probability for the j-th individual and $Nind$ is the number of people in the selected field. Finally, by adopting the roulette wheel selection technique [18], a person will be determined and will go to a random different field [16].

3.5. Finalization

After performing the abovementioned steps, the function value of all individuals is evaluated and the algorithm will repeat the processes until the consummation of all iterations [16].

4. Optimization of Fuzzy-PI with HBBO

Figure 4 represents the simulation diagram of Fuzzy-PI. The HBBO have been proposed to adjust scaling factors of membership functions (MFs) of the fuzzy system and the parameters of PI. A total of 15 triangular-type MFs and 25 rules were used in each FLC (see Figure 5).

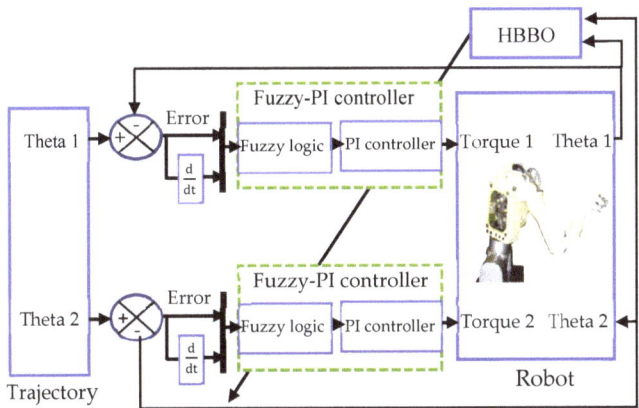

Figure 4. Control diagram for robot planar.

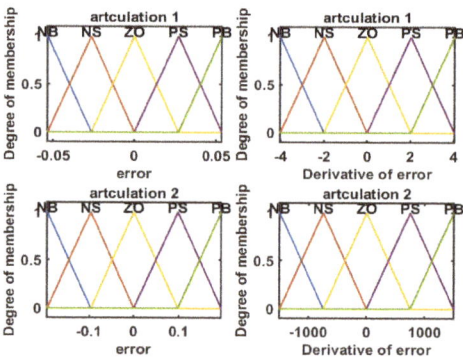

Figure 5. Memberships functions of links 1 and 2 after optimization by HBBO.

The optimization was performed under the following cost function of the absolute magnitude of the mean error (MAE):

$$\text{MAE} = \sum_{i=1}^{N} |e_1(i)| + |e_2(i)|, \tag{11}$$

where $e_1(i)$ is the error of the position of the i-th sample for the first angle, $e_2(i)$ is the error of the position of the i-th sample for the second angle, N is the number of samples. For the sake of examining the performances of the proposed algorithms, we engaged 50 individuals in 60 iterations and we set $k_1 = 0$, $k_2 = 2.5$ and $\sigma = 0.2$ to tune the parameters of Fuzzy-PI.

5. Results and Discussions

The purpose of the controller is to force the angles of the robot θ_1 and θ_2 to follow the desired trajectory defined by: $y_{d1,2} = 0.3 \cdot \sin t$ under the presence of a frictional force defined by: $F(q) = \begin{pmatrix} 10.\dot{\theta}_1 + 3.sign(\dot{\theta}_1) \\ 10.\dot{\theta}_2 + 3.sign(\dot{\theta}_2) \end{pmatrix}$. The robot parameters are: $m_1 = 1$ kg, $m_2 = 1.5$ kg, $l_1 = 1$ m, $l_2 = 0.8$ m.

The numerical simulation results of angle position, two link errors and control input obtained by Fuzzy-PI tuned by HBBO are represented in Figures 6–8. Figure 6 evidently shows that both angles for first and second links converge rapidly to their respective set point. It is clearer from Figure 7 that Fuzzy-PI exhibits height accuracy and was able to stabilize the errors around 10^{-4} and 10^{-3} for both the first and second links and cost function in 0.0056. Figure 8, meanwhile, highlights that the control signals acquire a periodicity form, which varies around 0 to 15 for the first link and -10 to 10 for the second link. It is obvious from the above discussions that HBBO was able to provide the best parameters of Fuzzy-PI and, consequently, the two positions (angles) of the robot perfectly follow the given reference positions.

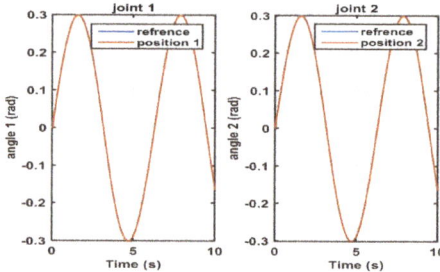

Figure 6. Results obtained for HBBO of two links of the robot.

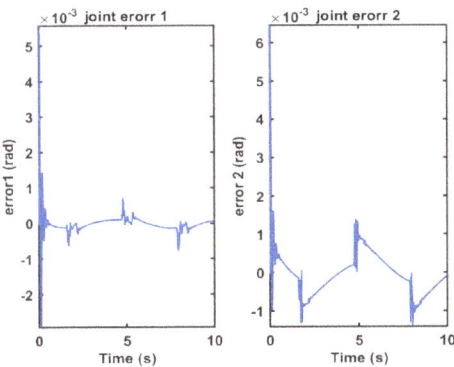

Figure 7. Results obtained for HBBO for errors of two angles of the robot.

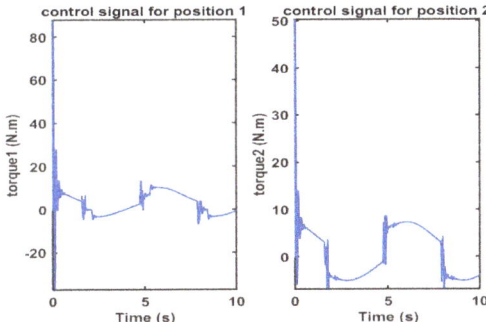

Figure 8. Results obtained for HBBO for errors of two angles of the robot.

6. Conclusions

Our study proposes the HBBO algorithm to determine the scaling factor of fuzzy membership and PI parameter in order to get a best convergence of a robot's state toward desired inputs. The proposed algorithm is capable of dealing with height-dimensional functions and bypassing local minimas. Furthermore, it relies on rather simple concepts and is easy to implement. The fuzzy system that we have opted is of the Takagi–Sugeno type. Future research should move in the direction of identifying additional cost functions and testing other algorithms.

Author Contributions: A.M. and Y.Z. propose in this paper a new architecture control design aims to control a 2 DOF robot manipulation with Fuzzy-PI in the presence of fractional force and to use HBBO in order to find the optimal parameters of this, later. All authors have read and agreed to the published version of the manuscript.

Funding: This research received no external funding.

Institutional Review Board Statement: Not applicable.

Informed Consent Statement: Not applicable.

Data Availability Statement: Not applicable.

Conflicts of Interest: The authors declare no conflict of interest.

References

1. Visioli, A. Tuning of PID controllers with fuzzy logic. *IEE Proc. Control Theory Appl.* **2001**, *148*, 1–8. [CrossRef]
2. Bingul, Z. A new PID tuning technique using differential evolution for unstable and integrating processes with time delay. *LNCS* **2004**, *3316*, 254–260.
3. Krohling, R.A.; Rey, J.P. Design of optimal disturbance rejection PID controllers using genetic algorithm. *IEEE Trans. Evol. Comput.* **2001**, *5*, 78–82. [CrossRef]
4. Mitsukura, Y.; Yamamoto, T.; Kaneda, M. A design of self-tuning PID controllers using a genetic algorithm. In Proceedings of the American Control Conference, San Diego, CA, USA, 2–4 June 1999; pp. 1361–1365.
5. Varol, H.A.; Bingul, Z. A new PID tuning technique using ant algorithm. In Proceedings of the American Control Conference, Boston, MA, USA, 30 June–2 July 2004.
6. BINGÜL. Zafer et KARAHAN, Oğuzhan. A Fuzzy Logic Controller tuned with PSO for 2 DOF robot trajectory control. *Expert Syst. Appl.* **2011**, *38*, 1017–1031. [CrossRef]
7. Zadeh, L.A. Information and Control. *Fuzzy Sets* **1965**, *8*, 338–353.
8. Qiao, F.; Zhu, Q.; Winfield, A.F.; Melhuish, C. Adaptive sliding mode control for MIMO nonlinear systems based on fuzzy logic scheme. *Int. J. Autom. Comput.* **2004**, *1*, 51–62. [CrossRef]
9. Mirjalili, S.; Lewis, A. The whale optimization algorithm. *Adv. Eng. Softw.* **2016**, *95*, 51–67. [CrossRef]
10. Pulasinghe, K.; Chatterjee, A.; Watanabe, K. A particle-swarm-optimized fuzzy-neural network for voice-controlled robot systems. *IEEE Trans. Ind. Electron.* **2005**, *52*, 1478–1489.
11. Chatterjee, A.; Watanabe, K. An optimized Takagi–Sugeno type neuro-fuzzy system for modeling robot manipulators. *Neural Comput. Appl.* **2006**, *15*, 55–61. [CrossRef]
12. Mourad, A.; Youcef, Z. Fuzzy-PI controller tuned with GWO for 2 DOF robot trajectory control. In Proceedings of the Conférence Nationale sur le Contrôle et la Sécurité des Systèmes Industriels, Skikda, Algeria, 6–7 October 2021; p. 6.
13. Mourad, A.; Youcef, Z. Fuzzy-PI Controller Tuned With GWO, WOA And TLBO For 2 DOF Robot Trajectory Control. In Proceedings of the International Conference on Advanced Engineering in Petrochemical Industry (ICAEPI'21), Skikda, Algeria, 23–25 November 2021; p. 6.
14. Chaima, K.; Youcef, Z.; Fernandez, L.J. Tuning non-linear controller by metaheuristics algorithms (ALO, ACO): Applied to control trajectory of mobile robot with HMI. In Proceedings of the International Conference on Advanced Engineering in Petrochemical Industry (ICAEPI'21), Skikda, Algeria, 23–25 November 2021; p. 6.
15. Chaima, K.; Youcef, Z.; Fernandez, L.J. Tuning non-linear controller by metaheuristics algorithms (HHO, WOA): Applied to control trajectory of mobile robot with HMI. In Proceedings of the International Conference on Advanced Engineering in Petrochemical Industry (ICAEPI'21), Skikda, Algeria, 23–25 November 2021; p. 6.
16. AHMADI. Seyed-Alireza. Human behavior-based optimization: A novel metaheuristic approach to solve complex optimization problems. *Neural Comput. Applications. Appl.* **2017**, *28*, 233–244. [CrossRef]
17. Griffiths, D.J. *Introduction to Electrodynamics*, 4th ed.; Cambridge University Press: Cambridge, UK, 2017; 620p.
18. Goldberg, D.E. *Genetic Algorithms in Search, Optimization and Machine Learning*; Addison-Wesley: Reading, UK; The University of Alabama, Addison-Wesley Publishing Company: Boston, MA, USA, 1989; 432p.

Adaptive Sliding Mode Control Improved by Fuzzy-PI Controller: Applied to Magnetic Levitation System [†]

Achouri Mourad [1] and Zennir Youcef [2,*]

[1] LRPCSI Laboratory Skikda, Université 20 Aout 1955 Skikda, Skikda 21000, Algeria; m.achouri@univ-Skikda.dz
[2] Automatic Laboratory of Skikda, Université 20 Aout 1955 Skikda, Skikda 21000, Algeria
* Correspondence: y.zennir@univ-Skikda.dz
[†] Presented at the 1st International Conference on Computational Engineering and Intelligent Systems, Online, 10–12 December 2021.

Abstract: This study mainly concerns the use of Fuzzy-PI adaptive sliding control (Fuzzy-ASMC) to force the stat space of MAGLEV to track a desired trajectory. The usage of adaptive sliding mode control allows the MAGLEV to operate in an uncertain environment and in the presence of external disturbances. The Fuzzy-PI schema is designed to improve the performance of adaptive sliding mode control and reduce the main drawback caused by the discontinuous term of this method, which is the well-known chattering phenomenon. The results of our study prove the effectiveness of the proposed approach in achieving desired performances.

Keywords: Fuzzy-PI; sliding mode control; MAGLEV; fuzzy logic; PI control; adaptive control

1. Introduction

Magnetic levitation (MAGLEV) systems have gained popularity because of their practical importance in many engineering fields, such as high-speed passenger trains, frictionless bearings, the centrifugation of nuclear reactors, levitated wind tunnel models, magnetic suspension and balance systems, the vibration isolation of sensitive machinery, the levitation of molten metal in induction furnaces and heart pumps, etc. [1]. The model that describes the dynamics of MAGLEV is the highly unstable, nonlinear state space model.

One of the most elegant strategies in the field of control is adaptive control. This method can treat systems with parametric variation when the operating conditions are degraded; however, this approach fails if they are affected by external perturbation later.

Several studies have been developed in the field of the control of non-linear systems, for example, adaptive control (Isidori 1989 [2], Slotine and Li 1991 [3]). However, sliding mode control (SMC) proposed by Utkin 1977 [4] has been the most popular approach for use in controlling uncertain, non-linear, single-input, single-output SISO systems (Drakunov and Utkin 1992 [5], Slotine 1984, 1987 [6,7]) because of its simplicity and its robustness against external disturbances. Sliding mode control is part of the family of controllers with variable structures, which can deal with uncertainties and unmodeled dynamics, insensitivity to external load disturbances, stability and a fast dynamic response [8–10]. The principle of this method is to constrain the trajectories of a system to achieve a given sliding surface and then stay there. However, in practice, control by sliding mode induced high-frequency switching known as chattering. These switches can excite unwanted dynamics that risk destabilizing, damaging or even destroying the system under study.

Many studies have proposed methods of dealing with chattering phenomena, which include replacing the sgn function by the saturation function or sigmoid function [11] and high-order sliding mode control, whose principle is to reject the discontinuities in higher derivatives of a system input [12,13]. Another method is to use an asymptotic observer via sliding mode, the aim of which is to generate ideal sliding modes in an auxiliary observation loop so that this observer loop does not integrate any unmolded dynamics [14].

Among these different proposed schemes, the Fuzzy-PI strategy has shown its effectiveness in alleviating the chattering phenomenon due to its smoothness, speed and the ease of implementation. Motivated by the above-mentioned discussion, we propose in this paper a new architecture control design based in adaptive sliding mode control (ASMC) to force the MAGLEV's to track a given desired trajectory, and the second part combination between Fuzzy-PI controller and ASMC controller used to reduce the chattering phenomenon caused by the dis-continuous term of the ASMC.

2. System Description

The dynamic model for the MAGLEV system as given as [15]:

$$\begin{cases} \frac{dp}{dt} = w \\ V = Ri + \frac{dL(p)i}{dt} \\ m\frac{dw}{dt} = mg - Q\left(\frac{i}{p}\right)^2 \end{cases}, \begin{cases} \frac{dp}{dt} = w \\ V = Ri + \frac{dL(p)i}{dt} \\ m\frac{dw}{dt} = mg - Q\left(\frac{i}{p}\right)^2 \end{cases}, \quad (1)$$

where p is the ball's position, w denotes the ball's velocity, i is the current in the electromagnet, V denotes the applied voltage, R and L are the coil's resistance and inductance, respectively, g is the gravitational constant, Q denotes magnetic force constant and m is the mass of the levitated ball.

The inductance L is assumed to be the nonlinear function of the ball's position p and is approximated as:

$$L(p) = L_1 + \frac{2Q}{p}, \quad (2)$$

where L_1 is a system parameter determined by the electromagnet coil inductance. Let us define $x_1 = p$, $x_2 = w$, $x_3 = i$ and $u = V$ and let us state that the vector is $x = (x_1\ x_2\ x_3)^T$; the state space model of the MAGLEV system can be expressed as [15]:

$$\begin{cases} \frac{dx_1}{dt} = x_2 \\ \frac{dx_2}{dt} = g - \frac{Q}{m}\left(\frac{x_3}{x_1}\right)^2 \\ \frac{dx_3}{dt} = -\frac{R}{L}x_3 + \frac{2Q}{L}\frac{x_2 \cdot x_3}{x_1^2} + \frac{u(t)}{L} \end{cases}. \quad (3)$$

3. Problem Formulation and Controller Design

3.1. Problem Formulation

The solution to the MAGLEV control problem is initiated by considering the nonlinear change of coordinates as follows:

$$\begin{cases} \xi_1 = x_1 - x_{1d} \\ \xi_1 = x_2 - x_{2d} \\ \xi_1 = g - \frac{Q}{m}\left(\frac{x_3}{x_1}\right)^2 \end{cases}. \quad (4)$$

Assuming $x_d = (x_{1d}, 0, x_{1d}\sqrt{gm/Q},)$ the dynamic model of the MAGLEV with external disturbance $d(t)$ in a new coordinate system can be re-written as [16]:

$$\begin{cases} \dot{\xi}_1 = \xi_2 \\ \dot{\xi}_2 = \xi_3 \\ \dot{\xi}_3 = f(\xi) + g(\xi)u(t) + d(t) \end{cases}, \quad (5)$$

where $f(\tilde{\xi})$ and $g(\tilde{\xi})$ are given by:

$$f(\tilde{\xi}) = 2(g - \tilde{\xi}_3)\left(\left(1 - \frac{2Q}{L(\tilde{\xi}_1 + x_{1d})}\right)\frac{\tilde{\xi}_2}{\tilde{\xi}_1 + x_{1d}} + \frac{R}{L}\right),$$
$$g(\tilde{\xi}) = \frac{-2}{L(\tilde{\xi}_1 + x_{1d})}\sqrt{\frac{Q(g - \tilde{\xi}_3)}{m}}$$
(6)

Consequently, the control objective is now modified to design the control input u, so that the closed loop system (5) states ($\tilde{\xi}_1, \tilde{\xi}_2, \tilde{\xi}_3$) converge to zero in finite time under the presence of disturbance $d(t)$.

After this, with some development in Equation (6), system (5) becomes:

$$\begin{cases} \dot{\tilde{\xi}}_1 = \tilde{\xi}_2 \\ \dot{\tilde{\xi}}_2 = \tilde{\xi}_3 \\ \theta_3\dot{\tilde{\xi}}_3 = (\sum_{i=1}^{3}\theta_i f_i(\tilde{\xi})) + g(\tilde{\xi})_1 u(t) + d(t) \end{cases},$$
(7)

where $f_i(\tilde{\xi})$ and $g_1(\tilde{\xi})$ are given by:

$$f_1(\tilde{\xi}) = \frac{-4(g - \tilde{\xi}_3)}{(\tilde{\xi}_1 + x_{1d})}\frac{\tilde{\xi}_2}{\tilde{\xi}_1 + x_{1d}},$$
$$f_2(\tilde{\xi}) = 2(g - \tilde{\xi}_3),$$
$$f_3(\tilde{\xi}) = 2(g - \tilde{\xi}_3)\frac{\tilde{\xi}_2}{\tilde{\xi}_1 + x_{1d}},$$
$$g_1(\tilde{\xi}) = \frac{-2\sqrt{(g - \tilde{\xi}_3)}}{\tilde{\xi}_1 + x_{1d}},$$
(8)

where θ_i are given by:

$$\theta_1 = \frac{\theta_3 Q}{L},$$
$$\theta_2 = \frac{\theta_3 R}{L},$$
$$\theta_3 = \frac{\sqrt{mL}}{\sqrt{Q}},$$
(9)

3.2. Controller Design

Considering the following sliding surface:

$$s(t) = \left(\frac{d}{dt} + \lambda\right)^{n-1} e(t),$$
(10)

where λ is a positive constant, n is the order of system and $e(t) = \tilde{\xi}_1 = x_1 - x_{1d}$ is tracking error.

Given that $n = $ 3rd sliding, this becomes:

$$s(t) = \lambda^2 \tilde{\xi}_1 + 2\lambda \tilde{\xi}_2 + \tilde{\xi}_3,$$
(11)

The derivative of sliding surface can be formulated as:

$$\dot{s} = f_1(\tilde{\xi}) + f_2(\tilde{\xi}) + f_3(\tilde{\xi}) + g_1(\tilde{\xi})u(t) + d(t) + \lambda^2 \tilde{\xi}_2 + 2\lambda \tilde{\xi}_3,$$
(12)

Note that in the conventional sliding mode control for system (5), the design of the control system will be as follows [5]:

$$\begin{cases} u = u_{eq} + u_s \\ u_{eq} = -\left[\frac{\partial s}{\partial \tilde{\xi}} g(\tilde{\xi})\right]^{-1} \frac{\partial s}{\partial \tilde{\xi}} f(\tilde{\xi}), \\ u_s = -\left[\frac{\partial s}{\partial \tilde{\xi}} g(\tilde{\xi})\right]^{-1} sgn(s) \end{cases}$$
(13)

where K is a positive constant, and u_{eq} and u_s are the equivalent control vector and the switching part of the control. sgn is the sign function defined by:

$$sgn(s) = \begin{cases} 1 & si\ s > 0 \\ 0 & si\ s = 0 \\ -1 & si\ s < 0 \end{cases}, \tag{14}$$

Now, let us design the control law for system (7) under the presence of parametric uncertainties and perturbation.

If we consider the following Lyapunov candidate function:

$$V = \frac{1}{2}(\theta_3 s^2 + \sum_{i=1}^{3} \frac{1}{\gamma_i} \tilde{\theta}_i^2), \tag{15}$$

where:

$$\tilde{\theta}_i = \theta_i - \hat{\theta}_i, \tag{16}$$

where $\hat{\theta}_i$ denotes the estimations used for uncertain terms θ_i, $\tilde{\theta}_i$ is the estimation error and γ_i denotes positive constants. After carrying out some mathematical manipulations, the derivative of the candidate Lyapunov function can be obtained as:

$$\dot{V} = \left(s\left(f_3(\xi) + +\lambda^2 \xi_2 + 2\lambda \xi_3 \right) - \frac{2}{\gamma_3} \dot{\hat{\theta}}_3 \right) \tilde{\theta}_3 + \left(f_2(\xi)s - \frac{1}{\gamma_2} \dot{\hat{\theta}}_2 \right) \tilde{\theta}_2 + \left(f_1(\xi)s - \frac{1}{\gamma_1} \dot{\hat{\theta}}_1 \right) \tilde{\theta}_1 - K|s| + d(t). \tag{17}$$

Assigning parameter update rules as:

$$\dot{\hat{\theta}}_3 = s\gamma_3 \left(f_3(\xi) + +\lambda^2 \xi_2 + 2\lambda \xi_3 \right), \tag{18}$$

$$\dot{\hat{\theta}}_2 = \gamma_2 f_2(\xi)s, \tag{19}$$

$$\dot{\hat{\theta}}_1 = \gamma_1 f_1(\xi)s, \tag{20}$$

$$\eta > k - D, \tag{21}$$

where $D = \max(d(t))$. Equation (17) turns out to be:

$$\dot{V} \leq -\eta|s| \leq 0, \tag{22}$$

The time derivative of the Lyapunov function defined in (15) is given in (22). Note that the function in (22) is negative semi-definite, ensuring the stability of the dynamical system given by (11) and (18) to (22). Moreover, this is proven according to the LaSalle–Yoshizawa theorem [5]. Thus, the existence of a sliding regime is proven.

Indeed, the discontinuous term $K\ sgn\ (s)$ of the sliding mode control excites strong oscillations around the surface, which causes the appearance of what is called "chattering". These can deteriorate the performance of the system and even lead to its instability [5]. In order to alleviate this problem, we suggest the Fuzzy-PI sliding mode controller [17] (see Figure 1).

In this case, the discontinuous term is replaced by a Fuzzy-PI regulator as follows:

$$u_s = K_p(K_s \cdot K \cdot sat(s)) + k_i \int K_s \cdot K \cdot sat(s) dt, \tag{23}$$

where K_s is the gain of the speed surface, K_p is the proportional factor, K_i is the integral factor, k is negative constant, sat is the saturation function and S is the speed surface.

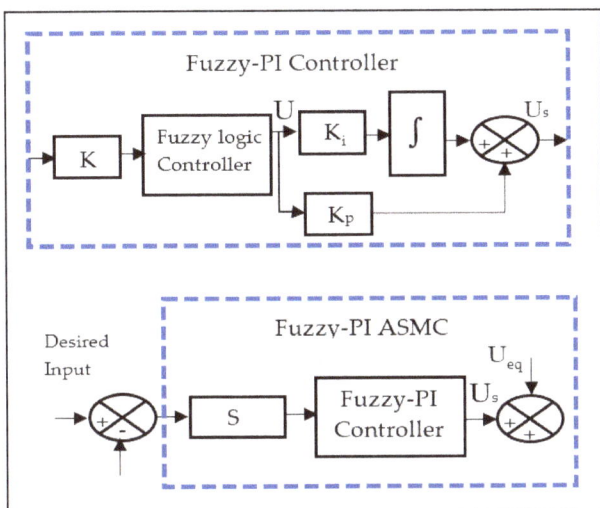

Figure 1. Control diagram for Fuzzy-PI ASMC.

4. Results and Discussion

In order to test the proposed controller, the model properties of the magnetic levitation system used in this study are R = 22 Ω, L = 0.5 H, Q = 0.003, m = 0.055 Kg and g = 9.81 m/s². System states are assigned as $[x_1\ x_2\ x_3]^T = [0\ 0\ 0.7]^T$, and $\theta_i = 1, \ldots, 3$ are set to 0. The values of the gains are taken as $k_p = 100$, $k_i = 100$ and $k = -100$. Adaptation gains are set as $\gamma_1 = 0.75$, $\gamma_2 = 1000$, $\gamma_3 = 1500$ and $\lambda = 50$. System states are assigned to track the following state values: $[x_{1d}\ x_{2d}\ x_{3d}]^T = [0.01\ 0\ 0.2884]^T$, under the disturbance $d(t) = 0.5 \cdot sin(0.2 \cdot t)$.

The membership functions for the input and output of the FL controller are obtained by trial and error to ensure optimal performance and are shown in Figure 2.

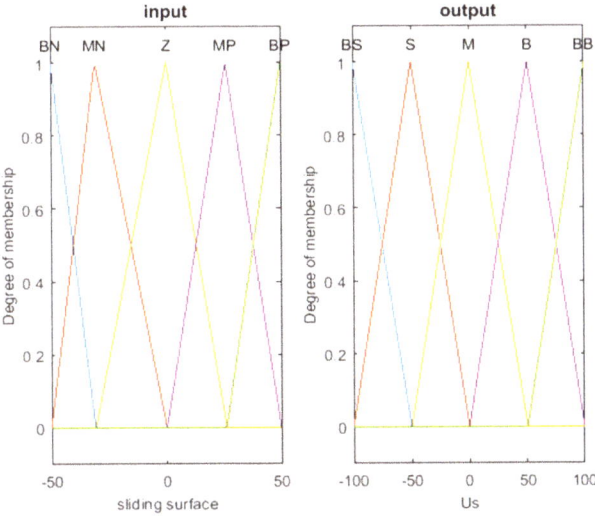

Figure 2. Fuzzy logic membership functions for input and output.

Then, the rules of the fuzzy logic controller can be written as:

$$\begin{aligned}&\text{If } s \text{ is BN then } u_s \text{ is BB}\\&\text{If } s \text{ is MN then } u_s \text{ is B}\\&\text{If } s \text{ is Z then } u_s \text{ is M}\\&\text{If } s \text{ is MP then } u_s \text{ is S}\\&\text{If } s \text{ is BP then } u_s \text{ is BS.}\end{aligned} \qquad (24)$$

The numerical simulation results of the ball position, ball velocity and current of coil obtained by Fuzzy-PI ASMC and ASMC are represented in Figures 3–9. Figure 3 evidently shows that both the Fuzzy-PI ASMC and ASMC provide fast convergence to their respective set point (0.01) in finite time of about 0.5 s. It is clear from Figure 4 that Fuzzy-PI ASMC exhibits height accuracy and precision without any chattering, whereas the ASMC depicts some chattering phenomenon. Figure 5 highlights that the both methods were able to stabilize the current coil in 0.2884 s; however, the ASMC creates some important oscillation, which can lead to some undesirable performance and instability.

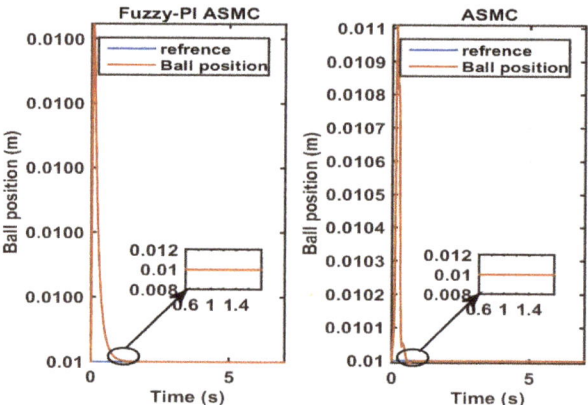

Figure 3. Results obtained via Fuzzy-PI ASMC and ASMC for ball position.

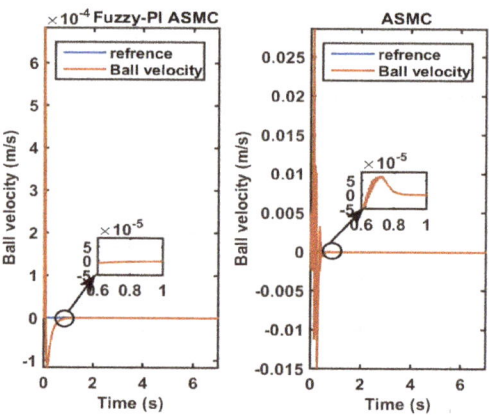

Figure 4. Results obtained via Fuzzy-PI ASMC and ASMC for ball velocity.

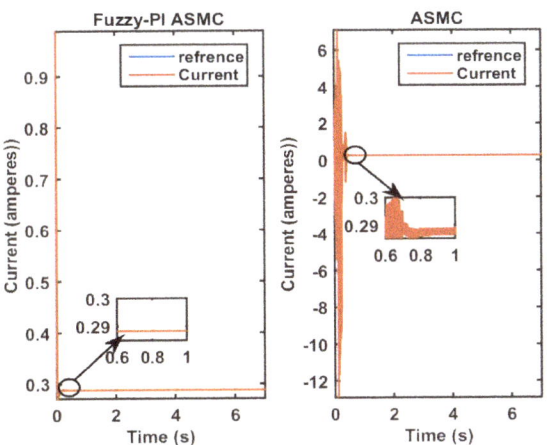

Figure 5. Results obtained via Fuzzy-PI ASMC and ASMC for current coil.

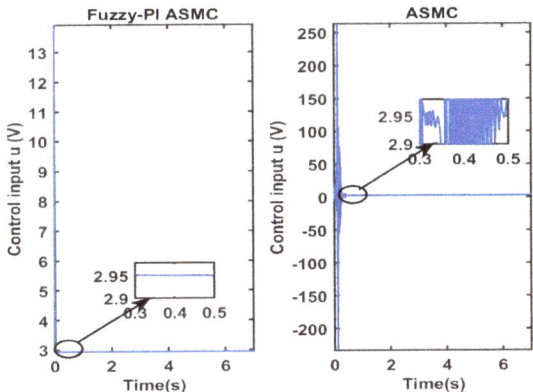

Figure 6. Control signal obtained via Fuzzy-PI ASMC and ASMC for control signal.

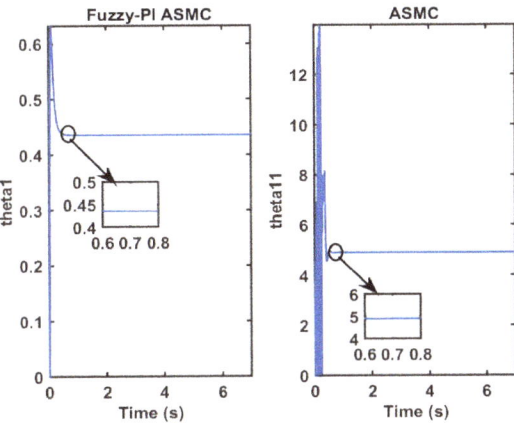

Figure 7. Parameter estimations obtained via Fuzzy-PI ASMC and ASMC for θ_1.

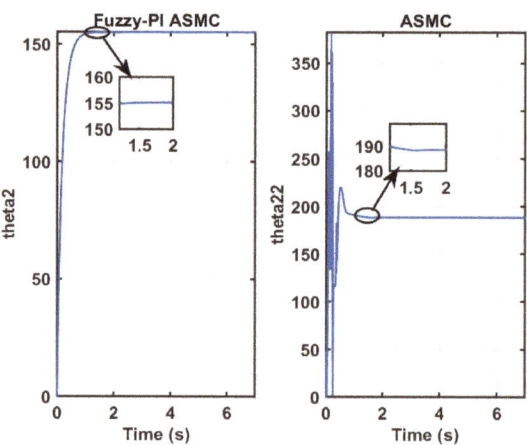

Figure 8. Parameter estimations obtained via Fuzzy-PI ASMC and ASMC for θ_2.

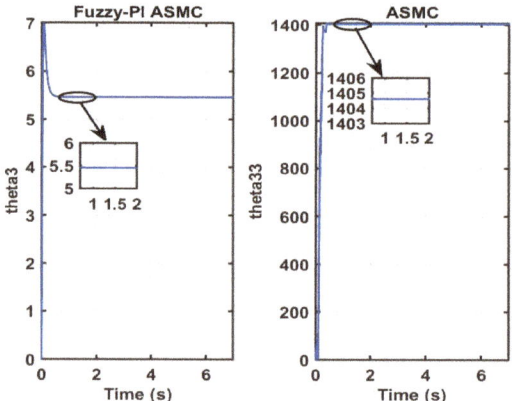

Figure 9. Parameter estimations obtained via Fuzzy-PI ASMC and ASMC for θ_3.

Figure 6 outlines the control signals of Fuzzy-PI ASMC and ASMC. One can see that Fuzzy-PI ASMC clearly outperform the ASMC approach by obtaining finite, continuous and smooth control input.

Figures 7–9 represent the estimated parameters for both Fuzzy-PI ASMC and ASMC. It is obvious from the results of those figures that the Fuzzy-PI ASMC was more successful in capturing those parameters and obtaining a lesser signals.

From the aforementioned discussion, we can simply conclude that Fuzzy-PI ASMC verifies our claims by obtaining fewer continuous signals and improving the ASMC.

5. Conclusions

This paper presented Fuzzy-PI adaptive sliding mode control to force the position of MAGLEV to track a given trajectory. The proposed approach takes advantages from ASMC in its high accuracy, fast dynamic response, stability, the simplicity of implementation and robustness for changes in internal or external parameters, and from Fuzzy-PI, it takes its capability to handle system uncertainty, as well as nonlinear situations, its smoothness, speed, ease of implementation and especially its performance in alleviating the chattering phenomenon caused by sliding mode control. The results obtained for the proposed controller were encouraging in terms of the application of MAGLEV in order to ensure the robustness and quality of the MAGLEV's performances.

Author Contributions: A.M. and Z.Y. propose in this paper a new architecture control design based in adaptive sliding mode control (ASMC) to force the MAGLEV's to track a given desired trajectory, and the second part combination between Fuzzy-PI controller and ASMC controller used to reduce the chattering phenomenon caused by the dis-continuous term of the ASMC. All authors have read and agreed to the published version of the manuscript.

Funding: This research received no external funding.

Institutional Review Board Statement: Not applicable.

Informed Consent Statement: Not applicable.

Data Availability Statement: Not applicable.

Conflicts of Interest: The authors declare no conflict of interest.

References

1. Goel, A.; Swarup, A. A novel high-order sliding mode control of magnetic levitation system. In Proceedings of the 2016 IEEE 59th International Midwest Symposium on Circuits and Systems (MWSCAS), Abu Dhabi, United Arab Emirates, 16–19 October 2016; pp. 1–4.
2. Isidori, A. *Nonlinear Control Systems*; Springer: Berlin, Germany, 1989.
3. Slotine, J.J.; Li, W. *Applied Nonlinear Control*; Prentice-Hall: Englewood Cliffs, NJ, USA, 1991.
4. Utkin, V. Variable structure systems with sliding modes. *IEEE Trans. Autom. Control* **1977**, *22*, 212–222. [CrossRef]
5. Drakunov, S.; Utkin, V. Sliding mode control in dynamic systems. *Int. J. Control* **1992**, *55*, 1029–1037. [CrossRef]
6. Slotine, J.J. Sliding controller design for nonlinear systems. *Int. J. Control* **1984**, *40*, 421–434. [CrossRef]
7. Slotine, J.J. *Applied Nonlinear Control*; Prentice-Hall: Englewood Cliffs, NJ, USA, 1987.
8. Barrero, F.; Gonzalez, A.; Torralba, A.; Galvan, E.; Franquelo, L.G. Speed control of induction motors using a novel fuzzy sliding-mode structure. *IEEE Trans. Fuzzy Syst.* **2002**, *10*, 375–383. [CrossRef]
9. Lin, F.; Chou, W.; Huang, P. Adaptive sliding-mode controller based on real-time genetic algorithm for induction motor servo drive. *IEEE Proc. Electr. Power Appl.* **2003**, *150*, 1–13. [CrossRef]
10. Barambones, O.; Garrido, A.J.; Maseda, F.J.; Alkorta, P. An adaptive sliding mode control law for induction motors using field oriented control theory. In Proceedings of the IEEE International Symposium on Intelligent Control (ISIC), Munich, Switherland, 4–6 October 2006; pp. 1008–1013.
11. Levant, A. Sliding order and sliding accuracy in sliding mode control. *Int. J. Control* **1993**, *58*, 1247–1263. [CrossRef]
12. Emel'yanov, S.V.; Korovin, S.V.; Levantovsky, L.V. Higher Order Sliding Modes in the Binary Control System. *Sov. Phys.* **1986**, *31*, 291–293.
13. Fridman, L.; Levant, A. *Higher-Order Sliding Modes, Sliding Mode Control in Engineering*; Control Engineering Series; Marcel Dekker Inc.: New York, NY, USA, 2002.
14. Bondarev, A.G.; Bondarev, S.A.; Kosteleva, N.E.; Utkin, V.I. Sliding Modes in Systems with Asymptotic State Observers. *Autom. Remote Control* **1985**, *46*, 49–64.
15. Al-Muthairi, N.; Zribi, M. Sliding mode control of a magnetic levitation system. *Math. Probl. Eng.* **2004**, *2004*, 93–107. [CrossRef]
16. Boonsatit, N.; Pukdeboon, C. Adaptive fast terminal sliding mode control of magnetic levitation system. *J. Control Autom. Electr. Syst.* **2016**, *27*, 359–367. [CrossRef]
17. Youcef, Z.; Sami, A. Comparison of PID and Fuzzy Controller for Path Tracking Control of Autonomous Electrical Vehicles. In Proceedings of the IEEE International Conference on Electrical Sciences and Technologies in Maghreb (CISTEM), Algiers, Algeria, 29–31 October 2018; p. 6.

Proceeding Paper

Mechanical Failure Detection in Induction Motors Using Stator Current and Stray Flux Analysis Techniques [†]

Remus Pusca [1], Salim Sbaa [2], Noureddine Bessous [3,*], Raphaël Romary [1] and Radouane Bousseksou [3]

1. Laboratory of Electrotechnical and Environmental Systems (EA-4025) Technology, University of Artois, F-62400 Béthune, France; remus.pusca@univ-artois.fr (R.P.); raphael.romary@univ-artois.fr (R.R.)
2. Department of Electrical Engineering, Faculty of Technology, University of Mohamed Khider, Biskra 07000, Algeria; s_sbaa@yahoo.fr
3. Department of Electrical Engineering, Faculty of Technology, University of El Oued, El Oued 39000, Algeria; bousseksou.rad@gmail.com
* Correspondence: nbessous@yahoo.fr
† Presented at the 1st International Conference on Computational Engineering and Intelligent Systems, Online, 10–12 December 2021.

Abstract: Because of its benefits, an induction machine is used in a variety of applications. The machine's robustness is one of its benefits. Generally, mechanical faults cause torque oscillations, eccentricity, and vibration, which affect the stator current value and magnetic field distribution. As a result, early warning of mechanical failures helps to prevent damage to the induction system or sudden stopping. In this sense, the accuracy of techniques in detecting rolling bearing failure is investigated in this article. The first method focused on stator current analysis and the second on stray flux signature analysis. The aim of this research is to compare the success of the stray flux technique and the stator current analysis in detecting inner raceway faults. In addition, this research suggests a novel method for determining the relationship between two signals based on a transfer function estimate and magnitude-squared coherence between current and flux. Experimental tests were realized in a laboratory to artificially create the bearing damage. After that, the analysis focused on characteristic harmonics related to the different harmonics.

Keywords: induction motors; rolling element bearing faults; motor current signature analysis; stray flux signature analysis; transfer function estimate; magnitude-squared coherence

Citation: Pusca, R.; Sbaa, S.; Bessous, N.; Romary, R.; Bousseksou, R. Mechanical Failure Detection in Induction Motors Using Stator Current and Stray Flux Analysis Techniques. *Eng. Proc.* 2022, 14, 19. https://doi.org/10.3390/engproc2022014019

Academic Editors: Abdelmadjid Recioui, Hamid Bentarzi and Fatma Zohra Dekhandji

Published: 11 February 2022

Publisher's Note: MDPI stays neutral with regard to jurisdictional claims in published maps and institutional affiliations.

Copyright: © 2022 by the authors. Licensee MDPI, Basel, Switzerland. This article is an open access article distributed under the terms and conditions of the Creative Commons Attribution (CC BY) license (https://creativecommons.org/licenses/by/4.0/).

1. Introduction

Induction motors (IMs) are commonly used in a variety of industrial uses. However, like all rotating electrical machines (REMs), they are vulnerable to a variety of faults. Monitoring is a crucial step in avoiding a sudden halt. Stator faults, rotor faults, bearing faults, and other faults are the most common fault classifications in IMs. The factor-bearing fault has a large proportion of fault distributions in IMs, reaching 41% [1]. Air-gap variance, torque oscillation, stator current over current, extreme loading, elevated losses, and others are some of the symptoms of this fault [2,3]. As a result, one of the most commonly used types of bearings in the mechanical method of REMs is the rolling element bearing (REB). Early detection of REB faults is essential in order to avoid a variety of damages, including economic losses, and they necessitate special supervision.

The fast Fourier transform (FFT) tool is one of the many that confirm a high level of efficiency in a stationary regime [4,5]. Researchers have recently used this method to study a variety of signals, including vibration, stator current, electromagnetic torque, and magnetic field signal [6–9]. Several faults have been detected using techniques such as artificial neural network (ANN), wavelet transform (WT), fuzzy logic (FL), Hilbert transform (HT), empirical mode decomposition (EMD), motor vibration signature analysis (MVSA), and motor current signature analysis (MCSA) [10–13]. Many scholars in the field of REM diagnosis have recently been interested in the stray flux signature analysis (SFSA) technique [14–16].

This paper examines the feasibility of using stray flux to detect REB faults in IM type. The main objective of this technique is to detect the REB fault. The IM used in the experimental test bench presented in Figure 1 has the following characteristics: P = 4 kW, p = 1. The fundamental frequency of the stator currents is f_s = 50 Hz.

Figure 1. Test bench dedicated to REB fault in IM.

2. REB Characteristic for Experimental Test

It is known that there are four elements of the REB. According to these elements, we can cite four REB faults:

1. Ball fault (BF);
2. Inner raceway fault (IRF);
3. Outer race fault (ORF);
4. Cage fault (CF).

The REB type used in this study has the serial number 6206. It contains ball numbers (N_b = 9) and diameter (D_b = 9.5 mm). The dimensions of the REB of serial number 6206 are: outer diameter (D_o = 62 mm), inner diameter (D_i = 30 mm), and thickness value (D_{th} = 16 mm) (see Figure 2). The inner raceway fault (IRF) was artificially created to study the IM behavior.

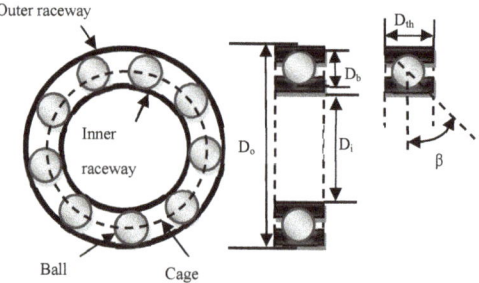

Figure 2. Schematic description of REB type.

3. Motor Current Signature Analysis (MCSA)

According to [17], the characteristic frequencies of the vibration signal for REBs, which has ball numbers between 6 and 12, can be approximated by:

$$f_{OR} = 0.4 N_b \times k \times f_r \tag{1}$$

$$f_{IR} = 0.6 N_b \times k \times f_r \quad (2)$$

where f_r is the mechanical rotor frequency given by:

$$f_r = \frac{(1-s)}{p} \cdot f_s \quad (3)$$

where s is the rotor slip.

Under REB faults, the spectral stator present includes the following additional harmonic components:

$$f^{\pm}_{charact-OR,IR,cage,ball} = |\nu f_s \pm k f_c| \quad (4)$$

where $f_c = f_{OR,IR,cage,ball}$ is the characteristic frequencies that can be found in the vibration signal spectrum, ν is the order of the stator time harmonics (ν = 1, 3, 5, etc.), and k is an integer.

Therefore, the characteristic frequencies that can be found in the stator current spectrum are:

$$f^{\pm}_{charact-IR-\nu,k} = |\nu f_s \pm k f_{IR}| \quad (5)$$

The IM runs with a nominal load (i.e., s = 3.66). In this case and according to Equation (3), the f_r value is 48.167 Hz. Table 1 summarizes some harmonics in the stator current spectrum caused by the IRF. It provides us a visual representation of the fault's several harmonics.

Table 1. Summary of some characteristic harmonics under IRF (s = 0.0366).

Formulas of Characteristic Harmonics in the Stator Current Spectrum	Theoretical Values (Hz)
$\|f_s + f_{IR}\|$	310.1018
$\|f_s - f_{IR}\|$	210.1018
$\|f_s + 2f_{IR}\|$	570.2036
$\|f_s - 2f_{IR}\|$	470.2036
$\|3f_s - f_{IR}\|$	110.1018
$\|5f_s - 2f_{IR}\|$	270.2036

The specific frequencies of the mixed rotor eccentricity fault are given by:

$$f_{mix-ecc} = |f_s \pm k f_r| \quad (6)$$

where k = 1, 2, 3, ...

It is known that these frequencies exist even in a healthy IM.

We can define the rotor slot harmonics (RSHs) given by:

$$f_{RSHs} = \left[\frac{k.N_{rb}(1-s)}{p} \pm \nu \right] \cdot f_s \quad (7)$$

where k is an integer. We can also define the saturation frequencies (f_{sat}) expressed as follows [18]:

$$f_{sat} = 3k f_s \quad (8)$$

where k is an odd number.

In all figures below, we will consider that the blue color represents the healthy state of an IM, and the red color represents the inner raceway fault.

Figure 3 presents characteristic frequencies of the IRF with low amplitude: 10, 110.3, 210.1, 270.4 Hz, and so forth. These frequencies verify Equation (5).

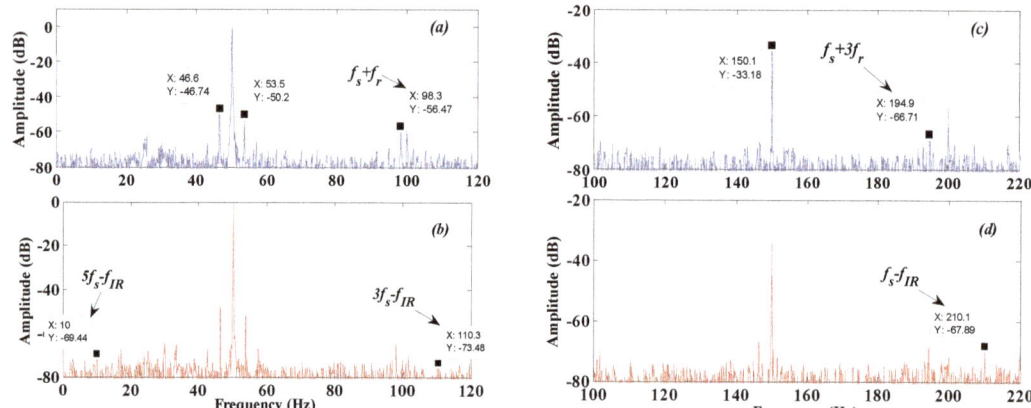

Figure 3. Stator current spectrum in healthy case (**a**,**c**) and IRF case (**b**,**d**) for 0–120 Hz and 100–220 Hz.

The frequency components of the mixed eccentricity fault are: $f_s + f_r$ and $f_s + 3f_r$. According to Figure 3, they have the values: 98.3 and 194.9 Hz respectively.

In the frequency band 250–550 Hz, we found the characteristic frequency which has the formula: $5f_s - 2f_{IR}$. In addition, the Lower Principal Slot Harmonics (L-PSH) and the Upper Principal Slot Harmonics (U-PSH) have the values 1195 and 1395 Hz respectively. They are clearly presented in the stator current spectra.

The distinction states of an IM under an IRF can be seen in the stator current spectra as we can see that the IRF frequencies have low amplitude.

4. Stray Flux Signature Analysis (SFSA)

For the study of rolling bearing faults, the SFSA is proposed as an alternative investigative technique [19]. It is based on the measurement of stray flux in various locations around the REM.

In Figures 4 and 5, the evolution of many types of amplitude, such as $s \times f_s$ and $3s \times f_s$ wavelength, can be seen and detected ($s = 0.0366$). In addition to $s \times f_s$ and $3s \times f_s$, the black arrow color represents new harmonics that tend to be inspired by the IRF.

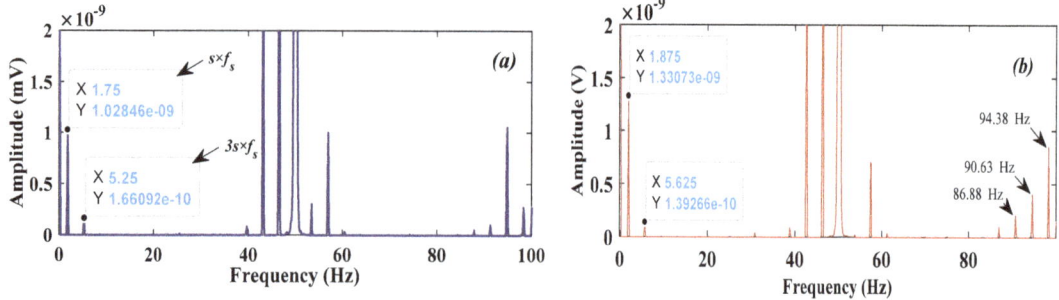

Figure 4. Flux spectrum: signal in healthy case (**a**) and IRF case (**b**) for 0–100 Hz.

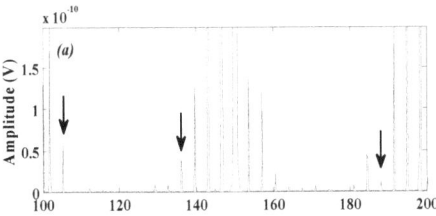 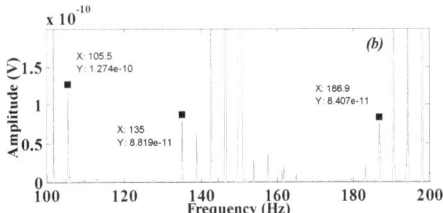

Figure 5. Flux spectrum: signal in healthy case (**a**) and IRF case (**b**).

In reality, rotor electrical and mechanical faults, as well as REB faults, have no effect on stator currents; however, they cause rotor eccentricity, which can deform the IM magnetic field's symmetry. The IRF can be detected in different range frequencies based on the flux spectra, which is determined using the coil sensors.

The analysis of SFSA-FFT allows us to find additional harmonics that appear at the same frequency given by Equation (5), which are $f_s - f_{IR}$ and $f_s + 2f_{IR}$.

These values correspond, respectively, at 209.8 H with Amp = 5.29×10^{-10} V and 569.4 Hz with Amp = 5.5×10^{-10} V. This confirms the results found in Table 1 (f_{IR} = 210.1018 Hz and $f_s + f_{IR}$ = 570.2036 Hz). In addition, other harmonics due to the mixed eccentricity of the rotor clearly appeared as $f_s + f_r$ = 98.13 Hz, $f_s + 2f_r$ = 146.3 Hz, $f_s + 3f_r$ = 194.3 Hz, and so forth.

It is interesting to note that these new frequencies are the same ones that were discovered in the stator current spectra. When one is the representation of the other, this verifies the relationship between current and flux (see Figure 6).

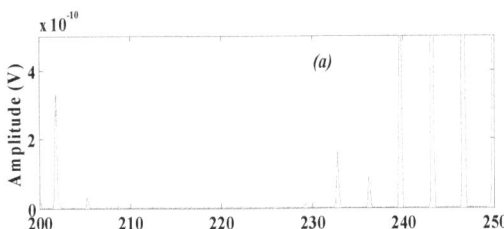 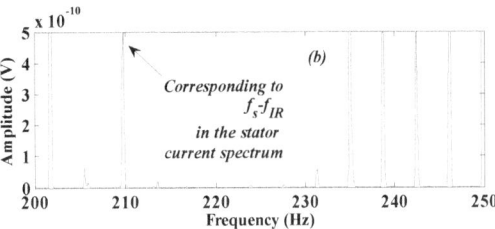

Figure 6. Flux spectrum: (**a**) healthy IM, (**b**) IRF.

Under the pole of the IM, which is equal to 1 ($p = 1$) when $sf_s = f_s - f_r$, we can denote the overlap between the frequencies sf_s and $f_s - f_r$. Table 2 shows the amplitude evolutions of certain $f_s + kf_r$ frequencies (3).

Table 2. Amplitude evolution of mixed eccentricity harmonics.

$f_s \pm kf_r$	Amp. Healthy IM (V)	Amp. Faulty IM (IRF) (V)
$f_s + f_r$	2.728×10^{-10}	8.547×10^{-10}
$f_s + 2f_r$	5.271×10^{-9}	1.576×10^{-9}
$f_s + 3f_r$	1.317×10^{-9}	7.401×10^{-10}

Finally, the SFSA-FFT study demonstrated the sensitivity of this technique in detecting the IRF. Furthermore, the amplitude variance of specific flux harmonics is related to current variations, as well as the appearance of certain new harmonics.

5. Transfer Function Estimate Analysis (TFEA)

The proposed method for system identification using a frequency analysis approach is briefly described below, followed by a detailed presentation of the theory. This method starts by finding a rough estimate of the relationship between signals (transfer function). This estimate is then mapped to a magnitude frequency representation. Information that is a physical realization of the system is retained, while information believed to be due to noise is discarded [20].

T_{xy} = tfestimate(x,y) finds a transfer function estimate (TF-estimate), and the input signal vector x (current or flux) and the output signal vector y (current or flux) are given to T_{xy}. The lengths of the vectors x and y must be equal. The linear, time-invariant transfer function T_{xy} models the relationship between input x and output y. The quotient of the cross power spectral density (P_{yx}) of x and y and the power spectral density (P_{xx}) of x is the transition function.

$$T_{xy}(f) = \frac{P_{yx}(f)}{P_{xx}(f)} \tag{9}$$

If x is real, tfestimate only estimates the transfer function at positive frequencies; in this case, T_{xy} is a column vector with lengths of nfft/2 + 1 for nfft even and (nfft + 1)/2 for nfft odd. Tfestimate calculates the transition function for both positive and negative frequencies if x or y is complex, and T_{xy} has length nfft [21].

This part will try to discuss the transfer function for the following two cases:
- Healthy IM: input (flux) and output (current).
- Faulty IM: input (flux) and output (current).

5.1. TF-Estimate for Healthy IM

The transfer function between flux and current for a healthy IM is shown in Figure 7.

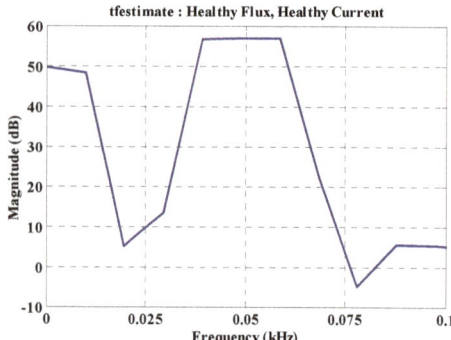 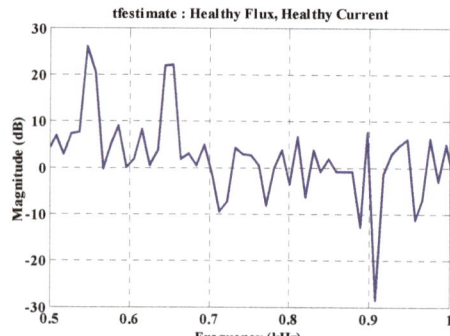

Figure 7. Transfer function estimate under different frequency bands (healthy IM).

Figure 7 shows the transfer function between two states of the IM. This information can help us to have a decision on the state of the induction machine. In addition, this information is considered as a new data which can exploit it for another analysis.

5.2. TF-Estimate for Faulty IM

The results that present the tfestimate between flux and current for a faulty IM is presented in Figure 8.

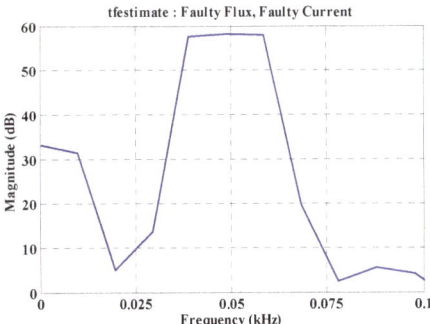 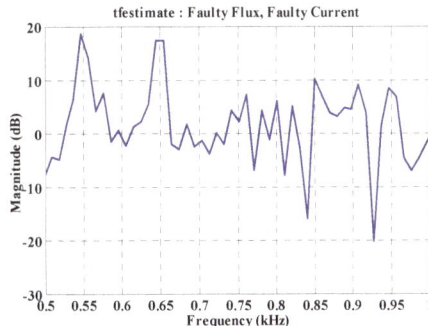

Figure 8. Transfer function estimate under different frequency bands (faulty IM).

The figures above show the transfer function between two signals. These signals can indicate very specific shapes for each fault. The exploitation of the transfer functions obtained can lead us to have a final decision on the state of the induction machine.

6. Mean-Squared Coherence Analysis (MSCA)

Carter and al. [22] developed the magnitude-squared coherence (mscohere) function, which used the weighted overlapped segmentation fast Fourier transform (FFT) approach.

Using Welch's averaged modified periodogram form, C_{xy} = mscohere(x,y) finds the magnitude squared coherence estimate, C_{xy}, of the input signals, x and y. The magnitude squared coherence approximation is a frequency function with values ranging from 0 to 1, and it shows how well x relates to y at each frequency. The magnitude squared coherence of x and y is a function of their power spectral densities, $P_{xx}(f)$ and $P_{yy}(f)$, as well as their cross power spectral densities, $P_{xy}(f)$:

$$T_{xy}(f) = \frac{P_{yx}(f)}{P_{xx}(f)} \quad (10)$$

The lengths of x and y must be equal. Mscohere returns a one-sided coherence approximation for real x and y. It returns a two-sided approximation for complex x or y [23].

Therefore, this technique can guide us to check the similarity between the spectra. This allows us to find the frequency zone affected by the fault.

It is important to put the principle of consistency between the signals studied as follows:

- Mscohere close to 1: The two signals have the same spectral content (similar).
- Mscohere close to 0: The two signals do not have the same spectral content.

Based on this strategy, we can easily define the area or frequency band where the new harmonics exist.

6.1. MS-Cohere for Healthy and Faulty IM (Currents)

First, we compared the current signals for a healthy and a faulty IM. According to Figures 9 and 10, the evolution of mscohere is clear. For different frequency bands between 0 and 5 kHz, the similarity of the frequencies corresponds to the similarity studied in the analysis of the current and the flux. The values of mscohere direct us directly to the affected frequency band.

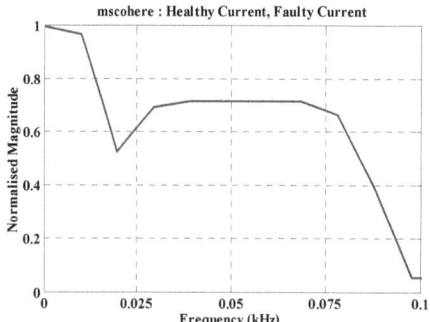
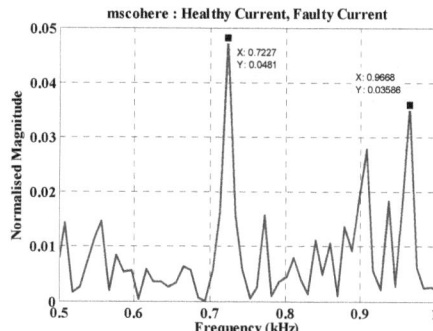

Figure 9. Magnitude-squared coherence of currents under different frequency bands (healthy and faulty IM).

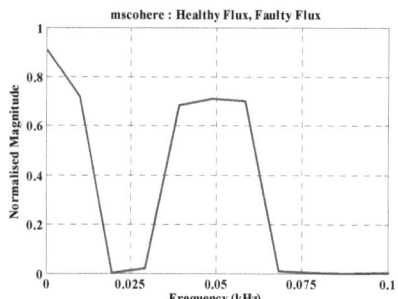
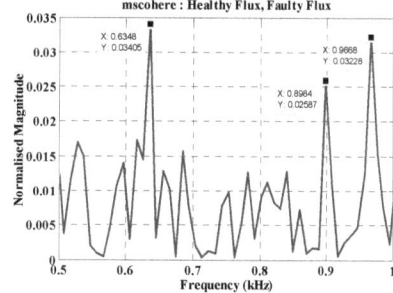

Figure 10. Magnitude-squared coherence of flux under different frequency bands (healthy and faulty IM).

It is clear that in certain frequency bands, the signals have the same spectral content. This indicates that this information can be used to analyze the affected bands.

6.2. MS-Cohere for Healthy and Faulty IM (Flux)

The results that compare two flux signals under a healthy and a faulty IM can be presented in Figure 10.

The evolution of the value of mscohere is between 0 and 1; the affected frequency band is clearly defined.

The advantages of this new proposal are to have a significant signal which can help us to detect the fault.

It is clear that in certain frequency bands, the signals have the same spectral content. In addition, all values close to 1 indicate the similarity in spectral content between the two signals. This information can help us to have a decision on the state of the induction machine.

7. Conclusions

The use of MCSA-FFT and SFSA-FFT to detect rolling element bearing faults in an IM is compared in this paper.

In summary, the MCSA-FFT analysis did not reveal any significant amplitude variation of mixed eccentricity or specific IRF frequencies in the stator current spectrum.

Stray flux signature analysis sensitive to the REB gave good information on the IRF. The use of SFSA-FFT in combination with at least one of the conventional techniques can be an advantageous method for increasing the reliability of the diagnosis.

The proposal of tfestimate in the diagnosis field of rotating electrical machines opens the door to have a relationship between signals. On the other hand, the transfer function can give important information on the behavior of the signals used.

We introduce a new indicator based on mscohere, which aims at characterizing a specific frequency band of the characteristic frequencies. This feature allows us to directly analyze the affected band frequency.

Author Contributions: Conceptualization, R.P.; methodology, R.R., N.B. and S.S.; validation, R.P., R.R. and N.B.; investigation, R.P., R.R., N.B. and S.S.; resources, R.P., R.R. and N.B.; data curation, R.P., N.B. and R.R.; writing—original draft preparation, R.P., N.B. and R.R.; writing—review and editing, R.R., R.P. and N.B.; visualization, R.R., R.P. and N.B.; supervision, R.R., R.P., N.B., S.S. and R.B. All authors have read and agreed to the published version of the manuscript.

Funding: Financial support from "Laboratory of Electrotechnical and Environmental Systems (EA-4025), Technology, University of Artois, F-62400 Béthune, France".

Institutional Review Board Statement: Not applicable.

Informed Consent Statement: Not applicable.

Data Availability Statement: Not applicable.

Acknowledgments: The technical and human support provided by Laboratory of Electrotechnical and Environmental Systems is gratefully acknowledged.

Conflicts of Interest: The authors declare no conflict of interest.

References

1. Bessous, N. Reliability Surveys of Fault Distributions in Rotating Electrical Machines: –Case Study of Fault Detections in IMs–. In Proceedings of the 2020 1st International Conference on Communications, Control Systems and Signal Processing (CCSSP), El Oued, Algeria, 16–17 May 2020; pp. 535–543.
2. Huang, X.; Wen, G.; Dong, S.; Zhou, H.; Lei, Z.; Zhang, Z.; Chen, X. Memory Residual Regression Autoencoder for Bearing Fault Detection. *IEEE Trans. Instrum. Meas.* **2021**, *70*, 3515512. [CrossRef]
3. Duan, N.; Wang, J.; Zhao, T.; Du, W.; Guo, X.; Wang, J. Novel Adaptive Fault Diagnosis Method for Wind Power Gearbox. *IEEE Access* **2021**, *9*, 11226–11240. [CrossRef]
4. Bessous, N.; Pusca, R.; Romary, R.; Sbaa, S. Rolling Bearing Failure Detection in Induction Motors using Stator Current, Vibration and Stray Flux Analysis Techniques. In Proceedings of the IECON 2020 The 46th Annual Conference of the IEEE Industrial Electronics Society, Singapore, 18–21 October 2020; pp. 1088–1095.
5. Puche-Panadero, R.; Martinez-Roman, J.; Sapena-Bano, A.; Burriel-Valencia, J.; Pineda-Sanchez, M.; Perez-Cruz, J.; Riera-Guasp, M. New Method for Spectral Leakage Reduction in the FFT of Stator Currents: Application to the Diagnosis of Bar Breakages in Cage Motors Working at Very Low Slip. *IEEE Trans. Instrum. Meas.* **2021**, *70*, 3511111. [CrossRef]
6. Capolino, G.A.; Romary, R.; Hénao, H.; Pusca, R. State of the art on stray flux analysis in faulted electrical machines. In Proceedings of the IEEE Workshop on Electrical Machines Design, Control and Diagnosis (WEMDCD), Athens, Greece, 22–23 April 2019; Volume 1, pp. 181–187.
7. Gyftakis, K.N.; Panagiotou, P.A.; Lee, S.B. The role of the mechanical speed frequency on the induction motor fault detection via the stray flux. In Proceedings of the IEEE 12th International Symposium on Diagnostics for Electrical Machines, Power Electronics and Drives (SDEMPED), Toulouse, France, 27–30 August 2019; pp. 201–207.
8. Samanta, A.K.; Routray, A.; Khare, S.R.; Naha, A. Minimum Distance-Based Detection of Incipient Induction Motor Faults Using Rayleigh Quotient Spectrum of Conditioned Vibration Signal. *IEEE Trans. Instrum. Meas.* **2021**, *70*, 3508311. [CrossRef]
9. Chirindo, M.; Khan, M.; Barendse, P. Analysis of Non-Intrusive Rotor Speed Estimation Techniques for Inverter-Fed Induction Motors. *IEEE Trans. Energy Convers.* **2020**, *36*, 338–347. [CrossRef]
10. Liu, Z.; Zheng, Z.; Li, Y. Enhancing fault-tolerant ability of a nine-phase induction motor drive system using fuzzy logic current controllers. *IEEE Trans. Energy Convers.* **2017**, *32*, 759–769. [CrossRef]
11. Guo, S.; Yang, T.; Gao, W.; Zhang, C.; Zhang, Y. An intelligent fault diagnosis method for bearings with variable rotating speed based on pythagorean spatial pyramid pooling CNN. *Sensors* **2018**, *18*, 3857. [CrossRef] [PubMed]
12. Khodja, A.Y.; Guersi, N.; Saadi, M.N.; Boutasseta, N. Rolling element bearing fault diagnosis for rotating machinery using vibration spectrum imaging and convolutional neural networks. *Int. J. Adv. Manuf. Technol.* **2020**, *106*, 1737–1751. [CrossRef]
13. Ding, J.; Xiao, D.; Li, X. Gear fault diagnosis based on genetic mutation particle swarm optimization VMD and probabilistic neural network algorithm. *IEEE Access* **2020**, *8*, 18456–18474. [CrossRef]
14. Lamim Filho, P.C.; Rabelo, L.M.; Batista, F.B.; Araújo, A.C. Orbit Analysis from a Stray Flux Full Spectrum for Induction Machine Fault Detection. *IEEE Sens. J.* **2021**, *21*, 16152–16161. [CrossRef]

15. Pusca, R.; Romary, R.; Bessous, N.; Sbaa, S. Comparative Study between Two Diagnostic Techniques Dedicated to the Mechanical Fault Detection in Induction Motors. In Proceedings of the 2020 International Conference on Electrical Engineering (ICEE), Istanbul, Turkey, 25–27 September 2020; pp. 1–8.
16. Park, Y.; Choi, H.; Lee, S.B.; Gyftakis, K.N. Search Coil-Based Detection of Nonadjacent Rotor Bar Damage in Squirrel Cage Induction Motors. *IEEE Trans. Ind. Appl.* **2020**, *56*, 4748–4757. [CrossRef]
17. Schoen, R.R.; Habetler, T.G.; Kamran, F.; Bartheld, R.G. Motor bearing damage detection using stator current monitoring. *IEEE Trans. Ind. Appl.* **1995**, *31*, 1274–1279. [CrossRef]
18. Bessous, N.; Sbaa, S.; Toumi, A. A detailed study of the spectral content in the stator current of asynchronous machines under broken rotor bar faults using MCSA technique. In Proceedings of the IEEE International Conference on Control Engineering & Information Technology (CEIT), Istanbul, Turkey, 25–27 October 2018; pp. 1–8.
19. Frosini, L.; Minervini, M.; Ciceri, L.; Albini, A. Multiple faults detection in low voltage inverter-fed induction motors. In Proceedings of the 2019 IEEE 12th International Symposium on Diagnostics for Electrical Machines, Power Electronics and Drives (SDEMPED), Toulouse, France, 27–30 August 2019.
20. Ilvedson, C.R. Transfer Function Estimation Using Time-Frequency Analysis. Doctoral Dissertation, Massachusetts Institute of Technology, Cambridge, MA, USA, 1998.
21. Soysal, A.O.; Semlyen, A. Practical transfer function estimation and its application to wide frequency range representation of transformers. *IEEE Trans. Power Deliv.* **1993**, *8*, 1627–1637. [CrossRef]
22. Carter, G.; Knapp, C.; Nuttall, A. Estimation of the magnitude-squared coherence function via overlapped fast Fourier transform processing. *IEEE Trans. Audio Electroacoust.* **1973**, *21*, 337–344. [CrossRef]
23. Sassaroli, A.; Tgavalekos, K.; Fantini, S. The meaning of "coherent" and its quantification in coherent hemodynamics spectroscopy. *J. Innov. Opt. Health Sci.* **2018**, *11*, 1850036. [CrossRef] [PubMed]

Proceeding Paper

Sliding Mode Control Based on Backstepping Approach for Microsatellite Attitude Pointing [†]

Halima Boussadia [1,*], Arezki Mohamed Si Mohammed [2], Nabil Boughanmi [1] and Abdelkrim Meche [3]

1. Department of Electronic, LARESI Laboratory, USTO-MB University, Oran 31000, Algeria; nabil.boughanmi@univ-usto.dz
2. Department of Space Mechanic Research, Centre of Satellite Development, Oran 31000, Algeria; masimohammed@asal.cds.dz
3. Department of Electronic, LSI Laboratory, USTO-MB University, Oran 31000, Algeria; meche_abdelkrim@yahoo.fr

* Correspondence: halima.boussadia@univ-usto.dz

† Presented at the 1st International Conference on Computational Engineering and Intelligent Systems, Online, 10–12 December 2021.

Abstract: The primary goal of this work is to present the design of sliding mode control, based on the backstepping approach, for the attitude tracking control of a micro-satellite, using reaction wheels. The presented technique is developed by combining sliding mode control with the backstepping technique, to achieve a fast and accurate tracking response. Firstly, backstepping and sliding mode controllers are developed. Then, the hybrid controller is designed. The selected controllers are applied to a Low Earth Orbit (LEO) micro-satellite, and they are compared in terms of accuracy, convergence time, power consumption, and maximum reaction wheel velocity. The simulation results clearly demonstrate the effectiveness of the presented technique.

Keywords: satellite; control; sliding mode; backstepping; satellite

1. Introduction

In recent years, satellites have become an important application area of new technological developments.

They are used in many fields, such as telecommunications, satellite surveillance, earth observation, and defense technologies. For the success of these missions, the satellite must be stabilized at a desired attitude.

The attitude is the orientation of the satellite in the space. In the absence of control, it evolves naturally under the effect of external disturbances [1]. Therefore, the attitude control problem is an interesting part of the research into new space technologies. It has attracted much attention in recent years because of the many types of space missions now being undertaken.

In satellite systems, the Attitude Determination and Control System (ADCS) is one of the most important systems, as it ensures the pointing of all satellite subsystems in the right direction during satellite missions (it ensures the pointing of the antenna into Earth's direction, solar array into sun direction, sensors into target direction, and thrusters into thrust direction).

In practical situations, satellites are subject to different external disturbances, which are characterized by coupled and nonlinear dynamics. Their tasks have become more complex and diverse, which put forward higher requirements for the accuracy and stability of the satellite attitude system [2]. Thus, the design of the attitude controllers is usually difficult.

Due to the above-mentioned problem, a large variety of nonlinear controllers have been proposed. These controllers include sliding mode control [3,4], fuzzy control [5], backstepping control and feedback control [6,7]. Among these control techniques, the backstepping and sliding mode are the most robust controls. The advantage of these two controls is that they are based on the Lyapunov theory, and particularly on the second method of Lyapunov (direct method), which ensures stability.

The backstepping control has been very useful in the space field over the past few years. In [8], this technique was used with the inverse optimal control to stabilize spacecraft attitude. In [9], backstepping was based on a similar skew-symmetric structure. In [1], it was developed based on the adaptive design of Lyapunov. Also, in [10], it was used based on adaptive design, to develop an attitude controller in the presence of the uncertainties of inertia parameters. In [11], the authors presented control by integrator backstepping with internal stabilization.

The sliding mode control is based on a sliding surface and the state trajectory is brought to this surface. This technique has been used in many studies for spacecraft attitude control. It was designed for spacecraft attitude tracking in [12], and for flexible spacecraft in [13]. In [14], the sliding mode control was developed based on the artificial neural network, adjusted by a genetic algorithm, to control the attitude of Alsat-1 (the first Algerian satellite). In [15], the authors presented control by sliding mode under body angular velocity constraints.

The main advantages of the sliding mode technique are its fast state convergence and its simplicity of implementation, in comparison with the backstepping technique, but the latter is more accurate than the sliding mode control. Therefore, the combination of these two techniques provides good performance.

In this work, we combine the two presented techniques (sliding mode and backstepping) to obtain a fast and accurate tracking response, with the presented controller developed using the technique presented in [16]. To demonstrate its effectiveness, we give a comparison between backstepping, sliding mode, and hybrid controller, in terms of accuracy, convergence time, power consumption, and maximum reaction wheel velocity.

The paper is organized as follows: Section 2 presents the dynamic and kinematic models used for the satellite; Sections 3–5 describe the design of the control laws that are presented in this work; in the next section, we present the simulation results, and finally, the conclusion of this paper is presented in Section 6.

2. Spacecraft Attitude Model

The dynamics of the spacecraft in inertial space, governed by Euler's equations of motion, can be expressed as follows, in vector form as [16,17]:

$$I\dot{\omega}_s^I = C_{ext} + I\omega_s^I \times \left(I\omega_s^I + h\right) - \dot{h} \quad (1)$$

where, $I = \begin{bmatrix} I_x & I_y & I_z \end{bmatrix}$ moment of inertia of spacecraft, $\omega_s^I = \begin{bmatrix} \omega_x & \omega_y & \omega_z \end{bmatrix}^T$ angular velocity vector in the inertial frame, $h = \begin{bmatrix} h_x & h_y & h_z \end{bmatrix}^T$ angular moment vector and $C_{ext} = \begin{bmatrix} C_x & C_y & C_z \end{bmatrix}^T$ external disturbance torque vector.

The kinematic equation, as follows, is expressed as:

$$\dot{q} = \frac{1}{2}\Omega q = \frac{1}{2}\Lambda(q) \quad (2)$$

where, $q = \begin{bmatrix} q_1 & q_2 & q_3 & q_4 \end{bmatrix}$ quaternion.

$$\Omega = \begin{bmatrix} 0 & \omega_{oz} & -\omega_{oy} & \omega_{ox} \\ -\omega_{oz} & 0 & \omega_{ox} & \omega_{oy} \\ \omega_{oy} & -\omega_{ox} & 0 & \omega_{oz} \\ -\omega_{ox} & -\omega_{oy} & -\omega_{oz} & 0 \end{bmatrix} \quad (3)$$

Equation (4) is as follows:

$$\Lambda(q) = \begin{bmatrix} q_4 & -q_3 & q_2 \\ q_3 & q_4 & -q_1 \\ -q_2 & q_1 & q_4 \\ -q_1 & -q_2 & -q_3 \end{bmatrix} \quad (4)$$

The angular body rates referenced to the orbit coordinates can be obtained from the inertial referenced body rates by using the transformation matrix A, in the following, as [18]:

$$\omega_s^o = \omega_s^I - A\omega_0 \quad (5)$$

where, $\omega_s^o = \begin{bmatrix} \omega_{ox} & \omega_{oy} & \omega_{oz} \end{bmatrix}^T$ is the angular velocity vector in the orbital reference frame.

The attitude matrix to transform any vector from the reference orbital to body coordinates in terms of quaternion is expressed in the following way, as:

$$A = \begin{bmatrix} q_1^2 - q_2^2 - q_3^2 + q_4^2 & 2(q_1q_2 + q_3q_4) & 2(q_1q_3 - q_2q_4) \\ 2(q_1q_2 - q_3q_4) & -q_1^2 + q_2^2 - q_3^2 + q_4^2 & 2(q_2q_3 + q_1q_4) \\ 2(q_1q_3 + q_2q_4) & 2(q_2q_3 - q_1q_4) & -q_1^2 - q_2^2 + q_3^2 + q_4^2 \end{bmatrix} \quad (6)$$

From Equations (1) and (2), the satellite mathematical model can be written in the following way, as:

$$\dot{x} = f(x) + Bu \quad (7)$$

$$y = Hx \quad (8)$$

where,

$x = [q_1, q_2, q_3, q_4, \omega_x, \omega_y, \omega_z]^T$ is the state vector;
$B = \begin{bmatrix} 0_{4\times3} & I_{3\times3} \end{bmatrix}^T$ is the control matrix;
$H = \begin{bmatrix} I_{4\times4} & 0_{4\times3} \end{bmatrix}$ is the observation matrix;
$U = -\dot{h}$ is the control input torque.

$$f(x) = \begin{bmatrix} 0.5(\omega_{oz}q_2 - \omega_{oy}q_3 + \omega_{ox}q_4) \\ 0.5(-\omega_{oz}q_1 + \omega_{ox}q_3 + \omega_{oy}q_4) \\ 0.5(\omega_{oy}q_1 - \omega_{ox}q_2 + \omega_{oz}q_4) \\ 0.5(-\omega_{ox}q_1 - \omega_{oy}q_2 - \omega_{oz}q_3) \\ I_x^{-1}(C_x - (I_z - I_y)\omega_y\omega_z - \omega_y h_z + \omega_z h_y) \\ I_y^{-1}(C_y - (I_x - I_z)\omega_x\omega_z + \omega_x h_z - \omega_z h_x) \\ I_z^{-1}(C_z - (I_y - I_x)\omega_x\omega_y - \omega_x h_y + \omega_y h_x) \end{bmatrix} \quad (9)$$

3. Backstepping Control Design

This section presents the design of the backstepping control technique, which is inspired by [19].

The presented algorithm is described in two steps, as follows:

3.1. Step 1

Firstly, we define the first and the second variable of backstepping, below:

$$z_1 = x_1 = q_e = q_c q \quad (10)$$

$$z_2 = x_2 - \alpha_1 \quad (11)$$

where, α_1 is a virtual control law.

The time derivative of z_1 is expressed, below, as:

$$\dot{z}_1 = \dot{x}_1 = \dot{q}_e = q_c\left(\frac{1}{2}\Lambda(q)\omega_s^o\right) \tag{12}$$

The first Lyapunov function is defined, below, as:

$$V_1(z_1) = z_1^T z_1 \tag{13}$$

Its time derivative is expressed, below, as:

$$\dot{V}_1 = 2z_1^T \dot{z}_1 = z_1^T G(q) z_2 + z_1^T G(q) \alpha_1 \tag{14}$$

where,

$$G(q) = q_c \Lambda(q) \tag{15}$$

To make $\dot{V}_1$ negative, α_1 is chosen as the following:

$$\alpha_1 = -k_1 G(q)^T z_1 \tag{16}$$

where, k_1 is a positive gain matrix.

The time derivative of V_1 becomes the following:

$$\dot{V}_1 = -z_1^T G(q) k_1 G(q)^T z_1 + z_1^T G(q) z_2 \tag{17}$$

The term $z_1^T G(q) z_2$ will be eliminated in the next step.

3.2. Step 2

The time derivative of z_2 is expressed in the following way, as:

$$\dot{z}_2 = \dot{\omega}_s^o - \dot{\alpha}_1 \tag{18}$$

where,

$$\omega_s^o = \omega_s^I - A\omega_0 \tag{19}$$

We replace Equation (18) in (17), obtaining the following:

$$\dot{z}_2 = \dot{\omega}_s^I - \dot{A}\omega_0 - \dot{\alpha}_1 \tag{20}$$

$$I\dot{z}_2 = I\dot{\omega}_s^I - I\dot{A}\omega_0 - I\dot{\alpha}_1 \tag{21}$$

The second Lyapunov function is defined, below, as:

$$V_2(z_1, z_2) = V_1(z_1) + \frac{1}{2} z_2^T I z_2 \tag{22}$$

Its time derivative is expressed, below, as:

$$\dot{V}_2 = \dot{V}_1 + z_2^T I \dot{z}_2 \tag{23}$$

$$\begin{aligned}\dot{V}_2 =& -z_1^T G(q) k_1 G(q)^T z_1 + z_1^T G(q) z_2 \\ &+ z_2^T \left[\left(C_{ext} - \omega_s^I \times (I\omega_s^I + h) - \dot{h}\right)\right] - I\dot{A}\omega_0 - I\dot{\alpha}_1\end{aligned} \tag{24}$$

To makes $\dot{V}_2$ negative, the control law $\dot{h}$ is chosen, seen below, as:

$$\dot{h} = k_2 z_2 + G(q)^T z_1 + \left(C_{ext} - \omega_s^I \times \left(I\omega_s^I + h\right)\right) - I\dot{A}\omega_0 - I\dot{\alpha}_1 \tag{25}$$

4. Sliding Mode Control Design

In this section, sliding mode control law is developed. The sliding mode control SMC (also called variable structure control) design can be divided into three steps, explained below.

4.1. Choice of Sliding Surface

The sliding surface has a linear form, defined below, as:

$$\mathbf{S} = \dot{\mathbf{q}}_e + \mathbf{W}\mathbf{q}_e \tag{26}$$

where, $\mathbf{q}_e = \mathbf{q}_c\mathbf{q}$ is quaternion error, $\mathbf{q}_c$ is quaternion command and $\mathbf{W}$ is diagonal gain matrix.

4.2. Convergence and Existence Conditions

The convergence and existence conditions force the dynamic of the system to converge to the sliding surface, which is presented in the first step. This condition can be characterized by the following:

$$\mathbf{S}\dot{\mathbf{S}} < 0 \tag{27}$$

4.3. Establishment of the Control Law

The sliding mode control law is divided into two main parts, seen in the following [18]:

$$\mathbf{U} = \mathbf{U}_{eq} + \mathbf{U}_d \tag{28}$$

The first component of the proposed controller is $\mathbf{U}_{eq}$, which will make sliding surface $\mathbf{S}$ invariant, is calculated by setting the derivate of the sliding surface to zero [20], shown below:

$$\dot{\mathbf{S}} = 0 \tag{29}$$

The second component is an extra control effort, which forces the quaternion and angular velocity component to reach the sliding surface in a finite time, in spite of disturbances, and it is computed according to constant reaching law, seen below, as [20]:

$$\mathbf{U}_d = -\mathbf{k}\,\text{sign}(\mathbf{S}) \tag{30}$$

where, $\mathbf{k}$ is a positive gain.

To eliminate the chattering phenomenon caused by the sign function, we can replace this function by a saturation function.

Finally, we obtain the command in the following way, as:

$$\mathbf{U} = -\mathbf{k}\,\text{sign}(\mathbf{S}) + \tfrac{1}{2}\mathbf{q}_c\mathbf{I}^{-1} \\ \left[\mathbf{W}\mathbf{q}_c\dot{\mathbf{q}} + \mathbf{q}_c\left(\tfrac{1}{2}\mathbf{\Lambda}\omega_s^o - \tfrac{1}{2}\mathbf{\Lambda}\dot{\mathbf{A}}\omega_0 + \tfrac{1}{2}\mathbf{\Lambda}\mathbf{I}^{-1}\left(\mathbf{C}_{ext} - \omega_s^I \times (\mathbf{I}\omega_s^I + \mathbf{h})\right)\right)\right] \tag{31}$$

where ω_0 is the mean orbital angular velocity.

$$\mathbf{\Lambda}(\mathbf{q}) = \begin{bmatrix} q_4 & -q_3 & q_2 \\ q_3 & q_4 & -q_1 \\ -q_2 & q_1 & q_4 \\ -q_1 & -q_2 & -q_3 \end{bmatrix} \tag{32}$$

5. Backstepping–Sliding Mode Control Design

In this section, we develop a sliding mode controller based on the backstepping approach, using the technique presented in [16]. The presented technique is designed from the fusion of the backstepping control presented in Section 3, and the sliding mode control presented in Section 4.

Firstly, we define the first variable of backstepping and the sliding surface as follows:

$$z_1 = x_1 = q_e = q_c q \tag{33}$$

$$S = \dot{q}_e + W q_e \tag{34}$$

The Lyapunov functions are defined in the following way, as:

$$V_1(z_1) = z_1^T z_1 \tag{35}$$

$$V_2(z_1, S) = V_1(z_1) + \frac{1}{2} S^T S \tag{36}$$

The time derivative of V_2 is expressed, below, as:

$$\dot{V}_2 = 2 z_1^T \dot{z}_1 + S^T \dot{S} \tag{37}$$

We chose the time derivative of the sliding surface, satisfying the condition $S^T \dot{S} \langle 0$ [1], shown below:

$$\dot{S} = -a_1 \text{sat}(S) - \beta_1 S \tag{38}$$

$$\dot{S} = q_c \ddot{q} + W q_c \dot{q} \tag{39}$$

$$\dot{S} = q_c \left[W q_c \dot{q} + q_c \left(\frac{1}{2} \dot{\Lambda} \omega_s^o - \frac{1}{2} \Lambda \dot{\Lambda} \omega_0 + \frac{1}{2} \Lambda I^{-1} (C_{ext} - \omega_s^I \times (I \omega_s^I + h)) - \frac{1}{2} \Lambda I^{-1} \dot{h} \right) \right] + W q_c \dot{q} \tag{40}$$

Finally, the control law is given as follows:

$$U = \left(\frac{1}{2} q_c \Lambda I^{-1} \right)^{-1} \left[\frac{1}{2} q_c \dot{\Lambda} \omega_s^o - \frac{1}{2} q_c \Lambda \dot{\Lambda} \omega_0 + \frac{1}{2} q_c \Lambda I^{-1} (C_{ext} - \omega_s^I \times (I \omega_s^I + h)) \right] + a_1 \text{sat}(S) + \beta_1 S \tag{41}$$

6. Simulation Results

The simulation results are obtained using the following parameters, in Table 1.

Table 1. Satellite Parameters.

Parameter	Value
Inertia [kgm²]	diag([12 14 10])
Orbit [km]	686
Inclination [deg]	98
Initial attitude [deg]	[5 10 −10]
Initial angular rate [deg/sec]	[0 −0.06 0]
External Torques [N.m]	$\begin{bmatrix} 10^{-7}(5\cos(\omega_0 t)+1) \\ 10^{-7}(5\cos(\omega_0 t)+2\sin(\omega_0 t)) \\ 10^{-7}(5\cos(\omega_0 t)+1) \end{bmatrix}$

The desired attitude for the Euler angles is [10 30 20]. And the Control parameters are presented in Table 2.

Table 2. Control Parameters.

Sliding Mode Prameters		Backstepping Prameters		Sliding Mode-Backstepping Prameters		
W	k	k_1	k_2	W	a_1	β_1
0.06EYE(3)	200EYE(3)	0.01EYE(3)	8EYE(3)	0.08EYE(3)	110EYE(3)	3EYE(3)

For a more detailed analysis, the RMS errors, the convergence time, the power consumption, and the maximum reaction wheel velocity were calculated, presented in Table 3.

Table 3. Performance evaluation of the different controllers.

	Sliding Mode	Backstepping	Hybrid
RMS errors [deg]	0.0013	0.00068	0.0007
Convergence time [sec]	Roll 50.85 Pitch 126.30 Yaw 127.30	Roll 95.75 Pitch 178.43 Yaw 178.06	Roll 66.47 Pitch 112.55 Yaw 108.89
Power consumption	2.45×10^{-5}	2.46×10^{-5}	0.065
Maximum reaction wheel velocity	233.29	526.64	729.85

Figures 1–3 show the simulation results of the backstepping, sliding mode and hybrid control. We clearly observed that the three controllers ensure the attitude tracking, but the Euler angles, calculated by the sliding mode and hybrid controllers, are converged after a short period, in comparison with Euler angles calculated by the backstepping controller. The analysis of Table 3 shows that the backstepping controller was characterized by a low convergence time (127.30 s), and the sliding mode controller was characterized by a good accuracy (0.00068). We conclude that the backstepping controller is better than the sliding mode, in terms of accuracy. But in terms of convergence time, the sliding mode controller is better than the backstepping. On the other hand, the backstepping–sliding controller was characterized by high performance, in terms of convergence time and accuracy (109 s and 0.0007 degrees respectively) because it combined the advantages of the two controllers (backstepping and sliding mode). We also observed that the two first controllers were characterized by the same energy consumption (2.45×10^{-5} W), but the maximum reaction wheel velocity of the sliding mode controller was higher than that of the backstepping controller. On the other hand, the hybrid controller was characterized by high power consumption and a high maximum reaction wheel velocity (0.065 W and 729.85 rpm respectively). This is due to the hybridization of the two techniques (backstepping and sliding mode).

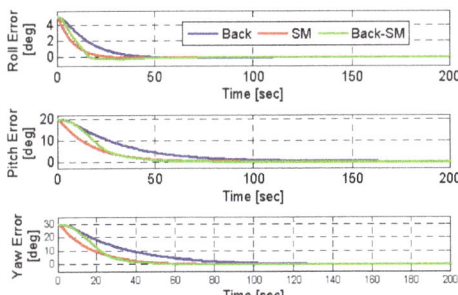

Figure 1. Euler angles errors.

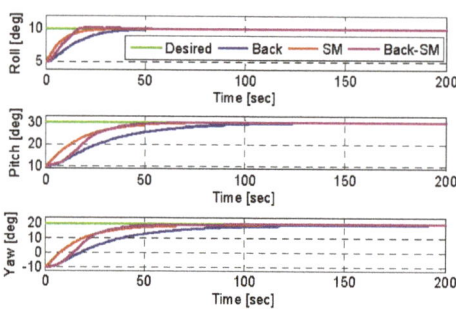

Figure 2. Attitude tracking control of Euler angles.

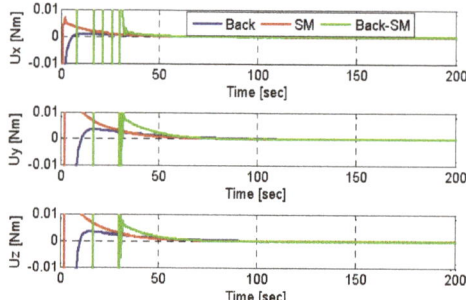

Figure 3. Control Torques.

7. Conclusions

In this work, we presented the design of sliding mode control, based on the backstepping approach, for Low Earth Orbit (LEO) micro-satellite attitude stabilization, using three axis controls by reaction wheels. The presented technique is developed by combining sliding mode control with the backstepping technique. Firstly, a nominal backstepping controller and nominal sliding mode controller were developed. Then, a combination of these two methods was designed to achieve fast and accurate tracking responses. The simulation results demonstrate the effectiveness of the presented technique. We found that the presented controller gives good performances because of the hybridization of the two techniques (backstepping and sliding mode).

Author Contributions: Writing—review and editing, H.B.; supervision, A.M.S.M. and N.B.; methodology, A.M. All authors have read and agreed to the published version of the manuscript.

Funding: This research received no external funding.

Institutional Review Board Statement: Not applicable.

Informed Consent Statement: Informed consent was obtained from all subjects involved in the study.

Data Availability Statement: The authors confirm that the data supporting the findings of this study are available within the article.

Conflicts of Interest: The authors declare that they have no conflict of interest.

References

1. Mohammed, M.A.S.; Boussadia, H.; Bellar, A.; Adnane, A. Adaptive backstepping control for three axis microsatellite attitude pointing under actuator faults. In Proceedings of the 13th European Workshop on Advanced Control and Diagnosis (ACD 2016), Lille, France, 17–18 November 2016.
2. Boskovic, J.D.; Li, S.M.; Mehra, M.K. Robust adaptive variable structure control of spacecraft under input saturation. *J. Guid. Control Dyn.* **2001**, *24*, 14–22. [CrossRef]
3. Lu, K.; Xia, Y.; Zhu, Z.; Basin, M.V. Sliding mode attitude tracking of rigid spacecraft with disturbance. *J. Frankl. Inst.* **2012**, *349*, 413–440. [CrossRef]
4. Zou, A.; Kumar, K.D. Adaptive fuzzy fault-tolerant attitude control of spacecraft. *Control Eng. Pract.* **2011**, *19*, 10–21. [CrossRef]
5. Costic, B.T.; Dawson, D.M.; Queiroz, M.S.; Kapila, V. Quaternion based attitude tracking control without velocity measurements. In Proceedings of the 39th IEEE Conference on Decision and Control, Sydney, Australia, 12–15 December 2000.
6. Wong, H.; de Queiroz, M.S.; Kapila, V. Adaptive tracking control using synthesized velocity from attitude measurements. *Automatica* **2001**, *37*, 947–953. [CrossRef]
7. Boussadia, H.; Mohammed, A.S.; Boughanmi, N.; Bellar, A. Adaptive Backstepping control for Microsatellite under Inertia Uncertainties. In Proceedings of the 39th IEEE Conference on Recent Advances in Space Technologies, Istanbul, Turkey, 19–22 June 2017.
8. Krstié, M.; Tsiotras, P. Inverse optimale stabilization of a rigid spacecraft. *IEEE Trans. Autom. Control* **1999**, *44*, 1014–1027.
9. Liu, Y.C.; Zhang, T.; Song, J.Y. Attitude controller design for larger angle maneuver based on similar skew-symmetric structure. *J. Astronaut.* **2009**, *30*, 1017–1023.
10. Doruk, R.Ö.; Kocaoğlan, E. Satellite attitude control by integrator backstepping with internal stabilization. *Aircr. Eng. Aerosp. Technol.* **2008**, *80*, 3–10. [CrossRef]
11. Crassidis, J.L.; Vadali, S.R.; Markley, F.L. Optimal Tracking of Spacecraft Using Variable-Structure Control. In Proceedings of the Flight Mechanics/Estimation Theory Symposium, NASA-Goddard Space Flight Center, NASA/CP-1999-209235, Greenbelt, MD, USA, 18–20 May 1999; pp. 201–214.
12. Hu, Q.; Xie, L.; Wang, Y. Sliding Mode Attitude and Vibration Control of Flexible Spacecraft with Actuator Dynamics. In Proceedings of the IEEE International Conference on Control and Automation, Guangzhou, China, 30 May–1 June 2007.
13. Mohammed, A.M.S. Three Axis Attitude Control Using Sliding Mode Based on the Artificial Neural Network for Low Earth Orbit Microsatellite. *Int. J. Syst. Appl. Eng. Dev.* **2012**, *6*, 223–233.
14. Azza El-S, I.; Tobal, A.M.; Sultan, M.A. Satellite Attitude Maneuver using Sliding Mode Control under Body Angular Velocity Constraints. *Int. J. Comput. Appl.* **2012**, *975*, 8887.
15. Bouadi, H.; Bouchoucha, M.; Tadjine, M. Sliding Mode Control based on Backstepping Approch for an UAV Type-Quadrotor. *World Acad. Sci. Eng. Technol.* **2007**, *26*, 22–27.
16. Wertz, J.R. *Spacecraft Attitude Determination and Control*; D. Reidel Publishing Company: Boston, MA, USA, 1986.
17. Sidi, M. *Spacecraft Dynamics and Control*; Cambridge University Press: Cambridge, UK, 1997.
18. Kanellakopoulos, I.; Kokotovic, P.V.; Morse, A.S. Systematic Design of Adaptive Controllers for Feedback Linearizable Systems. *IEEE Trans. Autom. Control* **1991**, *36*, 1241–1253. [CrossRef]
19. Young, K.; Utkin, V.; Özgüner, Ü. A control engineer's guide to sliding mode control. *IEEE Trans. Autom. Control* **1999**, *7*, 328–342. [CrossRef]
20. Slotine, J.J.E.; Li, W. *Applied Nonlinear Control*; Prentice-Hall Inc.: Hoboken, NJ, USA, 1991.

Proceeding Paper

Evaluation of Dimensionality Reduction Using PCA on EMG-Based Signal Pattern Classification †

Bouhamdi Merzoug [1,*], Mohamed Ouslim [1], Lotfi Mostefai [2] and Mohamed Benouis [3]

1. Department of Electronic, University of USTO MB Oran, Bir El Djir 31000, Algeria; ouslim@yahoo.com
2. Laboratory of Electrotechnics Engineering (LGE), University of Moulay Tahar, 20000 Saida, Algeria; latyfo@gmail.com
3. Department Computer Science, University of M'sila, M'sila 28000, Algeria; benouis.mohamed@univ-msila.dz
* Correspondence: merzougbouh@yahoo.fr
† Presented at the 1st International Conference on Computational Engineering and Intelligent Systems, Online, 10–12 December 2021.

Abstract: In this paper, we present a new low-cost system for surface electromyogram (sEMG) acquisition. developed and designed for rehabilitation application purposes. The noninvasive device delivers four-channel EMG bio-signals describing the electrical activity for the right upper limb muscles. The recorded EMG signals obtained from several healthy subjects were exploited to build a database for movement detection and to evaluate the mechanical properties of the upper limb muscles. The proposed study focuses mainly on the influence of the use of the principal component analysis (PCA) method on the movement classification performance based on the sEMG extracted signals. Several tests were conducted, and the simulation results clearly showed the positive impact of PCA as a dimensionality reduction approach with respect to two performance metrics: the classification rate (CR) and the system's response time. This advantage was confirmed via numerical tests using three different classifiers: K-nearest neighbor (KNN), probabilistic neural network (PNN), and learning vector quantization (LVQ), with and without PCA. The obtained classification rates highlighted the success of the proposed method since a clear improvement in the classification rates was achieved.

Keywords: electromyogram; principal component analysis; KNN; PNN; LVQ; classification rate

1. Introduction

Surface EMG signals are very powerful tools for modeling and measuring the electrical activity of the muscles in the human body; they are approved and well known to be useful in many disciplines such as rehabilitation, sports medicine, and biomechanical devices [1,2]. EMG devices are available on the market, but they are relatively expensive and are usually not based on open-source platforms. A part of this study is dedicated to a low-cost EMG system that we developed in our research laboratory.

The developed instrumentation system was designed using low-cost electronic parts, and is realized around passive components and dedicated integrated circuits that are reasonably cheap compared to other sophisticated systems for EMG signal acquisition, for example, Delsys products.

When an EMG signal is recorded from a muscle, various artifacts may contaminate it. Therefore, analyzing and classifying the EMG can be a very tedious and challenging task. In our case, the EMG signals were experimentally recorded from the proposed EMG hardware platform according to a specific protocol that was checked and approved by experienced medical staff from the local hospital. The extracted signals were compared with other EMG signals from standard databases available in the literature [3]. As a consequence, the obtained EMG database was considered suitable and ready for use in our experiments.

The proper analysis of myoelectrical signals can be correctly performed only if the acquired signals are of high quality and clean of noise. We should emphasize that the EMG system proposed in this paper considers signal processing in two parts: the analog signal processing achieved during the instrumentation stages and the digital part implemented in the form of a software algorithm.

In the remaining parts of this paper, we firstly present the design of the multi-channel EMG signal acquisition device for a rehabilitation application. Then, we discuss the methods used for preprocessing the bio-signal through a selection of the digital filtering processes for which the dimensionality reduction PCA (principal component analysis) is applied. We note here that the use of the PCA technique can be particularly efficient and advantageous since it leads to a reduction in the amount of data processed by the classifier, which will have a direct impact on the computation time. Then, different classification methods are described, followed by an explanation of various evaluation techniques and some comments on the obtained results. We conclude the paper by giving a summary of this research.

2. Description of the Overall System

A synoptic diagram for the EMG signal acquisition is shown in Figure 1. The bio-signals are acquired from the skin's surface by means of electrodes. In this case, standard, readily available Ag/AgCl electrodes were used.

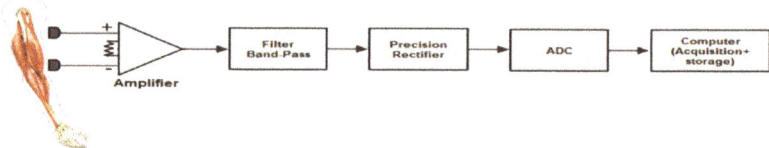

Figure 1. A synoptic diagram of acquisition and storage of EMG signals.

The EMG system consists of a four-channel bioamplifier module and a disposable biopotential electrode as a sensor.

The resulting signals have very low amplitude, from 50 µV to 1 mV.

An instrumentation amplifier was considered for the pre-amplifier, since it provides a high CMRR and low input bias current, ensuring high input impedance, which drastically reduces common-mode signals that can be higher than the EMG signal.

At the next stage, the signal is filtered by an active high-pass filter (cut-off frequency of 19.4 Hz) and an active low-pass filter (cut-off frequency of 482.28 Hz). After this, we utilized a precision full-wave rectifier, which rectifies the input signal at the output.

The data acquisition system used in this case was a multifunction DAQ device (NI USB-6210) from National Instruments, with a 16-bit resolution, and the EMG signal was digitized at 1000 samples per second.

Finally, at the data storage and processing stage, the acquired signal from the DAQ device is stored in a computer, and subsequently several processing tools are used, such as digital filtering, normalization, segmentation, and classification, as indicated in Figure 2.

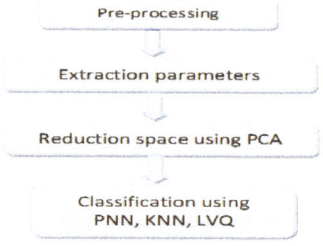

Figure 2. Steps of EMG signal processing to achieve better recognition.

3. Experiment and Data Collection

The EMG signals were acquired from four positions on the right upper limb, as shown in Figure 3a: the anterior deltoid (CH1), posterior deltoid (CH2), triceps brachii (CH3), and biceps brachii (CH4). G1 at the acromion and G2 at the olecranon are reference electrodes.

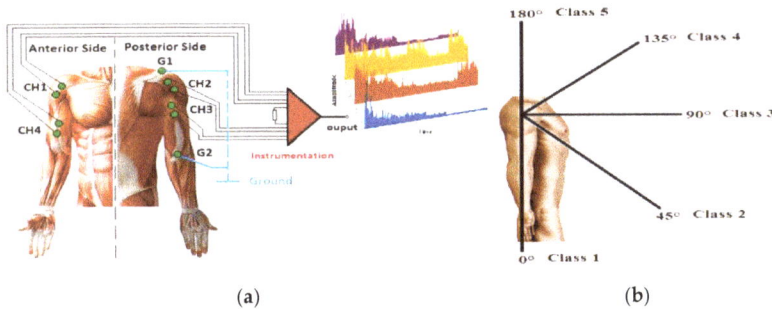

(a)   (b)

Figure 3. (a) EMG electrode placement on the right upper limb and instrumentation; (b) five motions (positions 0°, 45°, 90°, 135°, 180°).

The recorded signals from the four channels are classified to describe five positions at 0°, 45°, 90°, 135°, and 180°, as shown in Figure 3b. The database of EMG signals was collected from several participants aged between 20 and 42 years. The protocol followed during the acquisition experiments was: the subject makes a movement and stays steady at each position (equivalent to the five classes) for 30 s, then the upper limb is relaxed for 10 s.

4. Analyzing and Pre-Processing Data Signals

4.1. Digital Filtering

Two digital filtering algorithms were implemented:
- Digital notch filter to eliminate 50 Hz harmonic.
- Smoothing filter to reduce the high spatial frequencies in the EMG data.

4.2. Normalization

Data should be scaled to take values between 0 and 1. One possible formula to achieve this is given by Equation (1).

$$s_i = \frac{x_i - min(x)}{max(x) - min(x)} \tag{1}$$

where $x = (x_1, \ldots \ldots \ldots x_n)$ and s_i is the ith normalized data point.

4.3. Segmentation

All signals used in this study were segmented into segments of 200 samples, without overlapping.

4.4. Feature Extraction

A large amount of information can be extracted from the EMG signal. In our case only a small proportion was selected, according to the application targeted. In this study, we selected three types.

1. Integrated EMG (IEMG):

This is used as an onset detection index in EMG. It is defined by Equation (2).

$$IEMG = \sum_{n=1}^{N} |x_n| \tag{2}$$

N is the length of the signal and x_n represents the segment of the EMG signal.

2. Mean Absolute Value (MAV):

This is favored in prosthetic limb control. It is defined by Equation (3).

$$MAV = \frac{1}{N} \sum_{n=1}^{N} |x_n| \qquad (3)$$

3. Root Mean Square (RMS):

This is modeled as an amplitude-modulated Gaussian random process. It can be calculated using Equation (4).

$$RMS = \sqrt{\frac{1}{N} \sum_{n=1}^{N} x_n^2} \qquad (4)$$

4.5. Principal Component Analysis

In order to reduce the important dimensionality of the acquired segments of the EMG, we applied a PCA approach, so that we could retain only the discriminative features.

EMG Recognition Using PCA Approach

This step consists in defining the EMG data $\Gamma\_i; i = 1 \ldots M$. These data must be the same size and centered. We calculated the average of the dataset, represented as a vector.

$$\Psi = \frac{1}{M} \sum_{i=1}^{M} \Gamma_i \qquad (5)$$

The data are centered relative to their average.

$$\Phi_i = \Gamma_i - \Psi \qquad (6)$$

The construction of the global matrix A is obtained using Equation (7).

$$A = [\Phi_1 \Phi_2 \ldots \ldots \Phi_M] \quad (N^2 \times M) \qquad (7)$$

We calculate the covariance matrix of Φ using Equation (8).

$$C = \frac{1}{M} \sum_{i=1}^{M} \Phi_n \Phi_n^T = A \, X \, A^T \quad (N^2 \times N^2) \qquad (8)$$

Pentland et al. in [4] solved the problem mathematically to extract the values and eigenvectors.

$$CV_i = u_i V_i \qquad (9)$$

The eigenvalues of matrix C are selected in descending order, representing the variance of the original distribution space (EMG data).

$$u_i = \frac{1}{M} \cdot \sum_{i=1}^{M} var(U_i \cdot A_i^T) \qquad (10)$$

We denote the eigenvectors of C by AV_i.

We usually need to keep a smaller number of eigenvectors corresponding to the largest eigenvalues.

The two matrices AA^T and A^TA have the same values, and the eigenvectors are related as follows:

$$U_i = AV_i \qquad (11)$$

From this relationship, we use the matrix:

$$C = A^T A \qquad (12)$$

The weights of the original projection of the EMG vector on the new EMG data space are described as follows:

$$W_{ik} = U_k^T \phi_i \qquad (13)$$

for $k, i = 1, 2 \ldots M$.

The weights of the features of the EMG data in the resulting space, is supposed to have discriminative information and reduced size of data, given by:

$$\Omega_i^T = [W_{i1} W_{i2} \ldots \ldots W_{iM}] \qquad (14)$$

5. EMG Signal Classification

5.1. K-Nearest Neighbor Classification

The K-nearest neighbor (KNN) classifier is a conventional non-parametric classifier. It calculates the distances between a given point and all points in the training data set. Then, it assigns the considered point to the class among its K nearest neighbors (where K is an integer). The $K = 1$ case is a benchmark for other classifiers.

To appropriately conduct our tests, we considered the following parameters:

Ω_{test}: The weights of the features of the test EMG signal.

Ω_k: The weights of the features of the training EMG signal, where $K = 1 \ldots N$.

L1 is the Manhattan distance defined by Equation (15):

$$\varepsilon_k(\Omega_{test}; \Omega_k) = |\Omega_{test} - \Omega_k| = \sum_{i=1}^{k} |(\Omega_{test})_i - (\Omega_k)_i| \qquad (15)$$

L2 is the Euclidean distance defined by Equation (16):

$$\varepsilon_k(\Omega_{test}; \Omega_k) = \|\Omega_{test} - \Omega_k\| = \sum_{i=1}^{k} ((\Omega_{test})_i - (\Omega_k)_i)^2 \qquad (16)$$

The MahCosine distance is defined by Equation (17):

$$(\Omega_{test}; \Omega_k) = -\frac{\Omega_{test} \cdot \Omega_k}{\|\Omega_{test}\| \cdot \|\Omega_k\|} = -\frac{\sum_{i=1}^{k} (\Omega_{test})_i \cdot (\Omega_k)_i}{\sum_{i=1}^{k} ((\Omega_{test})_i)^2 \cdot ((\Omega_k)_i)^2} \qquad (17)$$

To perform the comparison, which is based on the calculation of the distance between two vectors, we take the minimum distance compared to an appropriate decision threshold value θ, as explained in the following.

$$\theta = \frac{1}{2} max\left(\|\Omega^i - \Omega^j\|\right) \qquad (18)$$

If $\min\{\varepsilon_k\} \geq \theta$ ($k = 1 \ldots M$) this is a defined class.
If $\min\{\varepsilon_k\} \leq \theta$ ($k = 1 \ldots M$) this is an unknown class.

5.2. Classification Using Neural Newtorks

Previous studies have shown improved EMG classification systems using neural networks, compared to classifications based on the Euclidean distance measure [5].

5.2.1. Probabilistic Neural Networks PNN

The PNN was proposed by D.F. Specht in 1988 for solving the problem of classification [6]. The theoretical foundation was developed based on Bayes decision theory, and it is implemented in a feed-forward network architecture.

A PNN is represented by Equations (19) and (20):

$$a = radbas(\| IW - x \| b) \quad (19)$$

$$y = compet(LWa) \quad (20)$$

where IW is the input weight and LW is the layer weight.

The PNN architecture shown in Figure 4 consists of two layers [6,7].

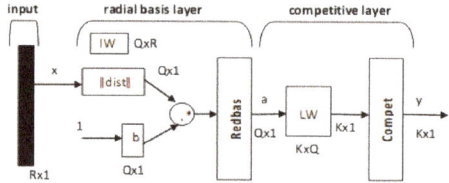

Figure 4. Architecture of the probabilistic neural network.

R is the number of elements in the input vector, Q represents the input/target pairs, and K represents the classes of the input data. The first layer computes distances from the input vector to the input weights (IW) and produces a vector whose elements indicate how close the input is to the IW. The second layer sums these contributions for each class of inputs to produce a vector of probabilities as an output. Finally, a transfer function on the output of the second layer picks up the maximum of these probabilities and produces a 1 for that class and a 0 for the other classes. Each hidden unit can approximate any continuous nonlinear function. In this study, we used the Gaussian function as the activation function, giving Equations (21) and (22).

$$radbas(n) = exp(-n^2) \quad (21)$$

$$compet(n) = e_i = [00001_i 0000]; n(i) = max(n) \quad (22)$$

5.2.2. Learning Vector Quantization Networks (LVQ)

The vector quantization technique was originally proposed by Tuevo Kohonen in the mid-1980s [5,7]. Both vector quantization networks and self-organizing maps are based on the Kohonen layer, which is capable of sorting items into appropriate categories of similar objects. These types of networks find their application in classification and segmentation problems. The architecture of the LVQ network is shown in Figure 5. It consists of three layers: the input layer, the competitive layer, and the linear output layer. The number of neurons in each layer depends on the input data and the number of classes handled. The number of input neurons is equal to the number of input matrix features of the training pattern, and the number of output neurons is equal to the number of class patterns. The number of hidden neurons is heuristic.

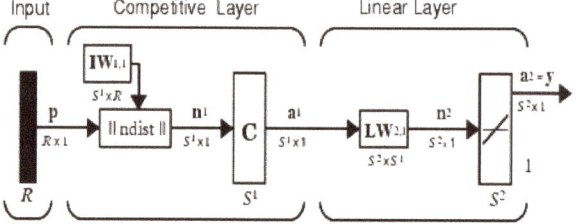

Figure 5. Architecture of learning vector quantization.

R is the number of elements in the input vector, S^1 is the number of competitive neurons, and S^2 is the number of linear neurons. The network functionality is defined by Equations (23)–(25).

$$n_j^1 = - \| IW_{1,1} - P \| \tag{23}$$

$$a^1 = compet(n^1) \tag{24}$$

$$a^2 = purline(LW_{2,1} a^1) \tag{25}$$

6. Results and Discussion

In order to evaluate and test the proposed approach for the EMG classification, we chose our own database, as previously described. In the first evaluation, the EMG vector was extracted using various statistical extraction methods. During this test, the Euclidean distance was selected for the classification stage. As a consequence, we computed the Euclidean distance between the input vector and the training set.

After a series of experiments, we obtained a better recognition rate based on the MahCosine distance, which achieved a rate of 75%. The comparison with other similarity measures used in this experiment is shown in Table 1.

Table 1. Recognition rate obtained by KNN with different types of similarity measures.

	L1	L2	cos	MahCosine
KNN	55%	62.5%	70%	75%

In the second evaluation, in order to enhance the results obtained in the previous experiment, we combined our system with two types of classifiers: the PNN and the LVQ. To achieve this, we selected the appropriate parameters of the system classifier architecture. In the case of the PNN network, the training algorithm does not require as many parameters as other neural networks (MLP, BP, LVQ, etc.); only the smoothing parameter σ parameter is needed for the network performance tuning. Usually, researchers and experts try different values of σ in a certain range, to obtain a suitable value that can reach the optimum accuracy [6].

The PNN used in our system was composed of two layers. The first layer is the input layer, and the number of hidden units is the number of independent variables. This layer receives the input data that correspond to the number of the extracted features. The output layer gives the number of states of EMG used in the training database. To obtain a higher recognition rate, we performed a series of experiments to choose the best smoothing parameter σ (σ < 120) for use in the PNN.

In the case of the LVQ, changes in the LVQ classifier parameters had a large effect on the classification results. We found that the best learning rate increased the system recognition rate. Therefore, we used different values of learning rates (0.1, 0.2, 0.3, and 0.6) with 800 epochs and 1000 hidden neurons in our experiments.

In the third experiment, after reducing the dimension of the EMG signal using statistical methods, we used the PCA approach to extract the EMG features in the new space, while considering the three classifiers, i.e., KNN, LVQ, and PNN.

After a series of experiments, we were able to choose the best parameter values to set up an appropriate choice of eigenvectors to give a better recognition rate. Feature vectors containing 7 components were obtained. Thus, the dimensionality of vectors to be input to the neural network was drastically reduced from 32 to 7. This indicates that there was significant redundancy present in the data set. These feature vectors were then applied at the input of a neural network classifier, i.e., LVQ or PNN.

The performances of the neural classifiers were evaluated by computing the classification rate (CR) and the running time (RT). In this experiment, we compared the performance of three approaches, namely, PCA-KNN, PCA-LVQ, and PCA-PNN, in terms of CR and RT.

We clearly verified the superiority of the PCA combined with a neural classifier compared to using a Euclidean distance classifier such as KNN.

The results obtained using our approach show that it reduced the training computation time and improved the recognition rate, as illustrated in Tables 2–4.

Table 2. The classification rate using different methods on our database (without PCA).

	LVQ	PNN	KNN
CR	80%	81%	75%

Table 3. The classification rate using different methods on our database (with PCA).

	LVQ	PNN	KNN
CR	82%	86%	78%

Table 4. Running time of performance classification.

	KNN	LVQ	PNN	PCA-KNN	PCA-LVQ	PCA-PNN
RT	0.032103	1.25	0.5	0.015338	1.05	0.45

7. Conclusions

In this paper, we proposed an approach for EMG classification based on a combination of two methods, with one used for the reduction of the space and feature extraction and the other used for classification and decision. The application of the proposed approach based on PCA combined with a probabilistic neural classifier succeeded in improving our system performance. Indeed, we achieved a better classification rate compared to other techniques described in this paper. Our choice of using PCA techniques as a pre-processing stage was successful in terms of many aspects of performance such as increasing the classification rate, decreasing the computation time, and reducing the memory required. As a continuation of this work, we propose to use the system in a real rehabilitation device.

Author Contributions: Basically, all authors have equally contributed to this work, under the supervision of M.O., and M.B. All authors have read and agreed to the published version of the manuscript.

Funding: This research received no external funding.

Institutional Review Board Statement: Not applicable.

Informed Consent Statement: Informed consent was obtained from all subjects involved in the study.

Data Availability Statement: Not applicable.

Conflicts of Interest: The authors declare no conflict of interest.

References

1. Clancy, E.; Horgan, N. Probabilistic Density of the Surface Electromyogram and its Relation to Amplitude Detectors. *IEEE Trans. Biomed. Eng.* **1999**, *46*, 730–739. [CrossRef] [PubMed]
2. Poo, T.S.; Sundaraj, K. Design and Development of a Low Cost EMG Signal Acquisition System using Surface EMG Electrode. In Proceedings of the 2010 IEEE Asia Pacific Conference on Circuits and Systems, Kuala Lumpur, Malaysia, 6–9 December 2010; pp. 24–27.
3. Atzori, M.; Gijsberts, A.; Castellini, C.; Caputo, B.; Hager, A.-G.M.; Elsig, S.; Giatsidis, G.; Bassetto, F.; Müller, H. Electromyography data for non-Invasive naturally-controlled Robotic Hand Prostheses. *Sci. Data* **2014**, *1*, 140053. [CrossRef] [PubMed]
4. Rokach, L. *Pattern Classification Using Ensemble Methods Series in Machine Perception and Artificial Intelligence*; World Scientific Publishing Co.: Singapore, 2010; Volume 75.
5. Sumathi, S.; Paneerselvam, S. *Computational Intelligence Paradigms: Theory & Applications Using Matlab*; Taylor and Francis Group: Abingdon, UK, 2010.

6. Specht, D. Probabilistic neural network and the polynomial adaline as complementary techniques for classification. *IEEE Trans. Neural Netw.* **1990**, *1*, 111–121. [CrossRef] [PubMed]
7. *Neural Network Toolbox Matlab, User's Guide*; MathWorks, Inc.: Natick, MA, USA, 1992.

Proceeding Paper

Performance Enhancement of Capon's DOA Algorithm Using Covariance Matrix Decomposition [†]

Naceur Aounallah

Department of Electronic and Telecommunications, Kasdi Merbah University, Ouargla 30000, Algeria; naceurcom@gmail.com

† Presented at the 1st International Conference on Computational Engineering and Intelligent Systems, Online, 10–12 December 2021.

Abstract: This paper deals with the problem of the direction of arrival (DOA) estimation for diverse systems of wireless communication using an antenna array. This study provides an improved version of Capon's direction of arrival algorithm. In fact, the proposed version uses an upper-triangular matrix extracted from the covariance matrix instead of the entire covariance matrix. The simulation results demonstrate that our proposed scheme can significantly improve the accuracy of direction of arrival estimation with low computation complexity.

Keywords: antenna array processing; DOA estimation; covariance matrix; QR factorization; Capon method

Citation: Aounallah, N. Performance Enhancement of Capon's DOA Algorithm Using Covariance Matrix Decomposition. *Eng. Proc.* **2022**, *14*, 7. https://doi.org/10.3390/engproc2022014007

Academic Editors: Abdelmadjid Recioui, Hamid Bentarzi and Fatma Zohra Dekhandji

Published: 29 January 2022

Publisher's Note: MDPI stays neutral with regard to jurisdictional claims in published maps and institutional affiliations.

Copyright: © 2022 by the author. Licensee MDPI, Basel, Switzerland. This article is an open access article distributed under the terms and conditions of the Creative Commons Attribution (CC BY) license (https://creativecommons.org/licenses/by/4.0/).

1. Introduction

In the field of wireless communications and their applications, estimating directions of arrival (DoA) is a very necessary task of paramount interest. For RADARs, SONARs, radio signal processing and smart antenna arrays, the beam-forming reflects the antenna performance; however, beam-forming cannot be achieved without estimating directions of arrival which makes it easier to focus the radiation in the desired direction while minimizing it in other directions [1,2]. In addition, new telecommunications standards ensure a good quality of service resulting from the extreme precision of the estimated directions of arrival.

Direction of arrival algorithms are used, in general, to estimate the number of incident plane waves on the antenna array and their angles of incidence. Several DOA estimation approaches have been designed, and their performances have been investigated thoroughly over the years; in addition, intensive studies in the area of DOA estimation were carried out to pinpoint the most convenient algorithm for the application of interest [3,4]. The most popular are: the Bartlett method [5], which is also known as the method of averaged periodograms; the Capon method [6], which determines an angular spectrum for each direction by minimizing the noise and the interference from other directions; the Maximum entropy method [7], which is based on the extrapolation of the covariance matrix; the Multiple Signal Classification (MUSIC) method [8], which determines the signal and noise subspaces and then searches the spectrum to find DOAs; the Minimum Norm technique [3], which is generally considered to be a high-resolution method that assumes a uniform linear antenna array geometry; and Estimation of Signal Parameters via Rotational Invariance Techniques (ESPRIT) [9] that determines the signal subspace from which the DOAs are determined in closed form.

Generally, the resolution of DOA algorithms that use a covariance matrix depends on the number of samples and the SNR level. Furthermore, despite having stepped in to face the limitations of the Bartlett method, such as to increase the resolving power of two sources spaced closer than a beamwidth [10], the traditional Capon method remains sensitive to the problem of limited samples and low SNR because it is based upon whole covariance matrix inversion. The presence of source correlation degrades the performance of Capon as compared to the MUSIC algorithm, which uses only an orthogonal projection to the signal subspace of the covariance matrix for estimating the DOA of incident signals.

The paper is organized in the following way. In the next section, we give the signal model and briefly describe the conventional Capon approach. The proposed algorithm is introduced in Section 3. The simulation results and analysis are given in Section 4. The last section deals with the conclusion.

2. Problem Formulation

This section firstly describes the general signal model that is considered for the DOA estimation problem and secondly, reviews the conventional DOA Capon algorithm.

For clarity sake, we consider a uniform linear geometry of the antenna array which is composed of M isotropic elements. The inter-element distance is taken to be half the wavelength. K narrowband signals $s_k(t)$, $1 \leq k \leq K$, impinge on the antenna array from different directions $(\theta_1, \theta_2, \cdots, \theta_K)$, as depicted in Figure 1. We also assume that the observed output is based on L snapshots.

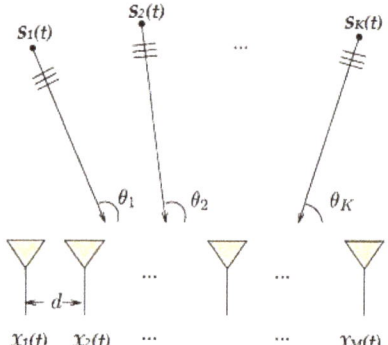

Figure 1. Example of a uniform linear antenna array.

The array output can be expressed according to the received signal vector as:

$$x(t) = \sum_{k=1}^{K} a(\theta_k) s_k(t) + n(t) \quad (1)$$

Under matrix notation, Equation (1) can be re-expressed as:

$$X(t) = A(\theta) S(t) + N(t) \quad (2)$$

where $X(t)$ is a $[M \times L]$ received array matrix, $S(t)$ is a $[K \times L]$ transmitted signal matrix, $N(t)$ is a $[M \times L]$ Gaussian white noise matrix with mean zero and covariance σ^2, and $A(\theta)$ is a $[M \times L]$ steering matrix containing the $[M \times 1]$ array response vectors $a(\theta_k)$ that can be expressed as:

$$a(\theta_k) = \left[1, e^{2j\pi(d/\lambda)\sin\theta_k}, \cdots, e^{2j\pi(M-1)(d/\lambda)\sin\theta_k}\right]^T \quad (3)$$

where λ is the wavelength of the signal, d is the distance between array elements and $[\cdot]^T$ is the transpose operator.

The $[M \times M]$ array covariance matrix R_x of the received signal can be written as [1]:

$$R_x = E\left[x(t) x^H(t)\right] = A . R_S . A^H + R_N \quad (4)$$

where $R_s = E[S(t) \cdot S(t)^H]$ is the $[K \times K]$ signal covariance matrix and R_N is the $[M \times M]$ noise covariance matrix.

In practice, the covariance matrix R_x is not known. Furthermore, it can be replaced by its sample estimated matrix $\widehat{R}_x$, which usually takes L number of snapshots in the form [4]:

$$\widehat{R}_x = \frac{1}{L} \sum_{l=1}^{L} x(l) x^H(l) \tag{5}$$

The Capon spectral-based method was originally developed for frequency-wave number estimation [6]. Then, for signal DOA estimation, this method was employed as a spatial filter that minimizes incoming power in all directions, with the constraint that its response is equal to unity gain in the direction of arrival under consideration. That is, the constraint imposed on this estimator is represented as:

$$\min_{\omega} E\left[|y(t)|^2\right] = \min_{\omega} \omega^H R_x \omega \text{ subject to } \omega^H a(\theta_1) = 1 \tag{6}$$

By exploiting the Lagrange optimization technique, when the number of snapshots is finite, the solution to (6) gives us the following Capon's weight vector:

$$\omega_{capon} = \frac{R_x^{-1} a(\theta)}{a(\theta)^H R_x^{-1} a(\theta)} \tag{7}$$

Hence, the Capon's output is given by the following spectral function:

$$P_{capon}(\theta) = \frac{1}{a(\theta)^H R_x^{-1} a(\theta)} \tag{8}$$

The directions of arrival can be determined through the highest peak location of the previous function. In other words, the estimated DOAs of all sources can be found as:

$$\hat{\theta}_m = \underset{\theta_m}{\arg\max} P_{capon}(\theta_m), m = 1, 2, \cdots, M \tag{9}$$

Therefore, to estimate DOA using the traditional Capon algorithm, we follow four fundamental steps which are: the estimation of the covariance matrix R_x, the calculation of its inversion R_x^{-1}, the determination of the spectrum function and the localization of the highest peaks. The complexities of these steps are $LM^2 + M^2$, $4M^2$, $M^2 + M$ and $4KP$, respectively. Thus, the overall Capon complexity is:

$$M^2(L+6) + M + 4KP$$

where M is the number of antennas, K is the number of sources, L the number of samples and P is the number of scan steps of theta.

3. New Proposed Algorithm

This section aims to propose a new scheme that can enhance the Capon algorithm performance in terms of DOA accuracy, and at the same time, reduce the computational complexity. In fact, the important contribution of the new method only consists of the inverse of the right upper triangle matrix instead of the inverse of the entire autocorrelation matrix.

The matrix used in the calculation of our improved Capon version is issued from the known QR factorization. This last can be applied on a matrix $A \in R^{m \times n}$ with linearly independent columns such as the estimated autocorrelation matrix $\widetilde{R}_x$. Thus, the factored matrix takes the following form:

$$\widetilde{R}_x = [q_1 \; q_2 \; \cdots \; q_n] \begin{bmatrix} R_{11} & R_{12} & \cdots & R_{1n} \\ 0 & R_{22} & \cdots & R_{2n} \\ \vdots & \vdots & \ddots & \vdots \\ 0 & 0 & \cdots & R_{nn} \end{bmatrix} \quad (10)$$

Here, we have a Q-factor that contains $q_1, \cdots, q_n$ orthonormal m-vectors and an R-factor which is $n \times n$ upper triangular with nonzero diagonal elements.

The procedure which is followed for the new DOA method can be summarized by the following steps:

- Estimate the autocovariance matrix using Equation (5).
- Decompose the estimated autocovariance matrix using QR factorization.
- Compute the inverse of the right upper triangle matrix R.
- Construct the improved spectral function as follows:

$$P_{new-capon}(\theta) = \frac{1}{\left| a(\theta)^H R^{-1} a(\theta) \right|} \quad (11)$$

- Find the highest peaks and their correspondent DOAs.

The complexity of this proposed algorithm can be deduced from the complete complexity of its above steps. These five steps require $LM^2 + M^2$, M^2, $2M$, $M^2 + M$ and $4KP$, respectively. Thus, the total new Capon complexity is: $M^2(L+3) + 3M + 4KP$. Consequently, the proposed new Capon method has a lower computational cost than the standard Capon method.

4. Simulation Results

In this section, simulation results are presented to show the performance of the proposed DOA method and to compare it to its original version, which is the conventional Capon technique. To this end, we use a linear uniform array with the parameters indicated in the table below.

Figure 2 depict curves of normalized spectrums, which correspond to three signals impinging on the uniform linear array. As seen from this figure, it is clear that the new algorithm gives the sharpest and clearest result among the three AOAs. It provides a perfect direction estimate and gives a very acceptable result compared to the conventional algorithm. As can be seen in this figure, for two very close sources located at $-12°$ and $-15°$, the standard Capon fails to correctly resolve the DOA where the large peak that is formed by the confusion of two neighboring peaks covers these directions simultaneously, whereas the proposed improved-Capon performs reasonably well and demonstrates its ability to separate the close sources.

As it is known in the theory and also in the practice of antenna arrays, the performances of most of algorithms that estimate the angles of arrival of the signals impinging on the array are mainly dependent on essential parameters, which are: the number of antenna elements, the spacing between these elements, the number of snapshots and the SNR value.

The following simulation example is based on the influence of the number of antennas on the performance of the new method proposed. In this example, we keep the same values of the parameters shown in Table 1, except that the noise covariance σ^2 is assumed to be 0.08, and we change the number of antennas for the comparison.

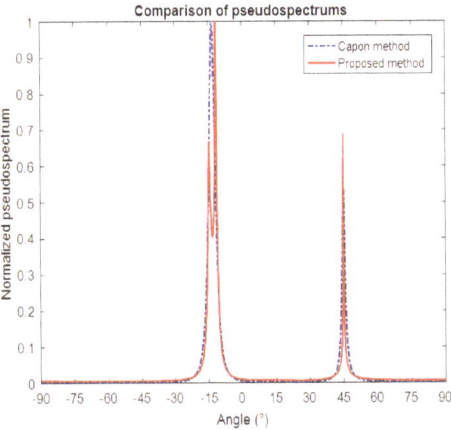

Figure 2. Comparison between normalized pseudo-spectrums of Capon and new Capon methods.

Table 1. Simulation parameters.

Parameters	Value
Number of elements (M)	8
Number of sources (K)	3
Number of snapshots (L)	200
Spacing between elements (d)	$\lambda/2$
Angles of arrival	$-12°, -15°$ and $45°$
NOise covariance σ^2	0.05

In Figure 3, a comparison of pseudospectra for varying numbers of array elements is displayed. As can be observed in this figure, when the number of array antennas grows, the accuracy in identifying very close sources increases. Indeed, for two signals that are close to each other, arriving exactly from $-15°$ to $-12°$ and impinging on an array of six elements, two peaks might be confused with a single one in the spectrum of the new Capon method. Furthermore, for an array of 9 or 12 elements, two peaks corresponding to exact DOAs are most easily identified. The peaks may become narrower with increasing antennas in the array, therefore, the angular accuracy of the method becomes more important.

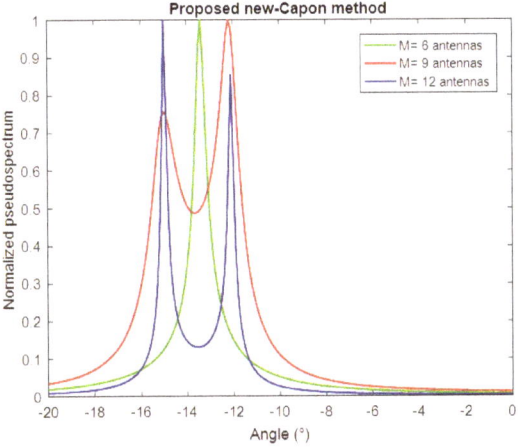

Figure 3. Comparison between normalized pseudo-spectrums of the new Capon method for a varying number of array elements.

To illustrate the effectiveness of the proposed scheme in terms of root mean square error (RMSE), we consider only one signal impinging on the eight-element ULA from the source direction $\theta = 10°$. In this simulation, we change the value of the SNR, and calculate the RMSE using Capon and the proposed method; 500 Monte Carlo trials are performed to obtain the statistical results.

The DOA accuracy is measured by the RMSE, which is defined as:

$$RMSE(\hat{\theta}) = E\{\varepsilon\} = E\left\{\sum_{i=1}^{Q}|\theta_i - \theta_{true}|^2\right\} \qquad (12)$$

where θ_i is the current estimated angle at the ith realization, θ_{true} is the true angle-of-arrival and Q is the number of Monte Carlo runs.

The root mean square error (RMSE) versus SNR is depicted in Figure 4. We can observe that the new algorithm always outperforms Capon for all values of SNR. In fact, the proposed algorithm has a reduced RMSE which indicates its accurate estimation performance. However, the slight additional estimation error of Capon certainly comes down to the need to compute the covariance matrix inversion, the geometry of the antenna array and the SNR value.

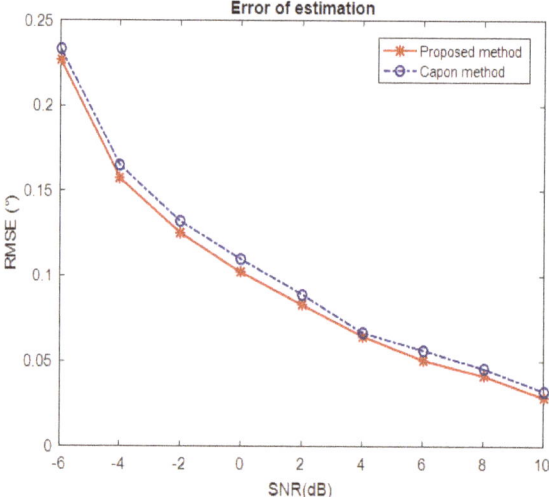

Figure 4. Variation of estimation error (RMSE) versus signal to noise ratio (SNR) of the standard Capon and the new Capon methods.

5. Conclusions

This paper has been devoted to the presentation of a new technique for estimating the direction of arrival of sources that are located in the far-field of a linear uniform antenna array. The performances of the proposed technique were compared to the basic Capon method through simulation examples. The superiority of this new technique lies in its precise estimation, even for closely spaced signals, and in its reduced complexity.

Funding: This research received no external funding.

Data Availability Statement: Not applicable.

Conflicts of Interest: The author declares no conflict of interest.

References

1. Constantine, A.B.; Panayiotis, I.I. *Introduction to Smart Antennas*; Morgan & Claypool Publishers: San Rafael, CA, USA, 2007.
2. Naceur, A.; Merahi, B.; Abdelmalik, T.A. Combined DMI–RLS Algorithm in Adaptive Processing Antenna System. *Arab. J. Sci. Eng.* **2014**, *39*, 7109–7116. [CrossRef]
3. Aounallah, N. Improving the resolution performance of min-norm and root-min-norm algorithms for adaptive array antenna. In Proceedings of the IEEE International Conference on Electrical Engineering-Boumerdes (ICEE-B), Boumerdes, Algeria, 29–31 October 2017; pp. 1–5.
4. Aounallah, N. Improved Polynomial Rooting of Capon's Algorithm to Estimate the Direction-of-Arrival in Smart Array Antenna. *J. Microw. Optoelectron. Electromagn. Appl.* **2018**, *17*, 494–508.
5. Bartlett, M.S. Periodogram analysis and Continuous spectra. *Biometrika* **1950**, *37*, 1–16. [CrossRef] [PubMed]
6. Capon, J. High-resolution frequency wave number spectrum analysis. *Proc. IEEE* **1969**, *57*, 1408–1418. [CrossRef]
7. Burg, J.P. The relationship between maximum entropy spectra and maximum likelihood spectra. *Geophysics* **1972**, *37*, 375–376. [CrossRef]
8. Schmit, O.R. Multiple emitter location and signal parameters estimation. *IEEE Trans. Antennas Propag.* **1986**, *34*, 276–280. [CrossRef]
9. Roy, R.; Kailath, K. Esprit-Estimation of signal parameter via rotational invariance techniques. *IEEE Trans. Acoust. Speech Signal Process.* **1989**, *37*, 984–995. [CrossRef]
10. Baig, N.A.; Malik, M.B. Comparison of Direction of Arrival (DOA) Estimation Techniques for Closely Spaced Targets. *Int. J. Future Comput. Commun.* **2013**, *2*, 654–659. [CrossRef]

Proceeding Paper

Blind Image Separation Using the JADE Method [†]

Khalfa Ali [1,*], Amardjia Nourredine [2] and Kenane Elhadi [1]

1. Department of Electronics, Faculty of Technology, Mohamed Boudiaf University, M'Sila 28000, Algeria; elhadi.kenane@univ-msila.dz
2. LIS Laboratory, Department of Electronics, Faculty of Technology, Ferhat Abbas University, Setif 19000, Algeria; amardjianour@univ-setif.dz
* Correspondence: ali.khalfa@univ-msila.dz; Tel.: +213-0664943391
† Presented at the 1st International Conference on Computational Engineering and Intelligent Systems, Online, 10–12 December 2021.

Abstract: Blind source separation (BSS) concerns the signal processing techniques that aim to find several elementary components of sources from linear combinations of these sources received on several sensors. This paper presents a method for the extraction of these independent components. It is called Joint Approximate Diagonalization of Eigenmatrices (JADE) and uses fourth-order cumulants. A simulation example shows the performance of the proposed algorithm by displaying its high separation accuracy. The proposed technique is compared to the Equivariant Adaptive Source Separation Algorithm (EASI).

Keywords: blind source separation; Joint Approximate Diagonalization of Eigenmatrices; fourth-order cumulants; EASI

Citation: Ali, K.; Nourredine, A.; Elhadi, K. Blind Image Separation Using the JADE Method. *Eng. Proc.* 2022, *14*, 20. https://doi.org/10.3390/engproc2022014020

Academic Editors: Abdelmadjid Recioui, Hamid Bentarzi and Fatma Zohra Dekhandji

Published: 28 February 2022

Publisher's Note: MDPI stays neutral with regard to jurisdictional claims in published maps and institutional affiliations.

Copyright: © 2022 by the authors. Licensee MDPI, Basel, Switzerland. This article is an open access article distributed under the terms and conditions of the Creative Commons Attribution (CC BY) license (https://creativecommons.org/licenses/by/4.0/).

1. Introduction

In signal and image processing, there are many cases where a set of observations are available and from which we wish to recover the sources that generated them. This problem, which has become a hotspot in the field of signal processing, is known as blind source separation (BSS). It has received great attention in several research fields such as speech, sound, image, telecommunications and biomedicine [1–4]. New research has significantly improved both the BSS theory and its practical applications. In biomedicine, the applications of BSS range from medical engineering to neuroscience. In image processing, BSS is a method of recovering the original images from the observed mixed images. This is referred to as blind image separation. One way to achieve the separation is to utilize relative motions of layers. Several technologies have been proposed to extract motions from image sequences [5,6]. They focus only on motion, whereas the layer restoration is not considered. Independent component analysis (ICA) has often been regarded as an attractive solution to the blind image separation problem. In biomedical applications, ICA has been applied to functional magnetic resonance imaging (fMRI) data analysis. In addition, some proposed image separation applications have taken a Bayesian approach [7]. In [4], Kayabol et al. approved a Markov random field (MRF) model to preserve the spatial dependence of neighboring pixels (e.g., sharpness of edges) in a 2-D model. They provided a full Bayesian solution to image separation using Gibbs sampling. Another MRF-based method has been proposed by Tonazzini et al. in [8]. In mechanical systems, BSS is used to evaluate complex mode shapes which may occur in the real world [9]. Also, evolutionary algorithms such as the Genetic algorithms (GA) [10–13], the Particle Swarm Optimization (PSO) algorithm [14–16], the Artificial Bee Colony (ABC) algorithm [17] and the JADE algorithm [18] are useful to solve optimization problems in diverse fields. They have been applied to find the optimal separation matrix in BSS techniques.

In this paper, the JADE algorithm [18] is used to solve the problem of blind source separation.

The rest of this paper is organized as follows: Section 2 describes the BSS model and the JADE algorithm. In Section 3 we present the simulation results. The conclusion and future work are given in the last section.

2. BSS Model

In a source separation situation, the observed data are composed of $\{X_i\} i = 1, \ldots, m$, where $\{X_i\}$ is a row-vector. The linear instantaneous mixed model of BSS can be indicated as:

$$Xi(t) = \sum_{j=1}^{n} a_{ji} s_j(t), \qquad (1)$$

where $a_{ji} (i = 1, \ldots, m, j = 1, \ldots, n)$ are mixing parameters, $s(t) = [s_1(t), \ldots, s_n(t)]^T$ are source signals, i.e., the observed signals. Then the Equation (1) can be written as:

$$X(t) = A.s(t) \qquad (2)$$

where A is the mixing matrix $A \in \mathcal{R}^{m \times n}$, and $s(t) \in \mathcal{R}^{m \times n}$ is the source vector. In this paper, we suppose that the number of sources, n, is equal to the number of mixtures, m. Our objective is to separate the signals from each other. The order of the estimated signals is not necessary. There are many different algorithms to accomplish blind source separation. The general concept to determine independent components is to compute the separating matrix W_i. The component signals are retrieved from the mixed signal by:

$$y = W_i.X \qquad (3)$$

The basic model of blind source separation is given in Figure 1.

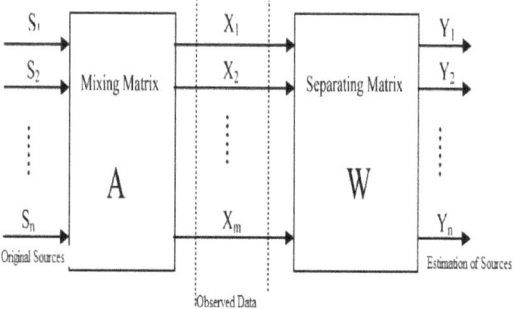

Figure 1. The basic model of blind source separation.

2.1. Joint Approximate Diagonalization of Eigenmatrices

An important contribution in blind source separation is the JADE algorithm [18] which optimizes a contrast function using a fourth-order cumulant. Our objective is to develop the approach relating to JADE. The algorithm is in several stages.

2.1.1. Whitening of X

The objective of whitening is transforming the observed vector X linearly so that we get a new vector $\widetilde{X}$ which is white, i.e., its components are uncorrelated, and their variances are equal to unity. In other words, the covariance matrix of $\widetilde{X}$ is equal to the identity matrix:

$$E(X.\widetilde{X}) = I \qquad (4)$$

2.1.2. Cumulant Calculations

In the previous step, X has been transformed into a set of principal components afflicted with equal variance, P_w. The objective of the JADE algorithm is to find the rotation of P_w, therefore its column vectors are independent. In this algorithm, for every observed signal, the cumulants of the signals are calculated, and are placed in a fourth-order tensor. If the signals are independent, their fourth-order cumulant will be zero.

The fourth-order cumulant of a vector X can be defined as:

$$cum_4\{x,x,x,x\} = E\{x^4\} - E^2\{x^2\} \quad (5)$$

2.1.3. Decompose the Cumulants

In the JADE method, the fourth-order cumulant is first decomposed into a set of $\frac{n(n+1)}{2}$ orthogonal eigenmatrices, $n.n$. This is done by forming a set of $\frac{n(n+1)}{2}$ symmetrical orthogonal matrices and projecting the cumulant tensors onto these planes. Every element of the cumulant j is then projected onto each M_i matrix:

for $i = 1$ to $\frac{n(n+1)}{2}$, matrix = M_i;
for $i_1 = 1$ to n, and for $i_2 = 1$ to n

$$M_i(i_1, i_2) = sum(sum(k(i_1, i_2, :, :) \times matrix)) \quad (6)$$

where cumulant.

2.1.4. Joint Diagonalization of the Eigenmatrices

The diagonalization of eigenmatrices is established on the Jacobi algorithm in order to minimize the sum of squares of the off-diagonal elements that correspond to the fourth-order cumulants between the different signals. Orthogonal diagonal eigenmatrices M_i are then acquired.

In Figure 2 we show the graphical representation of the JADE algorithm. The rotation matrix produces independent vectors by the diagonalization of the matrices derived from the fourth-order cumulant. A projection of the matrix of whitened scores U_w onto this space will therefore produce the separating matrix, W.

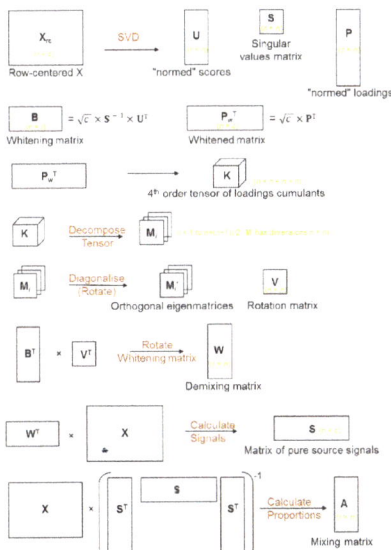

Figure 2. Graphical representation of the JADE algorithm [18].

2.2. Algorithm

In this section, a blind source separation method using JADE is proposed.

1. Normalize the N images.
2. Mixed images are formed by linearly mixing with a random matrix.
3. Initialization, estimate a Whitening matrix $\tilde{w}, z = \tilde{w}.X$.
4. Estimate a maximal set M_i of cumulants matrix.
5. Find the rotation matrix $\check{V}$ such that the simulants matrix are as diagonal as possible

$$\check{V} = \operatorname{argmin} \sum_i off(V^+ M_i V^-) \quad (7)$$

6. Estimate A as, $A = \check{V}.W^{-1}$, and estimate the components as $y = A^{-1}X$.

3. Simulation

With the purpose of explaining the proposed technique, two images, "Lena" and "Lynda", $N = 259 \times 194$, are mixed with

$$A = \begin{bmatrix} 0.6 & -0.4 \\ -0.4 & 0.6 \end{bmatrix} \quad (8)$$

The performance of separated images is evaluated by using peak signal to noise ratio (PNSR) [19], which is defined as follows, and shown in Tables 1–4.

$$PNSR = 10 \log \left[\frac{255}{\sum_{m=1}^{M} \sum_{n=1}^{N} s(m,n) - y(m,n)} \right] \quad (9)$$

Experience 1: Parrot.jpg and fruit.jpg.

Table 1. PNSR (dB) for the EASI algorithm.

estimated image1 EASI	6.4374
estimated image2 EASI	24.3083

Table 2. PNSR (dB) for JADE the algorithm.

estimated image1 JADE	17.3639
estimated image1 JADE	52.2668

Experience 2: barbara.jpg, lena.jpg.

Table 3. PNSR (dB) for the EASI algorithm.

estimated image1 EASI	18.5680
estimated image2 EASI	30.1416

Table 4. PNSR (dB) for the JADE algorithm.

estimated image1 JADE	31.0534
estimated image2 JADE	29.7526

4. Discussion

From the simulation results, we can deduce:

In Figures 3–6, we see that the images of the recovered images signal resemble the original ones. Second, we demonstrate the efficacy of the proposed algorithm by using the performance index PNSR.

Figure 3. EASI method.

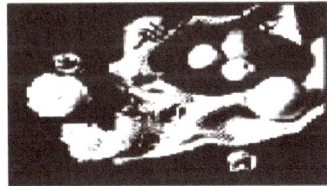

Figure 4. JADE method.

Figure 5. EASI method.

Figure 6. JADE method.

5. Conclusions

In this is paper, we have presented a powerful technique for natural mixtures accompanied by a blind separation of images. This technique utilizes the JADE algorithm that has low computational complexity. To evaluate the performance of the implemented JADE algorithm, a mixture of two images was used. In our future work, we will investigate other methods, such as optimization algorithms, in order to improve their performance accuracies.

Author Contributions: Conceptualization, K.A. and A.N.; methodology, K.A. and A.N.; software, K.A. and K.E.; validation, K.A., A.N. and K.E.; formal analysis, K.A.; investigation, K.A. and K.E.; resources, K.A.; data K.A.; writing—original draft preparation K.A. and A.N.; writing—review and editing, K.A., A.N. and K.E.; visualization, K.A.; supervision, K.A.; project administration, K.A.; funding acquisition, K.A., A.N. and K.E. All authors have read and agreed to the published version of the manuscript.

Funding: This research received no external funding.

Institutional Review Board Statement: Not applicable.

Informed Consent Statement: Not applicable.

Data Availability Statement: Not applicable.

Conflicts of Interest: The author declares no conflict of interest.

References

1. Hesse, C.W.; James, C.J. On semi-blind source separation using spatial constraints with applications in EEG analysis. *IEEE Trans. Biomed. Eng.* **2006**, *53*, 2525–2534. [CrossRef] [PubMed]
2. Kayabol, K.; Kuruoglu, E.E.; Sankur, B. Bayesian separation of images modeled with MRFs using MCMC. *IEEE Trans. Image Process* **2009**, *18*, 982–994. [CrossRef] [PubMed]
3. Lin, Q.H.; Yin, F.L.; Zheng, Y.R. Secure image communication using blind source separation. In Proceedings of the IEEE 6th Circuits and Systems Symposium on Emerging Technologies: Frontiers of Mobile (IEEE Cat. No. 04EX710), Shanghai, China, 31 May–2 June 2004; pp. 261–264.
4. Murata, N.; Ikeda, S. An on-line algorithm for blind source separation on speech signals. In Proceedings of the Nolta98, Crans-Montana, Switzerland, 14–17 September 1998; pp. 923–926.
5. Jung, T.P.; Makeig, S.; Humphries, C.; Lee, T.W.; Mckeown, M.J.; Iragui, V.; Sejnowski, T.J. Removing electroencephalographic artifacts by blind source separation. *Psychophysiology* **2000**, *37*, 163–178. [CrossRef] [PubMed]
6. Milles, J.; Van Der Geest, R.J.; Jerosch-Herold, M.; Reiber, J.H.; Lelieveldt, B.P. Fully automated motion correction in first-pass myocardial perfusion MR image sequences. *IEEE Trans. Med. Imaging* **2008**, *27*, 1611–1621. [CrossRef] [PubMed]
7. Ichir, M.M.; Mohammad-Djafari, A. Hidden Markov models for wavelet-based blind source separation. *IEEE Trans. Image Process.* **2006**, *15*, 1887–1899. [CrossRef] [PubMed]
8. Tonazzini, A.; Bedini, L.; Salerno, E. A Markov model for blind image separation by a mean-field EM algorithm. *IEEE Trans. Image Process.* **2006**, *15*, 473–482. [CrossRef] [PubMed]
9. Huang, W.; Wu, S.; Kong, F.; Wu, Q. Research on Blind Source Separation for Machine Vibrations. *Wirel. Sens. Netw.* **2009**, *1*, 453–457. [CrossRef]
10. Yang, Y.; Wang, X.; Zhang, D. Blind Source Separation Research, based on the Feature Distance Using Evolutionary Algorithms. *Int. J. Acoust. Vib.* **2014**, *19*, 276. [CrossRef]
11. Malhotra, R.; Singh, N.; Singh, Y. Genetic Algorithms: Concepts, Design for Optimization of Process Controllers. *Comput. Inf. Sci.* **2011**, *4*, 39. [CrossRef]
12. Burke, E.K.; Burke, E.K.; Kendall, G.; Kendall, G. *Search Methodologies, Introductory Tutorials in Optimization and Decision Support Techniques*; Springer: Berlin, Germany, 2005; pp. 97–125.
13. Zheng, P.; Liu, Y.; Tian, L.; Cao, Y. A Blind Source Separation Method Based on Diagonalization of correlation Matrices and Genetic Algorithm. In Proceedings of the Fifth World Congress on Intelligent Control and Automation, Hangzhou, China, 15–19 June 2004; Volume 3, pp. 2127–2131.
14. Zhou, H.; Chen, C.Z.; Sun, X.M.; Liu, H. Research on Blind Source Separation Algorithm Based on Particle Swarm Optimization. *Adv. Mater. Res.* **2014**, *989–994*, 1566–1569. [CrossRef]
15. Bai, Q. Analysis of particle swarm optimization algorithm. *Comput. Inf. Sci.* **2010**, *3*, 180. [CrossRef]
16. Tripathi, P.K.; Bandyopadhyay, S.; Pal, S.K. Multi-Objective Particle Swarm optimization with time variant inertia and acceleration coefficients. *Inf. Sci.* **2007**, *177*, 5033–5049. [CrossRef]
17. Ebrahimzadeh, A.; Mavaddati, S. A novel technique for blind source separation using bees colony algorithm. *Elsevier Swarm Evol. Comput.* **2014**, *14*, 15–20. [CrossRef]
18. Rutledge, D.N.; Bouveresse, D.J. Independent components analysis with jade algorithm. *Trac Trends Anal. Chem.* **2013**, *50*, 22–32. [CrossRef]
19. Jyothirmayi, M.; Kuzhali, E.S.; Selvi, S. Blind Source Separation Using Forward Difference Method (FDM). *Signal Image Process.* **2011**, *2*, 121.

Proceeding Paper

An Approach to Mitigate DDoS Attacks on SIP Based VoIP [†]

Warda Amalou *[ ] and Merouane Mehdi

DIC Laboratory, Department of Electronics, Faculty of Technology, University Blida 1, Soumâa Street No. 270, Blida 9068, Algeria; mmehdimerouane@gmail.com
* Correspondence: wardaamalou@gmail.com; Tel.: +213-698086200
† Presented at the 1st International Conference on Computational Engineering and Intelligent Systems, Online, 10–12 December 2021.

Abstract: Voice over Internet Protocol (VoIP) is a recent technology used to transfer video and voice over the Internet Protocol (IP). Session Initiation Protocol (SIP) is the most widely used protocol for signaling functions in VoIP networks. However, the VoIP service is vulnerable to several potential security threats. Distributed denial of service (DDoS) attack is a dangerous attack that prevents legitimate users from using VoIP services. In this paper, we propose a detection scheme based on the Deep Packet Inspection (DPI) method of analyzing packets to extract attack signatures for implementation in new VoIP DDoS attack detection rules with a low false negative rate. We have included experimental results to confirm the proposed scheme.

Keywords: DDoS; DPI; IP; SIP; VoIP

Citation: Amalou, W.; Mehdi, M. An Approach to Mitigate DDoS Attacks on SIP Based VoIP. *Eng. Proc.* **2022**, *14*, 6. https://doi.org/10.3390/engproc2022014006

Academic Editors: Abdelmadjid Recioui, Hamid Bentarzi and Fatma Zohra Dekhandji

Published: 26 January 2022

Publisher's Note: MDPI stays neutral with regard to jurisdictional claims in published maps and institutional affiliations.

Copyright: © 2022 by the authors. Licensee MDPI, Basel, Switzerland. This article is an open access article distributed under the terms and conditions of the Creative Commons Attribution (CC BY) license (https://creativecommons.org/licenses/by/4.0/).

1. Introduction

VoIP is an emerging voice communication technology. VoIP saw light after the appearance of the protocol of data network management. The voice is transformed into data that will then be transformed into IP packets and then transposed into the equipment of IP clients. This is how VoIP is present today on smartphones, tablets and PCs. This requires a VoIP phone, software or hardware.

Free software has caused havoc and an incursion into the world of telephony through PC-PBX solutions running under Linux or another free system and equipped with Open Source software such as Asterisk, Yate, VOCAL etc. [1].

Reliable, free and robust, Asterisk is probably the first Open Source solution of the VoIP for this we chose as solution for the realization of this work by also choosing a user-friendly and easy to use GUI named FreePBX and a multiplatform Softphone known as 3CX that allows users to make phone calls over the Internet. Like all computer systems, VoIP lines are exposed to the same attacks as your Internet connection and email. Cyber criminals develop attacks that specifically target VoIP. We have provided you with an update on the risks and best practices to know to secure your IP telephony.

2. Plateform Asterisk

2.1. VoIP: Protocols and Codecs

Today's voice networks, such as the public switched telephone network (PSTN), use digital switching technology to establish a dedicated link between the caller and the recipient.

H.323 is an ITU (International Telecommunication Union) standard originally developed for real-time multimedia conferencing and additional transfer. Technically, it is a container for several network and multimedia codec standards. The connection signaling part of H.323 is managed by protocol H.225, while the negotiation function is supported by H.245.

However, SIP is defined by the Internet Engineering Task Force (IETF) under RFC 3261. It has been developed specifically for IP telephony and other Internet services. SIP is used with the session description protocol for user discovery; it provides feature negotiation and call management. SDP (Session Description Protocol) is essentially a format to describe the initialization settings for multimedia streaming during the announcement and session invitation. The SIP/SDP pair is somewhat analogous to the H.225/H.245 protocol defined in H.323.SIP uses six basic methods to express its requests [2]:

1. SIP INVITE: This request indicates that the specified SIP Uniform Resource Locator URL (Uniform Resource Locator) user is invited to participate in a session.
2. SIP ACK: This request allows the caller to confirm that they have received a final response to a PROMPT request.
3. SIP OPTIONS: This request is used to query a SIP server, including the UAS (User Application Server) on different information.
4. SIP BYE: This request completes a communication.
5. SIP CANCEL: This request cancels all requests that have not yet been answered to the requester.
6. SIP REGISTER: This request allows the client to save its address to the server it is linked to [3].

2.2. Presentation of Asterisk

Asterisk implements the H.323 and SIP protocols as well as a specific protocol named IAX (Inter Asterisk eXcahnge). It allows communication between client and server as well as between two servers.

Asterisk derives its name from the asterisk symbol "*" found on telephone keyboards, implements the features and services of a PBX, allowing telephones to make calls and interconnect to the public switched telephone network and IP telephony networks. Thanks to its software nature and the GNU General Software License without GPL public license. Users can build telephone systems, add features to existing networks, or replace existing PBXs.

Although originally designed in the late 1990s for Linux, it can now be deployed on many other operating systems. What is more important is that because of its compact size code, it is possible to run it in an embedded system, while it can also boot from a flash drive, live CD or external drive [4].

2.2.1. Interface FreePBX

FreePBX is a simple-to-use GUI that controls and manages Asterisk. This interface offers pre-programmed features accessible via a user-friendly web interface to have a functional PBX without any programming [5].

2.2.2. Softphone 3CX

The 3CX phone system replaces a hardware IP phone. It supports SIP phones, VoIP providers and traditional PSTN lines. The simplicity of web-based management of the 3CX makes it easy to configure eliminating the need for costly maintenance [6].

3. Work Architecture

After presenting the Needs Identification section. This section presents the software environment by determining the different tasks performed. Figure 1 shows the working environment with the various machines installed.

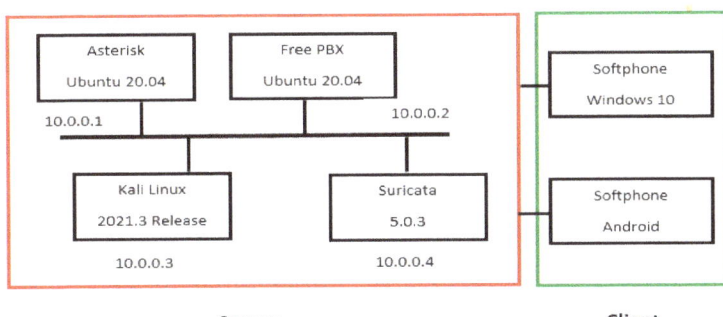

Figure 1. Overall diagram of the work carried out.

3.1. Astersik Server Setup

Implementation of Astersik and FreePBX

Create a new server by choosing Ubuntu 20.04 as the operating system with at least 2 GB of RAM.

FreePBX requires the Apache Web Server, MariaDB and PHP version 7.2 to be installed on your server. By default, Ubuntu 20.04 comes with PHP version 7.4, so you will need to install the Ondrej PHP repository on your server.

Thanks to the graphical interface one does not need to manage users manually with the file sip.conf of Asterisk, it is enough to access the FreePBX interface of administration after being identified. Among the FreePBX services the addition of SIP clients are shown in Figure 2.

Figure 2. Adding SIP clients to FreePBX.

This interface has the role of a well-defined database that undergoes each time an update of users, we have two types of customers, pjsip clients for softphones and chansip clients for Android devices, it is a convenient and easy to handle interface.

3.2. Implementation of 3CX Softphones

Each user has the option to download the Softphone (Android or Windows version) depending on the device used. Figure 3 shows a test of a successful call between two Softphone 3CX which are installed first on Windows XP and second on Windows 10.

Figure 3. Testing a call between two Softphones.

4. VoIP Security Risks and Methods

The VoIP is currently appearing and may be under attack. The VoIP.ms telephone service provider in Quebec implemented an aggressive denial-of-service attack that caused calls and telephone service interruptions. The incident began on or about 16 September and severely tested the VoIP provider's systems, websites and operations [7]. A second unprecedented coordinated cyber-attack hit voice-over-IP service providers in late October 2021. This type of distributed denial-of-service attack is intended to flood a website with Internet traffic in order to take it offline or expose it. The malicious campaign recently targeted VoIP providers that provide telephone services to businesses in the UK, including emergency services. VoIP.ms serves more than 80,000 out of 125 customers, most of whom are currently experiencing call problems [8].

DDoS is a form of cyber-attack in which computers, or bots, are simultaneously hired by an attacker to send a large number of Internet server requests that exceed the capacity of the server. As a result, an Internet server, faced with a sophisticated DDoS attack, can offer degraded performance or even complete collapse.

A SYN Flood occurs when the TCP layer is saturated, preventing the completion of the three-channel TCP negotiation between the client and the server on each port. Each connection using the TCP protocol requires the three-way handshake, which is a set of messages exchanged between the client and the serve as shown in Figure 4.

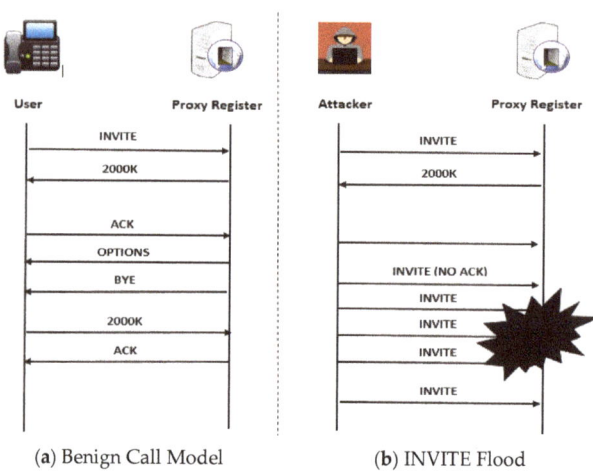

(a) Benign Call Model   (b) INVITE Flood

Figure 4. IP Call Models.

Different tools can be adapted to launch DoS/DDoS attacks, and others are explicitly designed for this purpose. Among these tools: (LOIC, Slowloris, Kali Linux etc....)

Kali Linux is a Debian-based GNU/Linux distribution with over 6008 pre-installed security analysis programs including Wireshark (a package analyzer), John the Ripper (a password-breaking tool) and Sipcrack (a software suite to crack the SIP protocol).

Security Solutions and Methods

In recent years, DDoS attacks against the VoIP have combined all these categories of attacks. This makes them even more dangerous and difficult. The adoption of an anti-DDoS solution is needed to strengthen the security of an IT infrastructure and applications. For this purpose, the monitoring of the health of the network is one of the essential tasks of the maintenance of infrastructures using an analysis tool such as: (tcpdump, caploader, Wireshark...). This part of work is dedicated to extracting digital fingerprints that characterize these offensives for this analysis is essential in our research before moving to detection. Wireshark captures packages and allows you to examine their contents [9].

To protect against computer attacks, firewalls are no longer enough. Intrusion detection systems are able to detect threats that the firewalls do not suspect. Like all IDS, Suricata has been developed for safety and performance as shown in Figure 5.

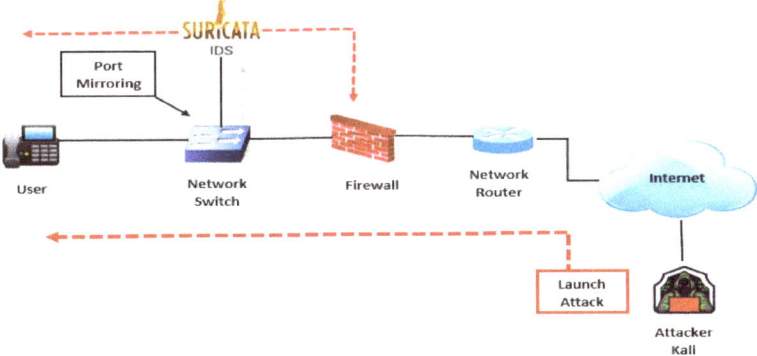

Figure 5. Network Intrusion Detection System Suricata Engine.

In terms of safety, good practices apply: dangerous functions are prohibited, defensive programming is the rule, a few thousand tests have been carried out.

Suricata can be configured to operate in four modes:

- Sniffer mode: in this mode, Suricata reads packets circulating on the network and displays them continuously on the screen;
- The "packet logger" mode: in this mode Suricata logs network traffic in directories on the disk.
- Network Intrusion Detection (NIDS) mode: in this mode, Suricata analyzes the network traffic, compares that traffic to rules already defined by the user and establishes actions to be performed.

5. Conclusions

VoIP is in danger. While voice communications (VoIP) have become more vulnerable to the same type of attacks that data has undergone over the past two decades, Organizations are constantly trying to ensure that precautions are taken to ensure the confidentiality and security of their communications. An IDS is an essential element for SIP user agents, but more SIP-based VoIP endpoints provide it. VoIP network administrators should consider implementing this technology within their SIP-based networks to benefit from the additional level of security that fire can provide. Using an IDS helps to keep the network safe from the real user and prevents DDoS, redirections and disconnections.

Author Contributions: Conceptualization, W.A. and M.M.; methodology, W.A. and M.M.; software, W.A. and M.M.; validation, W.A. and M.M.; investigation, W.A. and M.M.; resources, W.A. and M.M.; data curation, W.A. and M.M.; writing—original draft preparation, W.A. and M.M.; writing—review and editing, W.A. and M.M.; visualization, M.M.; supervision, M.M.; project administration, W.A. and M.M.; funding acquisition, W.A. and M.M. All authors have read and agreed to the published version of the manuscript.

Funding: This research received no external funding.

Data Availability Statement: Not applicable.

Conflicts of Interest: The authors declare no conflict of interest.

References

1. Kasse, B. Study and Implementation of a VoIP Communication System: Applied to an Open-Source IP PABX. Master's Thesis, University Cheikh Anta Diop de Dakar, Dakar, Senegal, 2011.
2. How VoIP Works: Protocols, Codecs and More. Available online: https://www.eetimes.com/how-voip-works-protocols-codecs-and-more/ (accessed on 21 September 2021).
3. What Is Session Initiation Protocol (SIP) & How Does It Work? Available online: https://www.nextiva.com/blog/sip-protocol.html (accessed on 5 September 2021).
4. Andreoulakis, I.I.; Pedini Ioannina, B. *VoIP and PBX Security and Forensics, a Practical Approach*, 2nd ed.; Springer Nature: Cham, Switzerland, 2016; pp. 154–196.
5. *ALEX Robar, FreePBX 2,5 Powerful Telephony Solution*; Packet Publishing: Birmingham, UK, August 2009; ISBN 9781847194725.
6. *DON Ayupo, Break Free from Outdated Phone*; 3cx Innovating Communications: Nicosia, Cyprus, 15 May 2020; pp. 1–8.
7. Canadian VoIP Provider Hit by DDoS Attack, Phone Calls Dropped. Available online: https://www.oxtero.com/2021/09/22/un-fournisseur-de-voip-canadien-touche-par-une-attaque-ddos-les-appels-telephoniques-interrompus/ (accessed on 29 October 2021).
8. DDoS Attack against VoIP Service Providers, the New Form Of Ransomware, November 2021 by Patrick LEBRETON. Available online: https://www.globalsecuritymag.fr/Attaque-DDoS-contre-des,20211104,117891.html (accessed on 9 November 2021).
9. Strengthen IT Security against DDoS Attacks. Available online: https://www.claranet.fr/expertises/cyber-securite/renforcer-la-securite-informatique-contre-les-attaques-ddos (accessed on 7 September 2021).

Proceeding Paper

Hilbert Fractal PIFA Antenna for DCS, PCS, UMTS and WiMAX Wireless Applications [†]

Youssouf Zemam *, Noureddine Boukli Hacene and Yamina Belhadef

Telecommunications Laboratory, Faculty of Technology, University of Tlemcen, BP 230, Pôle Chetouane, Tlemcen 13000, Algeria; bouklin@yahoo.com (N.B.H.); belhadef_y@yahoo.fr (Y.B.)
* Correspondence: youcef.optim@gmail.com
† Presented at the 1st International Conference on Computational Engineering and Intelligent Systems, Online, 10–12 December 2021.

Abstract: In this article, a novel quad-band fractal PIFA antenna design for DCS, PCS, UMTS, and WiMAX wireless communications systems is presented. The proposed antenna is a PIFA antenna where a slot having a Hilbert fractal shape at the third iteration has been inserted at the center of the radiating patch. The fractal shape of the implanted slot on the PIFA antenna was used in order to make the antenna operational at four frequency bands, according the required applications. The proposed antenna with the fractal shape of the slot offers quad-band operation with a miniaturized size compared to the initial PIFA antenna, such that the dimensions of the radiating patch become equal to 28 mm × 28 mm. This structure is operational in the following frequency bands: (1.73–2.08) GHz, (2.46–2.59) GHz, (3.39–3.47) GHz, and the band (4.56–5.02) GHz covering DCS, PCS, UMTS, and WiMAX mobile communications systems, respectively, with a gain ranging from 2 dB to 6 dB at the desired frequency bands. The fractal PIFA antenna design was carried out under CST MWs software with validation of the results made using HFSS software. There is good agreement between the obtained results by the two simulation software.

Keywords: Hilbert curve; fractal PIFA antenna; fractal shape; planar inverted F antenna; quad band antenna; CST MWs software; HFSS software

1. Introduction

Currently, most wireless communications devices operate in several frequency bands and provide different services. Additionally, because of the limited available space in these devices [1], in recent years, researchers have focused their work on the realization of miniature and multiband antennas. Usually, the planar inverted-F antenna (PIFA) is the most desirable design in many applications because of its low cost, simplicity of design, and low profile [2].

However, it is difficult to realize multiband applications from conventional PIFAs antenna. To meet these constraints, several techniques are reported in the literature, notably the use of different feeding techniques by coupling [3], the use of different slots forms [4–7], and also by the adding of parasitic elements at the antenna radiating patch [8]. Several antenna designs have been based on the use of different fractal shapes to achieve multiband antennas, due to their self-similarity and space-filling properties. The space-filling property of the Peano and Minkowski fractals [9,10] has been exploited to miniaturize the antennas., while the self-similarity property of the Hilbert, Koch, and Sierpinski curves can be used to have multiband behavior [11,12].

In this work, a novel Fractal PIFA antenna design was proposed. Parametric studies were made in order to well understand the effect of the implanted fractal shape at the radiating patch on the radio characteristics of the proposed antenna. The PIFA antenna with the fractal shape at the third iteration demonstrates many advantages where the clutter of the structure is very weak and the multiband operating serves to integrate it into the various mobile and wireless devices.

2. Design of the Proposed Antenna

2.1. Initial PIFA antenna Design

The initial antenna is a PIFA antenna with a radiating patch of dimensions Wp × Lp = 34 mm × 28 mm. The antenna is designed on an FR-4 type substrate with a permittivity εr = 4.4 and a thickness hs = 1.6 mm. The radiating element is located above the substrate with a height of H = 5.3 mm, and shorted to the ground plane with a tab of a width s = 4 mm. The initial antenna having overall dimensions of 38 mm × 60 mm and is fed by a 50 Ω microstrip line, as shown in Figure 1.

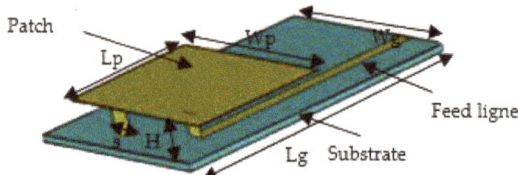

Figure 1. Structure of the initial PIFA antenna.

The resonant frequency *fr* of the initial antenna was determined from the following equation:

$$fr = \frac{C}{4(Wp \times Lp)\sqrt{\varepsilon r}} \quad (1)$$

where: C is the speed of light in the void, *Lp* and *Wp* are the length and width of the radiating patch

2.2. Quad-Band PIFA Antenna

Fractals have been widely used in the design and realization of multiband antennas due to the significant improvements in their performance. To improve the electromagnetic characteristics of the initial PIFA antenna, the Hilbert shaped fractal slot at the third iteration was implanted in the initial antenna radiating patch. The proposed antenna structure and the first four iterations of Hilbert's fractal form are shown in Figure 2.

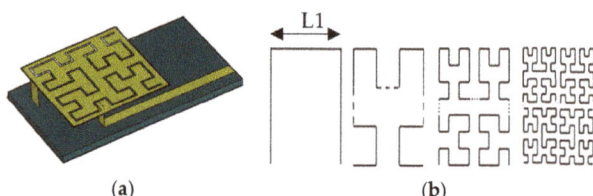

Figure 2. (**a**) Proposed antenna structure, (**b**) the first four iterations of Hilbert's fractal form.

The Figure 3 shows the return loss S11 of the initial antenna and the proposed antenna.

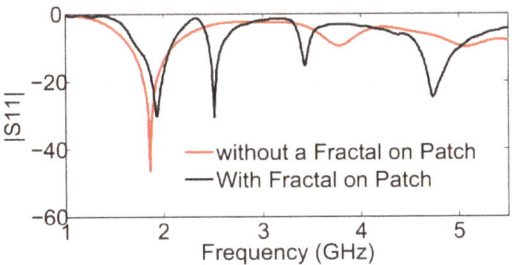

Figure 3. Return loss of the initial antenna and the proposed antenna.

3. Parametric Studies

In this part, parametric studies have been carried out to illustrate the effect of the fractal slot dimension on the radio electric characteristics of the proposed antenna.

Figures 4 and 5 represent the variation of the return loss S11 according to the frequency for different lengths (Ls) and widths (Ws) of the fractal slot.

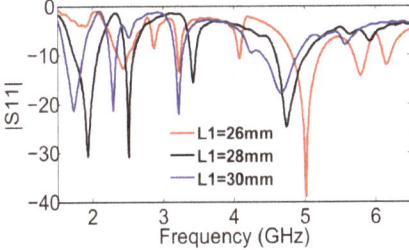

Figure 4. Return loss S11 of the proposed antenna for different lengths (Ls) of the fractal slot.

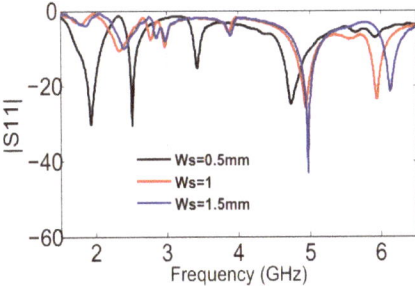

Figure 5. Return loss S11 of the proposed antenna for different widths (Ws) of the fractal slot.

Figure 6 shows variation of the return loss of the proposed antenna with different values of the height H between the radiating patch and the substrate.

From the results obtained in Figures 4–6, we can see that the width (Ws), the length (Ls) of the fractal shape, and the height (H) have remarkable influences on the radio electric characteristics of the proposed antenna. As a result, the antenna present a good performance with fractal slot width and length: Ws = 0.5 mm; Ls = 28 mm; and optimal height: H = 5 mm.

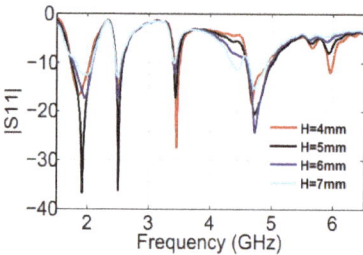

Figure 6. Variation of the return loss of the proposed antenna with different values of the height (H).

4. Discussion of Results

The parametric studies and the optimization of the geometric parameters of the proposed model were executed by CST Microwave Studio.

To validate the obtained result after the parametric study, we used the HFSS Ansys software, as shown in Figure 7.

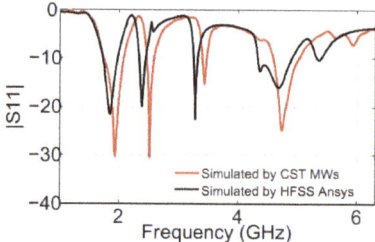

Figure 7. Return loss |S11| of the proposed antenna simulated under CST MWs and HFSS Ansys.

The Figure 8 shows the variation of the standing wave ratio (VSWR) of the proposed antenna according to the resonant frequency.

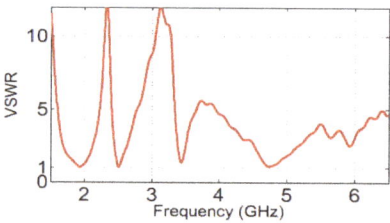

Figure 8. Variation of the VSWR of the proposed antenna according the resonant frequency.

Figure 8 shows that the standing wave ratio is between 1 and 1.4 at the four resonance frequencies. This gives a very good adaptation to the desired frequencies.

The radiation patterns in 2D (polar) of the proposed antenna on the two planes E and H are plotted at the four resonant frequencies 1.93 GHz, 2.51 GHz, 3.43 GHz, and 4.73 GHz, as shown in Figure 9.

To clearly see the radiation behavior of the designed antenna, we have plotted the 3D radiation patterns at the four chosen resonant frequencies, as shown in Figure 10.

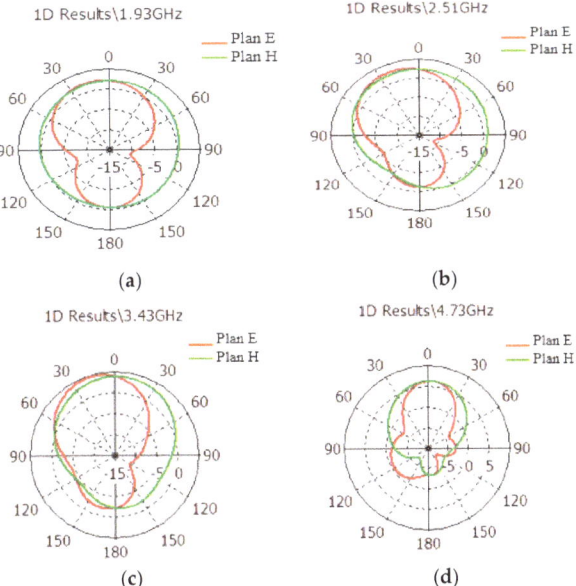

Figure 9. Radiation patterns in 2D of the proposed antenna on the two planes E and H plotted at the four resonant frequencies: (**a**) at 1.93 GHz, (**b**) at 2.51 GHz, (**c**) at 3.43 GHz and (**d**) at 4.73 GHz.

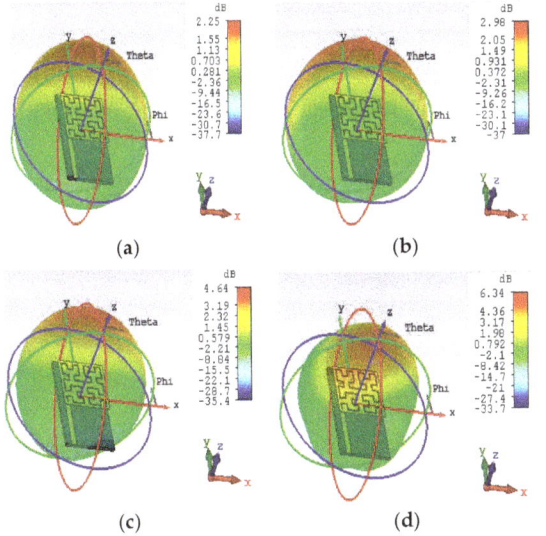

Figure 10. Three-dimensional radiation patterns of the proposed antenna at the four resonance frequencies: (**a**) at 1.93 GHz, (**b**) at 2.51 GHz, (**c**) at 3.43 GHz and (**d**) at 4.73 GHz.

From the polar radiation patterns, we notice that the proposed antenna present a gain ranging from 2 dB to 6 dB at the four resonant frequencies. The results found show well that the antenna is suitable at the four wireless communications systems: DCS, PCS, UMTS, and WiMAX, respectively.

5. Conclusions

In this paper, a fractal PIFA antenna for DCS, PCS, UMTS, and WiMAX wireless communications systems is studied.

The integration of the fractal slot at the center of the initial antenna radiating patch is a technique which was used to have multiband operating and also to miniaturize the proposed antenna. The Hilbert fractal slot at the third iteration, which was inserted at the center of the radiating element, allowed to allocate a multi-band operating of the proposed antenna and also contributed to reduce their size compared to the initial antenna with a miniaturization rate equal to 46.15%.

The proposed antenna simulation results with the two software CST and HFSS show a good agreement in terms of return loss S11. These obtained results was allowed to prove that the proposed antenna has good radiating characteristics and able to covering the frequency bands corresponding to the following four wireless communications systems: DCS, PCS, UMTS (1.73–2.08) GHz, WiMAX (2.46–2.59) GHz, WiMAX (3.39–3.47) GHz, and the WiMAX (4.56–5.02) GHz band, with compact dimensions occupy less space in wireless communications devices.

Author Contributions: All authors contributed to this proceeding paper article and All authors have read and agreed to the published version of the manuscript.

Funding: This research received no external funding.

Institutional Review Board Statement: Not applicable.

Informed Consent Statement: Informed consent was obtained from all subjects involved in the study.

Data Availability Statement: Not applicable.

Conflicts of Interest: The authors declare no conflict of interest.

References

1. Yadav, S.; Jain, P.; Choudhary, R. A novel approach of triangular-circular fractal antenna. In Proceedings of the 2014 International Conference on Advances in Computing, Communications and Informatics (ICACCI), Delhi, India, 24–27 September 2014; pp. 708–711.
2. Hang, W.; Kwai-Man, L.; Chi Hou, C.; Quan, X.; Kwok Kan, S.; HauWah, L. Small antennas in Wireless Communications. *Proc. IEEE J.* **2012**, *100*, 2109–2121. [CrossRef]
3. Kang, D.-G.; Sung, Y. Coupled-fed planar printed shorted monopole antenna for LTE/WWAN mobile handset applications. *IET Microwaves, Antennas Propag.* **2012**, *6*, 1007–1016. [CrossRef]
4. Guo, Y.-X.; Tan, H.S. New compact six-band internal antenna. *IEEE Antennas Wirel. Propag. Lett.* **2004**, *3*, 295–297. [CrossRef]
5. Manteghi, M.; Rahmat-Samii, Y. A novel miniaturized triband PIFA for MIMO applications. *Microw. Opt. Technol. Lett.* **2007**, *49*, 724–731. [CrossRef]
6. Naji, D.K.; Abdul-kareem, A. A dual-band U-slot PIFA antenna with ground slit for RFID applications. *J. Emerg. Trends Comput. Inf. Sci.* **2013**, *4*, 213–220.
7. Keerthika, M.A.; Balachandar, P.; Jaisree, S.; Silamboli, J. Design of Dual Tshaped PIFA antenna for multiband Wireless Applications. *Int. J. Eng. Sci. Res. Technol.* **2015**, *4*, 3.
8. Redzwan FN, M.; Ali, M.T.; Tan, M.M.; Miswadi, N.F. Dual-band Planar Inverted F Antenna with parasitic element for LTE and WiMAX mobile communication. In Proceedings of the 2014 International Symposium on Technology Management and Emerging Technologies, Bandung, Indonesia, 27–29 May 2014; pp. 62–67.
9. Sharma, N.; Singh, G.P.; Sharma, V. Miniaturization of fractal antenna using novel Giuseppe peano geometry for wireless applications. In Proceedings of the 2016 IEEE 1st International Conference on Power Electronics, Intelligent Control and Energy Systems (ICPEICES), Delhi, India, 4–6 July 2016; pp. 1–4.
10. Costanzo, S.; Qureshi, A.M. Miniaturized Planar Inverted-F Antenna Using Minkowski Pre-Fractal Structure. In Proceedings of the 2020 14th European Conference on Antennas and Propagation (EuCAP), Copenhagen, Denmark, 15–20 March 2020; pp. 1–4.
11. Tarbouch, M.; El Amri, A.; Terchoune, H.; Barrou, O. Compact PIFA Antenna with H-Tree Fractal for Mobile Handset Applications. In Proceedings of the 2nd International Conference on Computing and Wireless Communication Systems (ICCWCS'17), Larache, Morocco, 14–16 November 2017; pp. 1–6.
12. Sabban, A. Wearable Compact Fractal Antennas for 5G and Medical Systems. In *Wearable Systems and Antennas Technologies for 5G, IOT and Medical Systems*; CRC Press: Boca Raton, FL, USA, 2020; pp. 349–380.

Proceeding Paper

Design of a Miniature Dual-Band Patch Antenna Based on Meta-Materials for 5G and Wi-Fi Applications [†]

Yamina Belhadef [1,*], Fatima Zohra Moussa [2] and Souheyla Ferouani [3]

1. LTT Laboratory of Tlemcen, Department of Telecommunications, Abou-Bekr Belkaïd University, BP 230, Pôle Chetouane, Tlemcen 13000, Algeria
2. SSL Laboratory of Ain Temouchent, Department of Electronic and Telecommunications, Belhadj Bouchaib University, BP 284, Route de Sidi Bel Abbes, Ain Témouchent 46000, Algeria; moussafatima12@hotmail.com
3. LTT Laboratory of Tlemcen, Department of Electronic and Telecommunications, Belhadj Bouchaib University, BP 284, Route de Sidi Bel Abbes, Ain Témouchent 46000, Algeria; souhilaferouani@gmail.com
* Correspondence: belhadef_y@yahoo.fr
† Presented at the 1st International Conference on Computational Engineering and Intelligent Systems, Online, 10–12 December 2021.

Abstract: Our work consists of designing a dual-band planar antenna based on meta-materials for 5G applications. We propose a design approach consisting of a deposited patch antenna on an FR-4 type monolayer substrate placed above the CSRR cells based on the meta-materials working in millimeter wave. Thereafter, we will do a parametric study to extract the various parameters that influence its electromagnetic behavior. The studied and designed antenna aims to be used for 5G phone applications in the frequency band 3.3–3.8 GHz and Wi-Fi. The design is carried out by CST Microwave Studio software.

Keywords: design; patch antenna; bi-band antenna; miniature antenna; meta-materials; 5G; Wi-Fi; CST Microwave Studio

1. Introduction

The commercial use of 5G has arrived to meet the growing demands for low latency, big capacity, and ubiquitous mobile access, and will play a key role in connecting and enabling services. 5G must address, in addition to an increase in traffic volume, the challenge of connecting billions of devices to heterogeneous service needs [1]. 5G networks are expected to supply a lot of improvements [2].

The antenna is an essential element in 5G networks; however, it always occupies a higher volume in the communication chain, making it difficult to implement in small areas. Its miniaturization has become essential for an optimal design. Many antenna miniaturization techniques exist, and all go through a compromise between size and performance (bandwidth and/or radiation yield) [3], such as charging by passive elements, short circuit application, slots insertion, and use of a dielectric substrate of very high permittivity and meta-materials, etc.

Most materials found in nature (e.g., dielectrics) have positive constitutive parameters ($\varepsilon > 0$ and $\mu > 0$). For this reason, they are called doubly positive materials (DPS). Materials with negative permittivity and positive permeability ($\varepsilon < 0$ and $\mu > 0$) are called epsilon-negative materials (ENG), whose characteristics are presented by plasmas at certain frequencies [4]. On the other hand, materials with positive permittivity and negative permeability ($\varepsilon > 0$ and $\mu < 0$) are known as mu-negative materials (MNG), and ferrites exhibit this behavior at certain frequencies [5]. Materials that have negative constitutive parameters ($\varepsilon < 0$ and $\mu < 0$) are called doubly negative materials (DNG), or meta-materials. Until now, these materials have not been found in nature and they are obtained artificially.

Meta-materials have attracted great attention in recent years due to their unusual electromagnetic properties and their ability to guide and control electromagnetic waves where natural materials cannot [6]. The meta-materials used in the antennas field offer advantages such as reduction in weight and bulk, which is beneficial for their integration into electronic systems such as telecommunications systems in general, and telephone systems for the fifth generation (5G) in particular. In addition, the use of the latter aims to improve its characteristics in terms of resonance frequency (to have multi-band structures or rejected bands) and to make them reconfigurable, as well as for improved bandwidth, gain, directivity, mutual coupling minimization in an antenna array, polarization, and radiation pattern [7–9].

2. Design of a Patch Antenna for 5G

The geometry of the initial antenna is shown in Figure 1. This structure consists of a radiating element with length Lp and width Wp, with notches, fed by a microstrip line. It is deposited on an FR-4 type dielectric substrate with dielectric permittivity $\varepsilon r = 4.3$, of dimensions Ls and Ws and thickness h. The ground plane covers the substrate's whole rear face. Table 1 gives the dimensions of the initial antenna with notches using the given equations in [10–12].

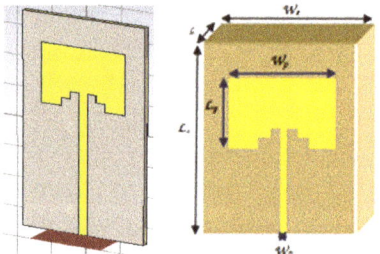

Figure 1. Geometry of the initial antenna.

Table 1. Dimensions of the initial antenna.

Dimensions	Size (mm)
L_s	70.68
W_s	34.9
h	1.595
L_p	19.722
W_p	24
W_0	2.5

Figure 2a,b represents, respectively, the return loss, the stationary wave rate VSWR, and the gain of the initial antenna.

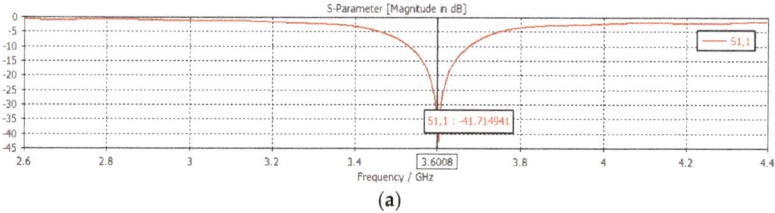

(a)

Figure 2. Cont.

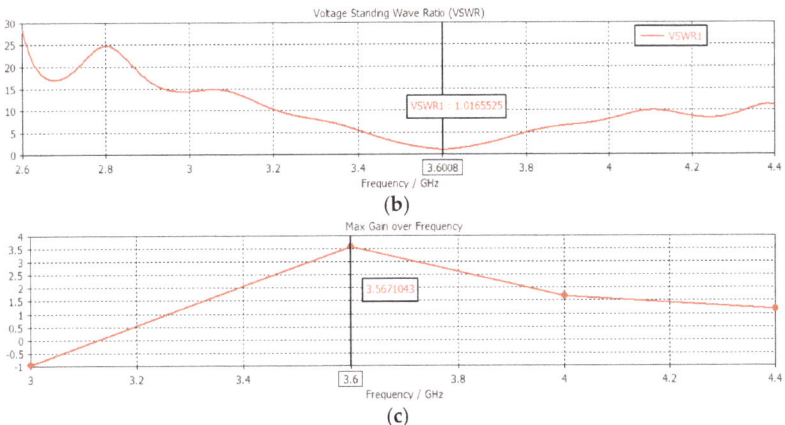

Figure 2. (a) Return loss. (b) Stationary wave rate. (c) Antenna gain.

Figure 2a shows that the adaptation is well-realized since the return loss S11 attains a level close to −41.86 dB at the resonant frequency 3.6 GHz, so the reflection at the antenna input is zero. We have also presented the stationary wave rate, which we notice is between 1 and 2 in the theoretical frequency band 3.53–3.67 GHz, which shows a good impedance match between the antenna and the feed line. The bandwidth is order 3.88%. The antenna gain is around 3.567dB at the resonance frequency 3.6 GHz.

Figure 3a–c represents, respectively, the polar radiation patterns, in 2D and 3D, of the antenna at the resonant frequency 3.6 GHz.

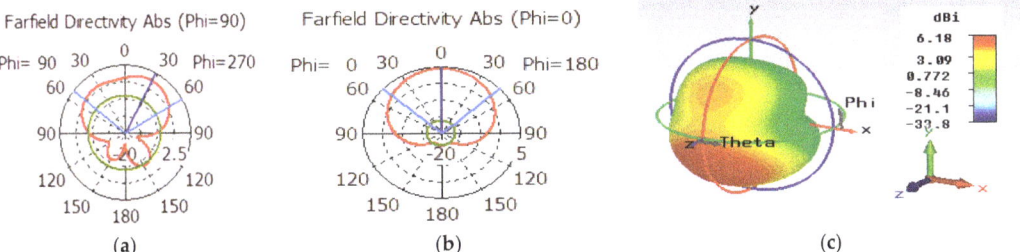

Figure 3. (a) Radiation pattern in 2D, plan H. (b) Radiation pattern in 2D, plan E. (c) Radiation pattern in 3D.

We notice that the exhibit antenna has almost omnidirectional radiation in the E-plane ($\varphi = 0°$) and in the H-plane ($\varphi = 90°$). These plots are verified on the radiation pattern plot in 3D.

3. Design of the CSRR Cell for 5G

The two-dimensional periodic structure of a complementary split-ring resonator (RAFC) is shown in Figure 4. The CSRR (complementary split-ring resonator) is placed on a lossy FR-4 type substrate characterized by a permittivity of 4.3, with a thickness of 1.56 mm. For the studied square RAFC, the external slot ring's external side is equal to (A = 4.9 mm), and the internal slot ring's external side is equal to (B = 4 mm). The two rings are concentric and spaced at 0.12 mm. Each ring is 0.33 mm wide, with a cut in the side of each ring presenting a gap of g = 0.59 mm.

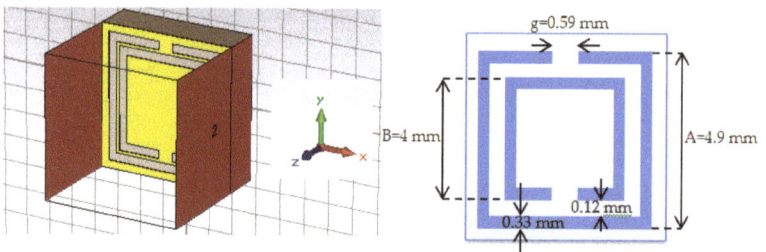

Figure 4. CSRR cell at the resonant frequency 3.6 GHz.

Figure 5 represents the modulus in dB of the return loss (S11) and transmission coefficient (S21) of the CSRR cell obtained by CST MWS software.

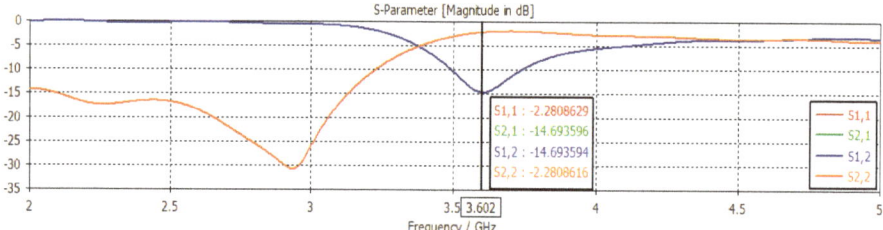

Figure 5. Transmission coefficient and return loss of the CSRR cell.

From the presented results in Figure 5, it can be seen that:
- The return loss S11 modulus presents a resonance at 3.602 GHz with a reflection of −2.28 dB.
- The transmission coefficient S21 modulus goes down to a value of −14.69 dB at the resonant frequency 3.602 GHz.

4. Design of a Dual-Band Antenna Based on Meta-Materials

Figure 6 presents three proposals for the radiating element of the initial antenna combined with CSRR cells. We have modified the number of CSRR cells on the radiating element in order to see their influences on the adaptation, while keeping the other antenna parameters unchanged.

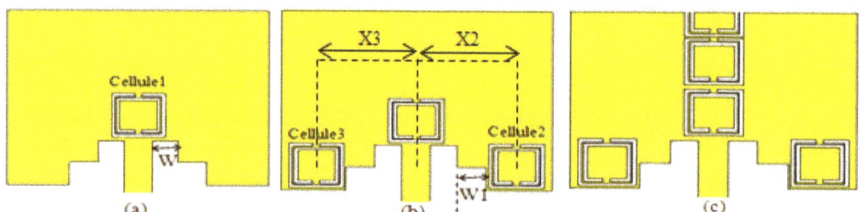

Figure 6. (a) Radiating element plus a CSRR cell. (b) Radiating element plus three CSRR cells. (c) Radiating element plus several CSRR cells.

Figure 7 represents, respectively, the return losses for the three structures proposed previously.

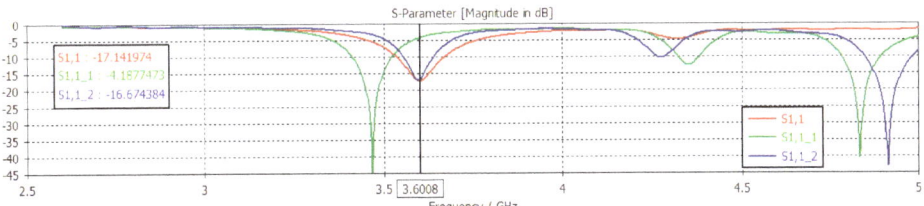

Figure 7. Return losses for the three structures, respectively.

The notes that can be extracted from these curves are:

The simulation result for the first structure of a CSRR cell (Figure 6a) gives a monofrequency operation with a return loss of −17.14 dB at the resonant frequency 3.6 GHz. For the second three-cell structure (Figure 6b), the antenna exhibits tri-band operation at the resonant frequencies 3.466 GHz, 4.352 GHz, and 4.834 GHz, with return loss levels below −44.73 dB, −12.55 dB, and −40.45 dB, respectively.

The design result for the last structure, where we inserted several CSRR cells on the radiating element (Figure 6c), shows that the reflected power contains three resonant frequencies—3.596 GHz, 4.275 GHz, and 4.91 GHz—with levels equal to −16.86 dB, 10.29 dB, and −43 dB, respectively.

Accordingly, the best structure one can choose to complete our study is the third structure because of its gives multi-band operation where the first peak of the return loss resonates almost at the desired resonance frequency of 3.6 GHz.

To show the effect of the different geometrical parameters of the chosen structure (the widths W and W1 of the notches, the location X2 of the second CSRR cell, the location X3 of the third CSRR cell, and the length Ls of the ground plane and of the substrate) on the antenna characteristics (Figure 5c), we carried out a parametric study to observe the influence of these elements on the antenna-matching.

4.1. Variation in Notch Width W

The curves shown in Figure 8 present a dual-band operation in which we observe two resonance frequencies: the first is at 3.59 GHz and the second is around 4.9 GHz.

We notice that the level of the return loss is inversely proportional to the notch width W for the first peak, where the decrease of the width W leads to an increase of the S11 level. For the second peak, the return loss increases when W increases. The best obtained result corresponds to W = 1.6 mm, such that the return loss reaches a value lower than −34.73 dB at the frequency 3.5912 GHz.

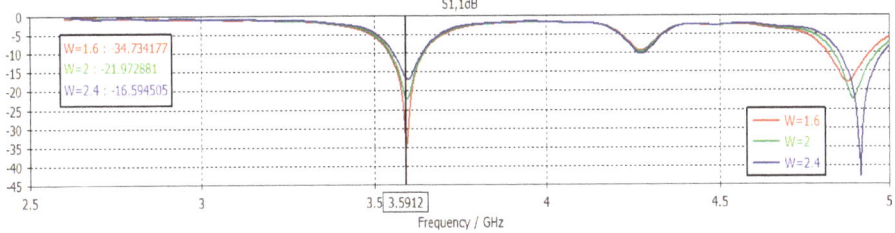

Figure 8. Influence of the notch width W on adaptation.

4.2. Variation of the Notch Width W1

The variation of the width W1 of the simulated antenna by CST MWS by fixing the width W to 1.6 mm is shown in Figure 9. This geometry appears as the most promising for W1 = 2.3 mm, where the amplitude of the reflected power is less than −47.66 dB at the desired frequency 3.5864 GHz. This variation provides a particular improvement in the adaptation of the antenna compared to the previous study.

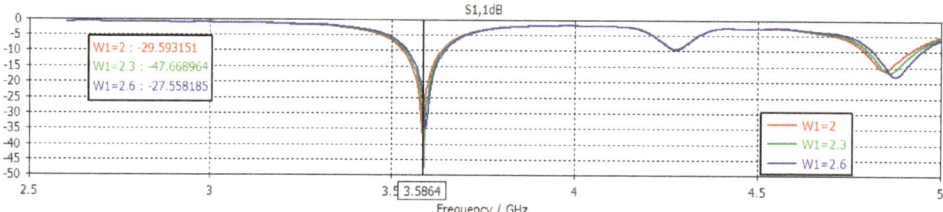

Figure 9. Influence of the notch width W1 on adaptation.

4.3. Variation of the X2 Distance of Second CSRR Cell

From the obtained results, we can visualize that the increase of the return loss level is inversely proportional to the X2 distance. We also observe a slight improvement in the resonance frequency that becomes to equal 3.5977 GHz, almost equal to the desired resonance frequency 3.6 GHz.

4.4. Variation of the X3 Distance of the Third CSRR Cell

In this phase, we made a slight variation to this distance by placing X2 at 8.29 mm. Figure 10 shows us that the curves are almost identical in the shape, but they have different levels of the return loss S11.

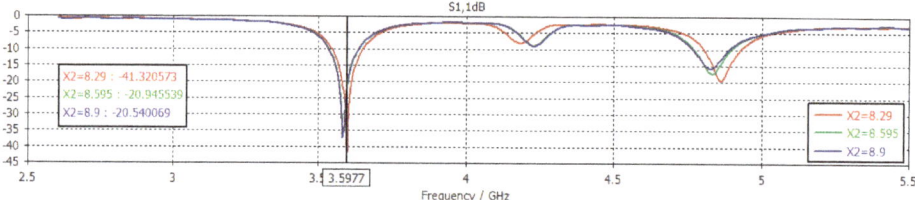

Figure 10. Influence of the X2 distance on adaptation.

4.5. Variation of the Length Ls of the Ground Plane and the Substrate

Now, we are interested in the influence of the length Ls of the ground plane and the substrate on the adaptation by fixing X3 at 8.29 mm (Figure 11).

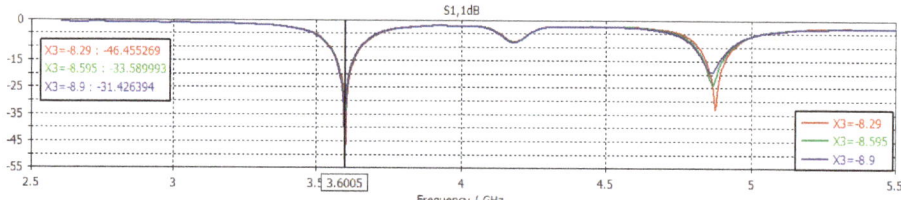

Figure 11. Influence of the X3 distance on adaptation.

According to Figure 12, the curves have identical shapes with different levels of the return loss. It is noticed that the reflection coefficient is inversely proportional to the length Ls of the ground plane and the substrate. The best result recorded corresponds to the length Ls = 65.68 mm.

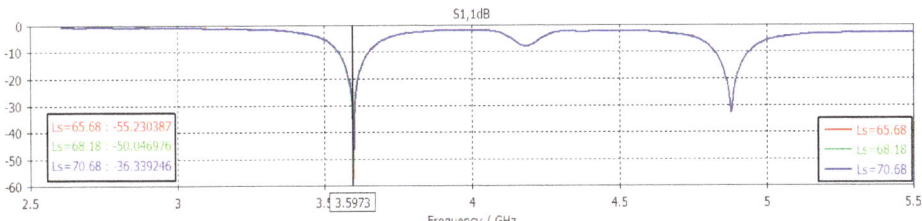

Figure 12. Influence of the length Ls on adaptation.

In Figure 13a–c, respectively, we represent the return loss, the VSWR, and the gain of the final dual-band antenna according to the last parametric study of the length Ls.

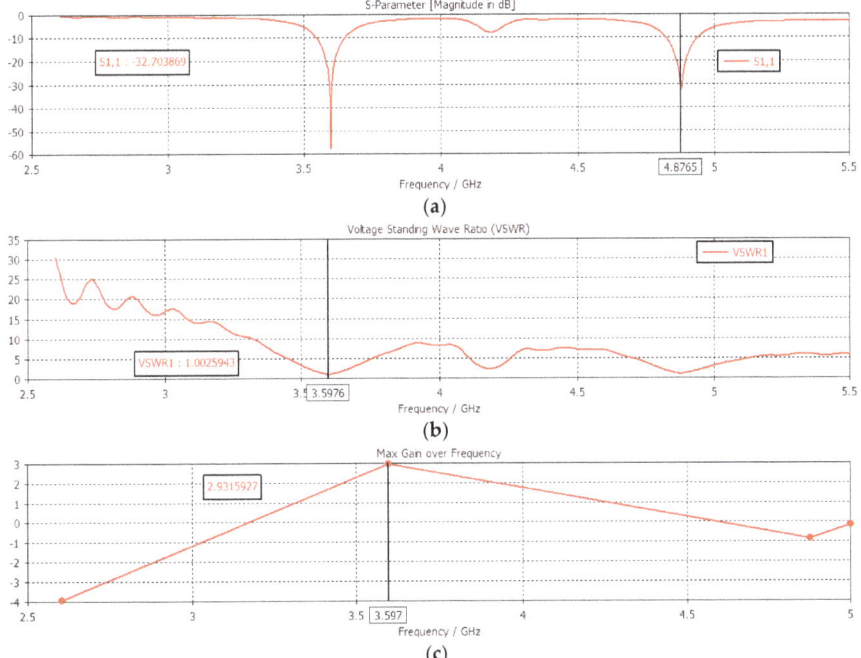

Figure 13. (**a**) Return loss. (**b**) Stationary wave rate. (**c**) Antenna gain.

According to the last study that we carried out and for Ls equal to 65.68 mm, the simulation results bring back a perfect adaptation to the resonance frequencies for a dual-band antenna. From Figure 13a, it can be said that the reflected power at the antenna input is zero since the two peaks reach values less than −55.23 dB and −32.70 dB at the frequencies 3.597 GHz and 4.876 GHz, respectively, according to the 5G and Wi-Fi systems. This result is very encouraging when comparing it with the initial result we recorded in our main antenna (Figure 1) with a miniaturization rate of around 07.07%.

We have also presented the stationary wave rate, which is of the order of one for each of the two resonance frequencies, which gives a good impedance match between the antenna and the feed line. The bandwidths are of the order of 101.5 MHz and 116 MHz for the two resonance frequencies, respectively. The antenna gain is around 2.93 dB at the 3.597 GHz resonance frequency.

Moreover, we find that the percentage of miniaturization of 07.07% is the best since it presents a perfect adaptation and a very satisfactory frequency band.

5. Conclusions

During this work, we have studied and designed a rectangular patch antenna intended for the new generation of mobile telephony, the fifth generation (5G). To learn about the effect of meta-material technology on printed antennas, we have inserted CSRR cells on the proposed rectangular patch antenna. The new geometry simulated by the CST Microwave Studio software presents a miniature bi-band antenna based on meta-materials according to the two 5G and Wi-Fi systems.

Author Contributions: All authors contributed to this proceeding paper article. All authors have read and agreed to the published version of the manuscript.

Funding: This research received no external funding.

Informed Consent Statement: Informed consent was obtained from all subjects involved in the study.

Data Availability Statement: Data sharing not applicable.

Conflicts of Interest: The authors declare no conflict of interest.

References

1. Hajri, S.E. L'amélioration des Performances des Systèmes sans fil 5G Par Groupements Adaptatifs des Utilisateurs. Ph.D. Thesis, Université Paris-Saclay, Paris, France, 2018.
2. Borhani Kakhki, M. Antennes à Formation de Faisceaux en Ondes Millimétriques Basées sur des Métamatériaux Pour les Applications 5G. Ph.D. Thesis, Université du Québec, Quebec City, QC, USA, 2020.
3. Kristou, N. Étude et Conception de Métamatériaux Accordables Pour la Miniaturisation D'antennes aux Fréquences Microondes. Ph.D. Thesis, Universite de Rennes 1, Paris, France, 8 June 2018.
4. Pendry, J.B.; Holden, A.J.; Robbins, D.J.; Stewart, W.J. Extremely Low Frequency Plasmons in Metallic Meso structures. *Phys. Rev. Lett.* **1996**, *25*, 4773–4776. [CrossRef] [PubMed]
5. Krowne, C.M.; Zhang, Y. *Physics of Negative Refraction and Negative Index Materials: Optical and Electronic Aspects and Diversified Approaches*, 1st ed.; Springer: Berlin/Heidelberg, Germany; New York, NY, USA, 2007.
6. Nacer, A. Etude et conception de structures à base de métamatériaux pour application aux circuits microondes et antennes. Ph.D. Thesis, University of Tlemcen, Tlemcen, Algeria, 22 December 2018.
7. Bilotti, F.; Toscano, A.; Vegni, L. Design of Spiral and Multiple Split-Ring Resonators for the Realization of Miniaturized Metamaterial Samples. *IEEE Trans. Antennas Propag.* **2007**, *55*, 2258–2267. [CrossRef]
8. Sahu, B.; Tripathi, P.; Singh, R.; Singh, S.P. Dual segment rectangular dielectric resonator antenna with metamaterial for improvement of bandwidth and gain. *Int. J. RF Microw. Comput.-Aided Eng.* **2014**, *24*, 646–655. [CrossRef]
9. Bait-Suwailam, M.M.; Siddiqui, O.F.; Ramahi, O.M. Mutual Coupling Reduction Between Microstrip Patch Antennas Using Slotted-Complementary Split-Ring Resonators. *IEEE Antennas Wirel. Propag. Lett.* **2010**, *9*, 876–878. [CrossRef]
10. Balanis, C.A. *Antenna Theory Analysis and Design*; Arizona State University: Tempe, AZ, USA, 2005.
11. Bahl, I.J.; Bhartia, P. *Microstrip Antennas*; Artech House: Norwood, MA, USA, 1980.
12. Balanis, C.A. *Advanced Engineering Electromagnetics*; John Wiley & Sons: New York, NY, USA, 1989.

Proceeding Paper

Coverage Analysis and Efficient Placement of Drone-BSs in 5G Networks [†]

Mohamed Amine Ouamri [1,2,3,*], Marius-Emil Oteşteanu [4], Gordana Barb [4] and Cedric Gueguen [3]

[1] Laboratoire D'informatique Médicale, Faculté de Technologie, Département d'ATE, Université de Bejaia, Bejaia 06000, Algeria
[2] Faculté de Génie Électrique et D'informatique, Département de Télécommunication, Université de Tizi Ouzou, Tizi Ouzou 15000, Algeria
[3] UFR Informatique et Électronique, University of Rennes 1/IRISA, 35000 Rennes, France; cedric.gueguen@irisa.fr
[4] Department of Communications, Politehnica University Timisoara, 300006 Timisoara, Romania; marius.otesteanu@upt.ro (M.-E.O.); gordana.barb@student.upt.ro (G.B.)
* Correspondence: ouamrimouhamedamine@gmail.com
† Presented at the 1st International Conference on Computational Engineering and Intelligent Systems, Online, 10–12 December 2021.

Abstract: The integration of drones as base stations has shown to be a potential approach for the future mobile communication systems. Hence, this emerging technology is currently being investigated within the 3GPP standardization community with the main objective of improving coverage and capacity in dense urban areas. Nevertheless, in order to provide adequate coverage for users, it is necessary to find the optimal location of the Drone-BS. This work proposes a novel approach for the Drone-BS in 5G communication systems, using the meta-heuristic algorithm. Firstly, we analyse the downlink coverage probability according to SINR by using stochastic geometry. Afterwards, we apply the Grey Wolf Optimizer algorithm in order to find the optimal Drone-BS placement under coverage probability constraint.

Keywords: drone-Base Station; coverage; 5G networks; Grey Wolf Optimizer

1. Introduction

The chronological progress and exponential growth of cellular networks has led the mobile communications community to suggest the use of drones as a Base Station (BS), with the incorporation of a transceiver, due to its massive potential in mobile communication systems [1]. This approach provides significant improved coverage, enhanced quality of service and increased capacity [2,3]. Furthermore, the high position of the drone-BS encourages Line-of-Sight (LOS) communication to grounds users [4], and consequently the optimal drone-BS deployment is paramount for the proper functioning of the network. On the other hand, with the significant increase in traffic volume, 5G mobile networks will exploit the vast amount of available spectrum in the millimeter wave (mmWave) band [5]. Simultaneously, a drone equipped with a mmWave base station offers considerable throughput. Several research projects are paying more attention to the drone-BS deployment. For instance, authors in [6] study the optimal Unmanned Aerial Vehicles (UAV) placement in order to analyse coverage with fixed UAV altitude. Similarly, in [7], the authors investigate the optimal placement of drone-cells by taking into consideration the backhaul requirements. In addition, the authors propose the robustness solution of drone-BS placement under the user's movement. A heuristic approach based on Particle Swarm Optimization (PSO) is introduced in order to find the optimal 3D location of drone-cells in [8]. The study aims to maximize coverage and limit interference while reducing the drone's altitudes. More recently, in [3], the authors propose a novel 3D UAV-BS placement using exhaustive search (ES) and maximal weighted area algorithms. They maximize coverage under the quality-of-service requirement constraint. The efficient UAVs deployment in order to provide coverage is suggested in [4]. The authors study the downlink coverage probability as function of altitude and antenna gain and apply circle packing theory in order to maximize the coverage area. Authors in [9] present UAVs-BS placement based on the location of users. In this paper we investigate the drone-BS placement by assuming random distribution and mmWave Path Loss model. We analyse the downlink coverage probability based on altitude and antenna gain. We apply a Grey Wolf Optimizer (GWO) algorithm [10] in order to find the optimal 3D position that satisfies coverage under interference constraint. The rest of this paper is organized as follows: Section 2 presents the system model adopted for our work, Section 3 describes the downlink coverage probability and Section 4 provides the proposed optimal drone-BSs placement algorithm using GWO. Simulation and numerical results are given in Section 5. Finally, conclusion and future work are discussed in Section 6.

2. System Model

In this section we present the system model adopted for our work. We consider an urban scenario where N users are distributed randomly in the area represented by (x_j, j). The M drones-BSs are randomly distributed with fixed power transmission. Each drone is defined by its altitude h and location (x_i, i). Geometrically, the coverage area of the drone is given by $C_{drone} = (R^2 - h^2)$, where R represents the radius of the transmitter drone [11]. Figure 1 depicts a possible scenario of drone-BSs deployment. Additionally, we assume that the propagation environments are both LOS and Non-Line-of-Sight (NLOS). On the other hand, the metric for satisfying quality of service is based on the determination of the Signal-to-Interference Plus Noise Ratio (SINR), which should be above a certain threshold $SINR > SINR_{thr}$. According to [3], the probability of the mean path loss is given by:

$$PL(h, d_{ji}) = PL_{LOS} P_{LOS} + PL_{NLOS} P_{NLOS} \tag{1}$$

where P_{LOS} represents the probability of the LOS link given by Equation (2) and $P_{NLOS} = 1 - P_{LOS}$. As discussed in [12], the path loss between drone-BSs and users for the LOS and NLOS propagation in dB is given by Equation (3).

$$P_{LOS} = \frac{1}{1 + a \exp\left(-b\left(\left(\frac{180}{\pi}\right) \tan^{-1}\left(\frac{h}{\sqrt{(x_j - x_i)^2 + (y_j - y_i)^2}}\right) - a\right)\right)} \tag{2}$$

$$\begin{aligned} PL_{LOS} &= 20\log\left(\frac{4\pi f_c d_{ji}}{c}\right) + \eta_{LOS} \\ PL_{NLOS} &= 20\log\left(\frac{4\pi f_c d_{ji}}{c}\right) + \eta_{NLOS} \end{aligned} \tag{3}$$

where f_c represents the carrier frequency, $d_{ji} = \sqrt{(x_j - x_i)^2 + (y_j - y_i)^2 + h^2}$ is the distance between the drone-BSs and user i. Furthermore, η_{LOS} and η_{NLOS} are the average additional losses for LOS and NLOS, respectively. The probability mean path loss can be further rewritten as:

$$PL(h, d_{jt}) = (\eta_{LOS} - \eta_{NLOS}) P_{LOS} + 10 \log\left(\sqrt{\frac{h^2 +}{(x_j - x_i)^2 + (y_j - y_i)^2}}\right) + B \tag{4}$$

with $B = 20 \log\left(\frac{4\pi f_c}{c}\right) + \eta_{NLOS}$.

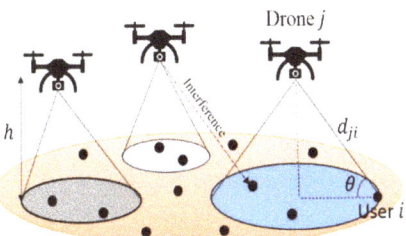

Figure 1. System Model.

As shown in Figure 1, the blue circles represent the drone's coverage area, and the black points indicate the users in the area. At this point, there are two major binary decisions to be conducted. The first one is to determine the deployment of drone-BSs and the second one is to determine the users covered by drone-BSs. The procedure can be developed mathematically as follows: let $D = \{1 \ldots M\}$ represent the set of the candidate drone-BSs and $U = \{1 \ldots N\}$ the set of the users. For the first case, the binary decision can be formulated as:

$$\omega_{xyh}^i = \begin{cases} 1, & if\ the\ drone - BS\ is\ deployed\ at\ (x_i, y_i, h) \\ 0, & otherwise \end{cases} \quad (5)$$

Then, for the second case (user's coverage):

$$\varphi_j^i = \begin{cases} 1, & if\ user\ j\ is\ covered\ by\ one\ drone - BS\ i \\ 0, & otherwise \end{cases} \quad (6)$$

3. Downlink Coverage Probability Calculation

In this section we study the downlink coverage probability. When evaluating channel performance, a typical user in the area is associated with a drone-BS when the SINR is greater than a predefined threshold. According to [3], the received power at the user j from its drone-BS is given by:

$$p_r^{ji} = p_t - PL(h, d_{ji}) - \vartheta \quad (7)$$

where p_t is the power transmission and ϑ is the shadow fading with Gaussian random variable in dB for LOS and NLOS environments. The SINR ratio is given by the following formula:

$$SINR = \frac{p_r^{ji}}{\sum_{i' \in D,\ i' \neq i} p_r^{i'j} + N} \quad (8)$$

$$\mathbb{P}[SINR > SINR_{thr}] = \mathbb{P}\left[\frac{p_r^{ji}}{\sum_{i' \in D,\ i' \neq i} p_r^{ji'} + N} \geq SINR_{thr}\right] \quad (9)$$

Lemma 1. *In the drone-BS network, the downlink coverage probability for a ground user located at a distance d_{ji} from drone-BS can be expressed as:*

$$p_c = Q\left(\frac{\left(PL(h, d_{ji}) + SINR_{thr}\left(\sum_{i' \in D,\ i' \neq i} p_r^{ji'} + N\right) - p_t + \mu\right)}{\sigma}\right) \quad (10)$$

where $Q(.)$ is the Q function.

Proof.

$$p_c = \mathbb{P}\left[\frac{p_r^{ji}}{\sum_{i' \in D,\ i' \neq i} p_r^{ji'} + N} \geq SINR_{thr}\right]$$

$$= \mathbb{P}\left[p_r^{ji} \geq SINR_{thr}\left(\sum_{i' \in D,\ i' \neq i} p_r^{ji'} + N\right)\right]$$

$$= \mathbb{P}\left[p_t - PL(h, d_{ji}) - \vartheta \geq SINR_{thr}\left(\sum_{i' \in D,\ i' \neq i} p_r^{ji'} + N\right)\right] \quad (11)$$

$$= \mathbb{P}\left[\vartheta \leq p_t - PL(h, d_{ji}) - SINR_{thr}\left(\sum_{i' \in D,\ i' \neq i} p_r^{ji'} + N\right)\right]$$

$$Q\left(\frac{\left(PL(h,d_{ji}) + SINR_{thr}\left(\sum_{i' \in D,\ i' \neq i} p_r^{ji'} + N\right) - p_t + \mu\right)}{\sigma}\right)$$

where $\vartheta \sim N(\mu_{LOS}, \sigma^2_{LOS})$ and $\vartheta \sim N(\mu_{NLOS}, \sigma^2_{NLOS})$ represent the shadow fading with normal distribution, in dB, for LOS and NLOS cases, respectively. However, the Complementary Cumulative Distribution Function (CCDF) of a Gaussian random variable as show in Equation (12) below gives the downlink coverage probability for LOS environment.

$$p_c = Q\left(\frac{\left(PL_{LOS}P_{LOS} + SINR_{thr}\left(\sum_{i' \in D,\ i' \neq i} p_r^{ji'} + N\right) - p_t + \mu_{LOS}\right)}{\sigma_{LOS}}\right) \quad (12)$$

4. Optimal Drone-BSs Placement

In this section we propose to solve the 3D deployment of drone-BSs using GWO [10], where the goal is to maximize coverage by increasing the number of users covered by drone-BSs. Generally, the drone-BSs placement constitutes a NP-hard problem. For this reason, evolutionary algorithms can be a suitable alternative. Mathematically, the coverage problem can be formulated using Mixed Integer Non-Linear Programming (MINLP), as follows:

$$\max_{x_i,\ y_i,\ h,\ \varphi^i_j} \sum_{j=1}^{N} \sum_{i=1}^{M} \varphi^i_j \quad (13)$$

Subject to:

$$\min \sum_{i=1}^{M} \omega^i_{xyh} \quad (14)$$

$$h_{min} \leq h \leq h_{max} \quad (15)$$

$$\sum_{j=1}^{N} b_j\ \varphi^i_j \leq BW \quad (16)$$

The first constraint assumes that the coverage must be met with a minimum number of drone-BSs deployed. Indeed, a considerable deployment of drones leads to a reduction in the distance between them and hence, the interference from the adjacent drone-BSs increases [4]. The variables h_{min}, h_{max} in the second constraint represent the minimum and maximum drone-BS's altitude, respectively. Nevertheless, as the altitude of drone-BS increases, the coverage radius also increases, and energy performance of drone-BSs decreases. The last proposed constraint indicates the total limiting available bandwidth, where b_j is the bandwidth required by user j and BW denotes the total bandwidth of the drone-BS [7]. Now we apply GWO in order to find the optimal 3D drone-BSs placement. Proposed by [10], GWO is a meta-heuristic algorithm inspired by the Grey Wolf hunting mechanism. The GWO algorithm takes into consideration the search, encircling and attacking prey by Grey Wolf. Notwithstanding, the algorithm classifies wolf into four groups to find leadership: α is the most optimal solution and β, are the second and third best solutions, respectively. X represents the alternative solutions. The process is mathematically modelled as follows:

$$X(t+1) = \frac{1}{3}(X_1(t) + X_2(t) + X_3(t)) \quad (17)$$

where:
$$X_1(t) = X_\alpha - A_1 \times D_\alpha \quad (18)$$
$$X_2(t) = X_\beta - A_2 \times D_\beta \quad (19)$$
$$X_3(t) = X_\theta - A_3 \times D_\theta \quad (20)$$

From the equations above, $X_1(t)$, $X_2(t)$, $X_3(t)$ are the position vectors of the prey, and $X(t+1)$ represents the grey wolf position vector. Grey wolves encircle prey during the hunt. The mathematically model-encircling behaviour is given by the following formula:

$$D = |C \times X_p(t) - X(t)| \quad (21)$$

where: $C = 2 \times r_2$ and $A = 2a \times r_2 - a$ are two coefficient vectors, and r_1, r_2 are vectors randomly generated between $[0, 1]$. The Algorithm 1 of GWO is given by:

Algorithm 1: GWO for drone-BS deployment.

Initializing the drone-BSs population $X_i = (i = 1, 2, \ldots n)$
Initialize α, A and C
for $i = 1 : n$ do
$j = 1 : m$ do
Calculate a distance, pathloss and evaluate coverage probability in each user
end for
Find the fitness of each search agent $X_\alpha, X_\beta, X_\theta$
while $t < Max_{iter}$
for each search agent
$\quad X(t+1) = \frac{1}{3}(X_1(t) + X_2(t) + X_3(t))$
end for
Update α, A and C
Calculate the fitness of all search agents
Update $X_\alpha, X_\beta, X_\theta$
$t = t + 1$
end while
return X_α

---

5. Simulation Results

The simulation and numerical results for the downlink coverage probability and optimal drone-BSs placement are presented in this section. 200 users and 10 drone-BSs are randomly distributed within a 2×2 km^2 area. The simulation parameters are illustrated in Table 1. Our goal is to serve the maximum number of users based on a reduced number of drone-BSs using a mmWave carrier frequency.

Table 1. Simulation parameters adopted for our work.

Parameters	Value
f_c	28 GHz
$h_{min} \leq h \leq h_{max}$	$1000 \leq h \leq 3000$ m
M (number of drone-BSs)	10
N (number of users)	200
P_t	30 dBm
$SINR_{thr}$	5 dBm
B	20 MHz

Figure 2 depicts the downlink coverage probability considering different altitudes for the drone-BSs. We observe that the coverage probability increases when the altitude of the drone-BSs also increases. However, as mentioned above, a very high altitude can influence the energy performance of the drone. Figure 3 shows the optimal drone-BSs placement and the minimum required number of drone-BSs to ensure that all users are covered. The results indicate that in order to satisfy 0.76 of downlink coverage probability, it is necessary to deploy five drone-BSs. On the other hand, a coverage probability can be improved by increasing the number of drones, although this would lead to a decrease in the distance between the drones and consequently the interference at user level would be higher.

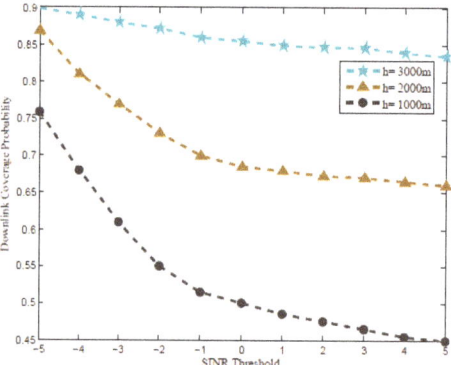

Figure 2. Coverage probability versus SINR threshold, at different altitudes.

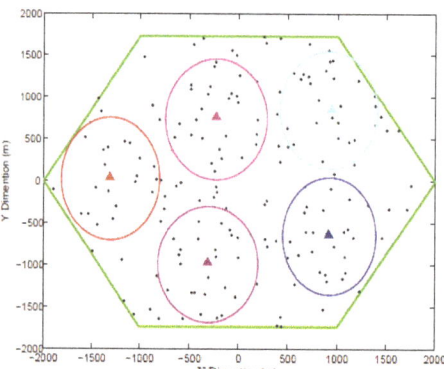

Figure 3. Drone-BSs placement at the end of the GWO iteration.

Furthermore, the number of users served by the deployed drone-BSs are illustrated in Figure 4. We observe a decrease in the number of users covered by the network when the number of drone-BSs is reduced. Moreover, the results obtained indicate that the drone-BSs are separated in distance, leaving uncovered areas. Besides, the optimal altitude selected for the drone-BSs can be improved to increase the coverage radius and get more users covered, but with reduced energy performance.

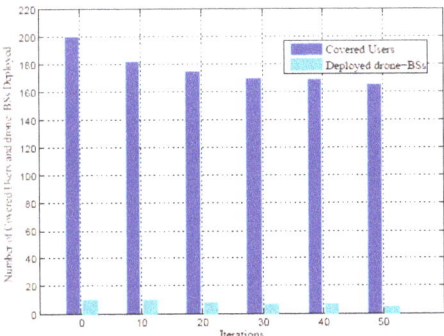

Figure 4. Number of covered users and drone-BSs deployment at each iteration.

6. Conclusions

Drone-BSs deployment in 5G networks is currently an important subject with extreme potential in the mobile communication networks industry. Placement optimization is a complicated task that requires automation algorithms to find the optimal solution for the placement of drone-BSs. In this work, we studied a 3D deployment of drone-BSs in a 5G network using GWO algorithm. Firstly, we analysed the downlink coverage probability according to SINR and altitude. Next, we proposed a mathematical model in order to maximize coverage under a minimum number of drone-BSs, altitude and total limiting available bandwidth. The results obtained showed a minimization of the total number of drone-BSs deployed with a coverage reaching 82.5%. Our study does not take into consideration the blocking effect and overlap between drones that are important for the handoff, but these factors will be the focus of research in future work.

Author Contributions: Conceptualization, M.A.O. and G.B.; methodology, C.G.; software, M.A.O.; validation, M.-E.O. and C.G.; formal analysis, M.A.O.; investigation, G.B.; resources, G.B.; writing—review and editing, C.G. and M.-E.O.; supervision, M.-E.O.; All authors have read and agreed to the published version of the manuscript.

Funding: This Project is financed by Politehnica University Timisoara, Timisoara 300006, Romania.

Institutional Review Board Statement: Not applicable.

Informed Consent Statement: Not applicable.

Data Availability Statement: Not applicable.

Acknowledgments: The authors wish to acknowledge the technical support, infrastructure and documentation provided by Nokia Networks.

Conflicts of Interest: The authors declare no conflict of interest.

References

1. Bor-Yaliniz, I.; Yanikomeroglu, H. The New Frontier in RAN Heterogeneity: Multi-Tier Drone-Cells. *IEEE Commun. Mag.* **2016**, *54*, 48–55. [CrossRef]
2. Mozaffari, M.; Kasgari, A.T.Z.; Saad, W.; Bennis, M.; Debbah, M. Beyond 5G With UAVs: Foundations of a 3D Wireless Cellular Network. *IEEE Trans. Wirel. Commun.* **2019**, *18*, 357–372. [CrossRef]
3. Alzenad, M.; El-Keyi, A.; Yanikomeroglu, H. 3-D Placement of an Unmanned Aerial Vehicle Base Station for Maximum Coverage of Users with Different QoS Requirements. *IEEE Wirel. Commun. Lett.* **2018**, *7*, 38–41. [CrossRef]
4. Mozaffari, M.; Saad, W.; Bennis, M.; Debbah, M. Efficient Deployment of Multiple Unmanned Aerial Vehicles for Optimal Wireless Coverage. *IEEE Commun. Lett.* **2016**, *20*, 1647–1650. [CrossRef]
5. Chen, S.; Zhao, J. The requirements, challenges, and technologies for 5G of terrestrial mobile telecommunication. *IEEE Commun. Mag.* **2014**, *52*, 36–43. [CrossRef]

6. Li, X.; Guo, D.; Yin, H.; Wei, G. Drone-assisted public safety wireless broadband network. In Proceedings of the 2015 IEEE Wireless Communications and Networking Conference Workshops (WCNCW), New Orleans, LA, USA, 9–12 March 2015; pp. 323–328.
7. Kalantari, E.; Shakir, M.Z.; Yanikomeroglu, H.; Yongacoglu, A. Backhaul-aware robust 3D drone placement in 5G+ wireless networks. In Proceedings of the 2017 IEEE International Conference on Communications Workshops (ICC Workshops), Paris, France, 21–23 May 2017; pp. 109–114.
8. Kalantari, E.; Yanikomeroglu, H.; Yongacoglu, A. On the Number and 3D Placement of Drone Base Stations in Wireless Cellular Networks. In Proceedings of the 2016 IEEE 84th Vehicular Technology Conference (VTC-Fall), Montreal, QC, Canada, 18–21 September 2016; pp. 1–6.
9. Bor-Yaliniz, R.I.; El-Keyi, A.; Yanikomeroglu, H. Efficient 3-D placement of an aerial base station in next generation cellular networks. In Proceedings of the 2016 IEEE International Conference on Communications (ICC), Kuala Lumpur, Malaysia, 23–27 May 2016; pp. 1–5.
10. Mirjalili, S.; Mirjalili, S.M.; Lewis, A. Grey Wolf Optimizer. *Elsevier Adv. Eng. Softw.* **2014**, *69*, 46–61. [CrossRef]
11. Al-Turjman, F.; Lemayian, J.P.; Alturjman, S.; Mostarda, L. Enhanced Deployment Strategy for the 5G Drone-BS Using Artificial Intelligence. *IEEE Access* **2019**, *7*, 75999–76008. [CrossRef]
12. Al-Hourani, A.; Kandeepan, S.; Lardner, S. Optimal LAP Altitude for Maximum Coverage. *IEEE Wirel. Commun. Lett.* **2014**, *3*, 569–572. [CrossRef]

Proceeding Paper

UIS Characterization of LOCOS-Based LDMOS Transistor Fabricated by 1 μm CMOS Process [†]

Ali Houadef [1,*] and Boualem Djezzar [2]

[1] Signals and Systems Laboratory (LSS), Institute of Electrical and Electronic Engineering (IGEE), M'Hamed Bouguerra University of Boumerdés (UMBB), Boumerdés 35000, Algeria
[2] Reliability of Semiconductor Components Team (FCS), Microelectronics and Nanotechnology Division (DMN), Centre de Développement des Technologies Avancées (CDTA), Algiers 16000, Algeria; bdjezzar@cdta.dz
* Correspondence: a.houadef@univ-boumerdes.dz
† Presented at the 1st International Conference on Computational Engineering and Intelligent Systems, Online, 10–12 December 2021.

Abstract: This paper investigates the ruggedness of an n-type LDMOS under single shot unclamped inductive switching (UIS) stress conditions. We present a detailed method to define the electrothermal safe operating area (SOA), and the physics of the failure mechanism is described. We conclude that the device robustness depends mainly on the gate bias, much less on the pulse duration on millisecond range, the inductive load value, or the initial operating temperature, although the Kirk effect is always present under all conditions. However, the failure mechanism fundamentally changes to pure avalanche breakdown under short pulses.

Keywords: LDMOS; TCAD; UIS; ruggedness

1. Introduction

Laterally diffused MOSFET transistors (LDMOS) are the primary choice for high-voltage (HV), RF/microwave applications. Even when the process nodes are downscaled, and variants of LDMOS designs are reported, the usage of older, much more robust technologies are still adopted in the market [1–6].

Such technologies rely on the extension of the drift region, the reduced surface field principle (RESURF), the local oxidation of silicon (LOCOS), and the separation field oxide (FOX) to achieve a balance between the off-state breakdown voltage (BV) and the on-state resistance (R_{ON}). That balance is commonly known as the figure of merit (FoM), which is calculated often using Baliga's equation. Additionally, by using a standard CMOS process, the integration of such devices along the high-performance (HP) circuits is possible with little additional effort [7].

However, that integration comes with the cost of a low BV, as is the case in the device under test (DUT). The low BV value; of 21 V; raises the concern of catastrophic failure during switching, because LDMOS transistors have primarily an inductive load, which stresses the device at the switching moment under a high-power value, in addition to small parasitic inductive loads, which could have the same effect [8]. The purpose of this study is to assess whether the DUT could sustain such sudden power dissipation. The LDMOS design is a conflicting process between a wide SOA, high BV, and low R_{ON}.

Defining the SOA depends heavily on the final application, as the final implementation requires different standards, as such, the breakdown mechanism will change accordingly [9]. Under short pulses, the device unavoidably will be under electrostatic discharge (ESD), as a charge device model (CDM), human body model (HBM) conditions, machine model (MM), and/or transmission line measurement (TLP), or even high-power electromagnetic interference (EMI) [10,11]. The stress time range is of several pico, nano, or microseconds.

In this case, the breakdown is purely electrical. The SOA upper-boundary is when the device shows negative resistance [12,13], which is due to the electrical onset of the NPN transistor [14,15].

Under pulses of a few milliseconds and up to tens of seconds ranging in values, such as the polarity reversal of an H-Bridge in smart-power ICs [16], the breakdown is electrothermal, which is due to the impact-ionization and thermal generation, a consequence of the onset of the parasitic NPN transistor and its Kirk effect [17].

Furthermore, longer pulses, hundreds of seconds up to years of stress, are often categorized as hot carrier injection (HCI) degradation, which affects the electrical parameters non-catastrophically [18–20], although, it also could be a combination of HCI and a thermal degradation component called bias temperature instability (BTI) [21]. This work addresses some aspects of the former two cases, as the layout does affect the robustness.

This paper is organized as follows: Section 2 describes the device and the simulation setup. Section 3 we presents the various stress results and discusses the physics of the failure mechanism, and concludes in Section 4.

2. Device and UIS Set-Up

The DUT is obtained from a process simulation, using Sentaurus tool [22], following a 1 µm CMOS flow, adopted in CDTA's cleanroom [23,24]. It uses a 15 nm thick gate oxide and 787 nm FOX using the LOCOS separation feature. We shorted the source and the body to reduce the effect of parasitic BJTs, which is one of the causes of avalanche generation. The DUT, shown in Figure 1a, is where we added the thermodes required for the electrothermal simulation. We extended the simulated substrate thickness to 100 µm, unlike regular simulations to allow a realistic dissipation of heat.

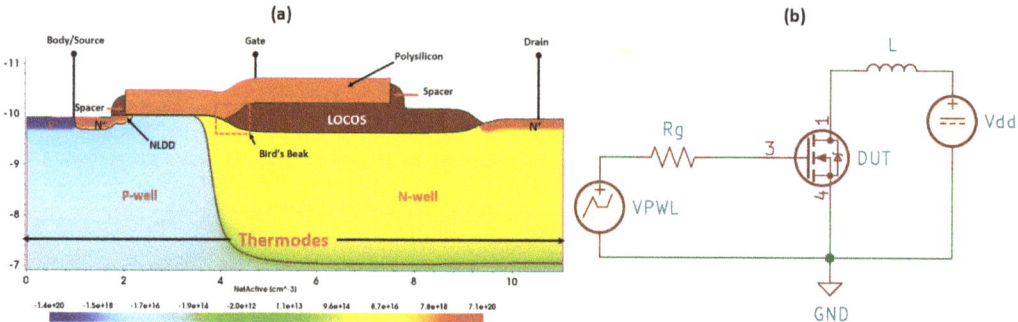

Figure 1. (a) DUT final doping distribution and (b) UIS test circuit.

In practice, integrated LDMOS devices are tested under clamped inductive switching (CIS), done by adding a Zener diode. This is to ensure that the thermal runway of nearby devices and/or nearby cells does not underestimate the safe operating area (SOA) by a premature thermal breakdown. Nonetheless, it is not the case in this TCAD simulation, and a UIS set-up, shown in Figure 1b, gives us an SOA that extends the device lifetime by reducing other degradation mechanisms [18]. Apart from the DUT, we used SPICE compact models for the other components, hence it is a mixed-mode simulation. The drain is attached to a variable inductive load; the gate is attached to a 10 Ω resistor, to approximate the single-cell metallic resistance, with voltage pulses of variables durations. The contact thermal resistance at the gate was set to 10^3 cm^2 KW^{-1} as an approximate boundary condition of the DUT width [25], although in practice, dealing with surface resistances is much more complicated [26].

3. Results & Discussion

After the quasi-stationary ramp that sets V_{DS} to 15 V, a transient simulation that applies the pulse, shown in Figure 2, is performed for up to 1 s to check the thermal runaway. The failure mechanism could either be: a localized excess in temperature at the bird's beak, which is due to high impact-ionization, due to hot-carriers caused by the high electric field, or an excess in current that triggers *NPN* parasitic transistor.

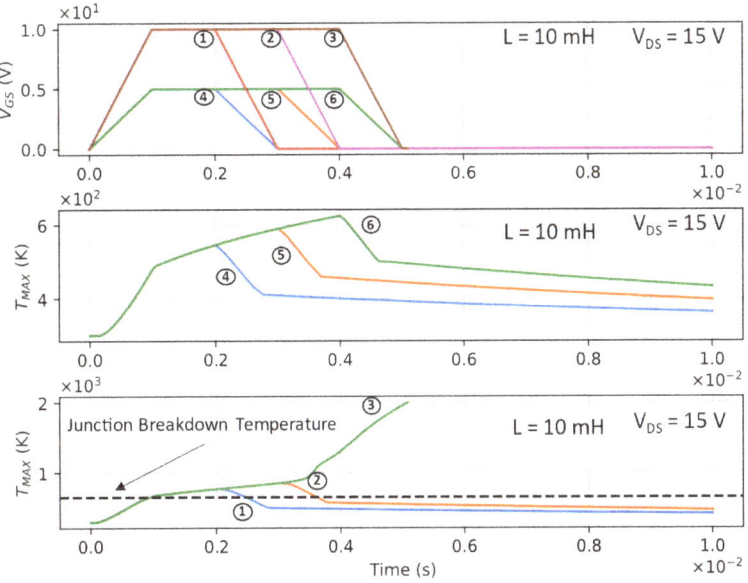

Figure 2. DUT temperature response to millisecond pulses of various durations and gate voltage amplitudes.

First, we noticed that the inductive load values, which were $L = [10-2, 10-1, 1, 10]$ mH, under millisecond pulses, do not have a main impact on the characteristics, so we kept only a 10 mH value for the following results. Second, we tested the DUT under peak a V_{GS} pulse of 5 V and 10 V, the pulse duration is PW = [1, 2, 3] ms. There was no significant voltage overshoot that could reach the drain BV value under all variations or a critical excess in temperature. I_{DS} remains under nominal values when V_{GS} = 5 V. The electric field peak of 2.88 MV/cm is at the bird's beak, and the lattice temperature peak range is between 546 K and 623 K, which is considerably lower than the 650 K limit [27], especially when the temperature hot spot is in the bottom of the substrate and not in the active area. It is at V_{GS} = 10 V that the device fails under all pulses, and the current value is well over the nominal values.

To better define the SOA, we checked T_{MAX} under various V_{GS} values, from 5 V to 10 V with a 1 V step at V_{DS} = 15 V. We noticed that the device does not fail if V_{GS} < 7 V. Next, we checked T_{MAX} again, under various V_{DS} values, from 10 V to 20 V (sub-BV) while V_{GS} = 7 V. The results are summarized in Figure 3. The device is safe as long as V_{GS} < 7 V, irrespective of V_{DS}. Therefore, the device failure location is located near the gate. Precisely for this particular structure, at the bird's beak.

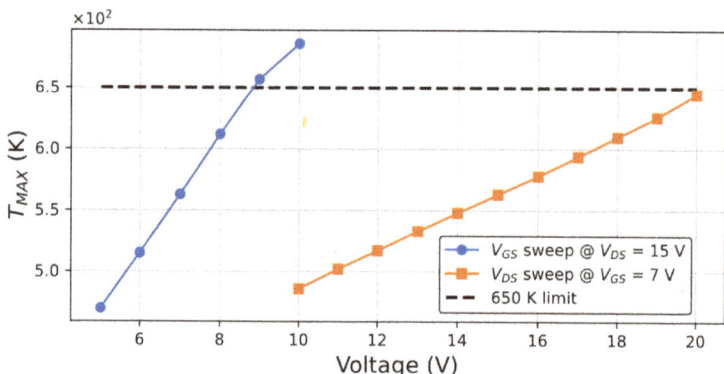

Figure 3. DUT thermal SOA and voltage dependency.

The physics of the failure mechanism is as follows. We noticed that the electron velocity, under all scenarios, is ~10^7 cm/s, which is a saturation velocity v_{sat}. We also noticed that the electron density n and the donor concentration (ionized impurity concentration) N_D have the same scalar distribution. Finally, the space charge is extended towards the drift region. The aforementioned conditions meet the expected Kirk effect (or base-push-effect) triggered by the parasitic NPN BJT. Under all biases, a strong inversion regime is reached, and the electrons that created the channel (Δn) also create a space charge region (SCR). The SCR by definition extends towards the least doped region, which, in this case, is the drift region. As Δn gets bigger, the SCR extends deeper into drift region until it reaches the drain. Since the Kirk effect is always present in the DUT, the high energetic carriers accelerated by the high electric field created by the drain potential always cause a significant impact ionization rate. If this electric field exceeds ~0.55 MVcm^{-1} in the silicon, the impact ionization rate peaks at 3.15×10^{28} cm^{-3} s^{-1}, and thus increases the probability of creating additional electron-hole pairs (EHP). The new EHPs are as energetic—or more energetic—as the loss in energy occurs due to the collisions with the lattice atoms, which is compensated by the thermal runaway. Since the SCR covers most of the drift region and the drain, a critical value of EHPs is reached that causes avalanche breakdown. Therefore, the failure mechanism is a thermal runaway followed by an avalanche breakdown [17].

In practice, however, such an HV transistor is likely to be near a significant source of heat. Therefore, we must consider the initial temperature (T_{init}). The results in Figure 4, show a sweep at V_{DS} = 15 V, V_{GS} = 7 V, where T_{init} is varied from 300 K to 420 K with a 20 K step. The behavior is linear; T_{MAX} increases by the same amount as T_{init}. With all parameters considered, the primary electrothermal SOA is $V_{DS} \leq 15$ V, $V_{GS} \leq 7$ V, and $T_{init} \leq 380$ K (105 °C). However, it is worth noting that the thermal runaway does not stop at the first cycle of the pulse. Figure 5, shows that the thermal breakdown is easily reached under repetitive UIS, hence the necessity of the protection circuit even under SOA.

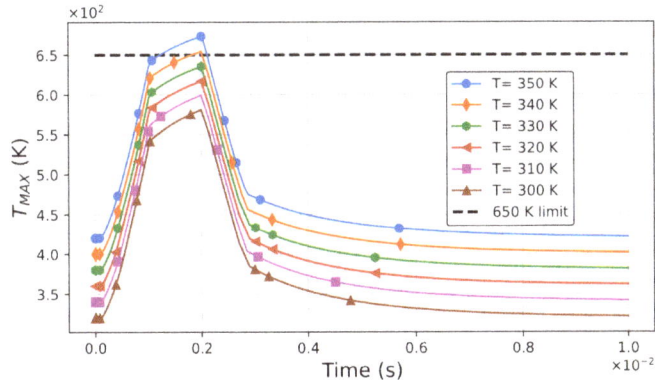

Figure 4. DUT thermal SOA against initial thermal conditions.

The qualitative failure mechanism described above does not hold under all scenarios. The shorter pulses change the breakdown mechanism from an electrothermal one to a purely electrical breakdown (avalanche only). The device under short pulses does not have the time to generate a significant current, thus heat, as plotted in Figure 6A. On the other hand, the drain voltage overshoot exceeds BV, as illustrated in Figure 6B. This causes a snap-back and current crowding as the relatively high doping profile of the drift region, which is meant for the CMOS logic n-well, reduces the parasitic collector ballast resistance. The latter will increase the gain of the parasitic BJT and thus, the early onset of a premature failure. The failure has also a component of a very high electric field at the edges. Finally, in practice, there will be a probability of premature oxide breakdown, and current filamentation between the device cells [15].

The presented DUT, obtained from a process meant for HP circuitry, got a low BV, but a wide SOA under millisecond pulse UIS stress. The range of drain and gate biases should be enough to achieve an unconditional stable gain in a power amplifier, which is a subject for future studies. Depending on the layout, the type of cooling (passive or active), and the final application, the SOA could be extended, especially under sub-millisecond pulse stress, as well as the lifetime of the device.

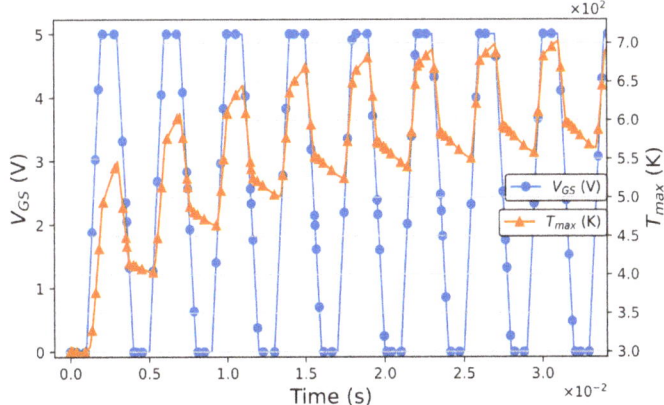

Figure 5. DUT thermal SOA against repetitive UIS.

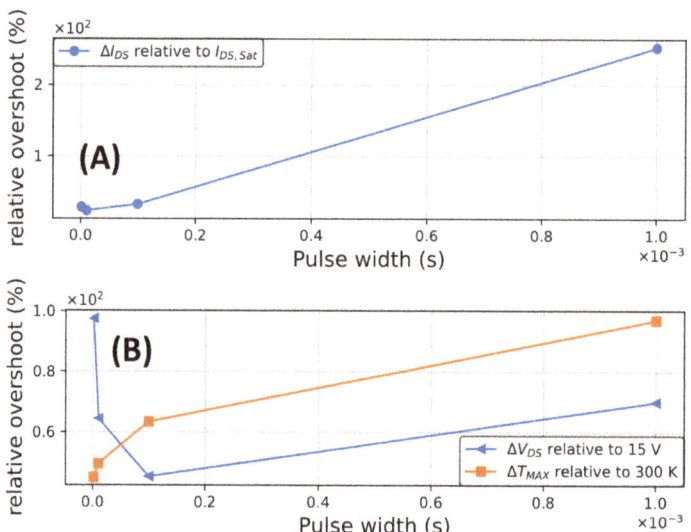

Figure 6. Failure mechanism physics towards short and mid-long UIS pulses. (**A**) Due to the short pulse, the device could not generate a lot of drain to source current, (**B**) shows the consequence in terms of temperature and drain to source potential.

4. Conclusions

A detailed setup of UIS stress to evaluate the SOA of a LOCOS-based LDMOS made with a 1 µm CMOS process is presented. The failure mechanism is a thermal runaway followed by an avalanche breakdown. Replying on such a process allows a wide SOA at the expense of a relatively low BV even when the Kirk effect is always present under nominal bias conditions. However, under sub-millisecond pulses durations, the breakdown becomes purely electrical, and the SOA narrows down. Which requires additional technological and design efforts to avoid failure.

Author Contributions: A.H. created the scripts of the TCAD simulations, extracted and visualized the results, and wrote the paper. B.D. provided the necessary process parameters, examined the numerical values of the results, and assisted in the paper's correction. All authors have read and agreed to the published version of the manuscript.

Funding: This work was supported by the Directorate-General for Scientific Research and Technological Development/Ministry of High Education and Scientific Research of Algeria (DGRSDT/MESRS).

Institutional Review Board Statement: Not applicable.

Informed Consent Statement: Not applicable.

Data Availability Statement: Not applicable.

Conflicts of Interest: The authors declare no conflict of interest.

References

1. Theeuwen, S.; Mollee, H.; Heeres, R.; van Rijs, F. LDMOS technology for power amplifiers up to 12 GHz. In Proceedings of the 2018 13th European Microwave Integrated Circuits Conference (EuMIC), Madrid, Spain, 23–25 September 2018; pp. 162–165.
2. Mehrotra, S.; Radic, L.; Grote, B.; Saxena, T.; Qin, G.; Khemka, V.; Thomas, T.; Gibson, M. Towards ultimate scaling of LDMOS with Ultralow Specific On-resistance. In Proceedings of the 2020 32nd International Symposium on Power Semiconductor Devices and ICs (ISPSD), Vienna, Austria, 13–18 September 2020; pp. 42–45.
3. Pjenčák, J.; Agam, M.; Šeliga, L.; Yao, T.; Suwhanov, A. Novel approach for NLDMOS performance enhancement by critical electric field engineering. In Proceedings of the 2018 IEEE 30th International Symposium on Power Semiconductor Devices and ICs (ISPSD), Chicago, IL, USA, 13–17 May 2018; pp. 307–310.

4. Kumar, B.S.; Paul, M.; Shrivastava, M.; Gossner, H. Performance and reliability insights of drain extended FinFET devices for high voltage SoC applications. In Proceedings of the 2018 IEEE 30th International Symposium on Power Semiconductor Devices and ICs (ISPSD), Chicago, IL, USA, 13–17 May 2018; pp. 72–75.
5. Vigneau, M.; Ercoli, M.; Maroldt, S. Fully integrated three-way LDMOS Doherty PAs for 1.8–2.2 GHz dual-band and 2.6 GHz m-MIMO 5G applications. *Int. J. Microw. Wirel. Technol.* **2021**, 1–18. [CrossRef]
6. Houadef; Djezzar, B. Process and performance optimization of Triple-RESURF LDMOS with Trenched-Gate. *Int. J. RF Microw. Comput.-Aided Eng.* **2021**, *31*, e22745. [CrossRef]
7. Erlbacher, T. *Lateral Power Transistors in Integrated Circuits*; Springer: Berlin/Heidelberg, Germany, 2014.
8. Fu, Y.; Li, Z.; Ng, W.T.; Sin, J.K. *Integrated Power Devices and TCAD Simulation*; CRC Press: Boca Raton, FL, USA, 2014.
9. Moens, P.; van den Bosch, G. Characterization of total safe operating area of lateral DMOS transistors. *IEEE Trans. Device Mater. Reliab.* **2006**, *6*, 349–357. [CrossRef]
10. Vashchenko, V.A.; Shibkov, A. *ESD Design for Analog Circuits*; Springer Science & Business Media: Berlin/Heidelberg, Germany, 2010.
11. Bayram, Y.; Volakis, J.L.; Myoung, S.K.; Doo, S.J.; Roblin, P. High-power EMI on RF amplifier and digital modulation schemes. *IEEE Trans. Electromagn. Compat.* **2008**, *50*, 849–860. [CrossRef]
12. Ridley, B. Specific negative resistance in solids. *Proc. Phys. Soc. (1958–1967)* **1963**, *82*, 954. [CrossRef]
13. Hower, P.L.; Pendharkar, S. Short and long-term safe operating area considerations in LDMOS transistors. In Proceedings of the 2005 43rd Annual IEEE International Reliability Physics Symposium, San Jose, CA, USA, 17–21 April 2005; pp. 545–550.
14. Volkov, A.F.; Kogan, S.M. Physical phenomena in semiconductors with negative differential conductivity. *Sov. Phys. Uspekhi* **1969**, *11*, 881. [CrossRef]
15. Denison, M.; Blaho, M.; Rodin, P.; Dubec, V.; Pogany, D.; Silber, D. Moving current filaments in integrated DMOS transistors under short-duration current stress. *IEEE Trans. Electron Devices* **2004**, *51*, 1331–1339. [CrossRef]
16. Smith, B.; Xu, J.; Devore, J.; Chellamuthu, A.; Amey, B.; Pendharkar, S.; Efland, T. Peripheral motor drive PIC concerns for integrated LDMOS technologies. In Proceedings of the 2004 16th International Symposium on Power Semiconductor Devices and ICs, Kitakyushu, Japan, 24–27 May 2004; pp. 159–162.
17. El-Kareh, B.; Hutter, L.N. *Silicon Analog Components*; Springer: Berlin/Heidelberg, Germany, 2015.
18. Houadef, A.; Djezzar, B. HCI Degradation of LOCOS-based LDMOS Transistor fabricated by 1 µm CMOS Process. In Proceedings of the 2020 International Conference on Electrical Engineering (ICEE), Istanbul, Turkey, 25–27 September 2020; pp. 1–6.
19. Houadef, A.; Djezzar, B. Evaluation of Hot Carrier Impact on Lateral-DMOS with LOCOS feature. *Alger. J. Signals Syst.* **2021**, *6*, 16–23.
20. Houadef, A.; Djezzar, B. Hot Carrier Degradation in Triple-RESURF LDMOS with Trenched-Gate. In Proceedings of the 2021 IEEE 32nd International Conference on Microelectronics (MIEL), Nis, Serbia, 12–14 September 2021; pp. 141–144.
21. Tyaginov, S.; Grasser, T. Modeling of hot-carrier degradation: Physics and controversial issues. In Proceedings of the 2012 IEEE International Integrated Reliability Workshop Final Report, South Lake Tahoe, CA, USA, 14–18 October 2012; pp. 206–215.
22. Sentaurus™ Process User Guide. Mountain View, CA. September 2017. Available online: https://www.synopsys.com (accessed on 15 September 2021).
23. Djezzar, B.; Bellaroussi, M.T. Process and Device Simulation of 1.2 µm- Channel N- well C-MOS Technology. In Proceedings of the 5th International Conference on Microelectronics (ICM'93), Dhahran, Saudi Arabia, 14–16 December 1993; pp. 28–32.
24. Boubaaya, M.; HadjLarbi, F.; Oussalah, S. Simulation of Ion Implantation for CMOS 1 µm Using SILVACO Tools. In Proceedings of the 24th International Conference on Microelectronics (ICM'12), Algiers, Algeria, 16–20 December 2012; pp. 1–3.
25. Modeling the Unclamped Inductive Switching Capabilities of Silicon Power Devices Using TCAD Sentaurus. Mountain View, CA. 2017. Available online: https://www.synopsys.com (accessed on 15 September 2021).
26. Williams, T. *The Circuit Designer's Companion*; Elsevier: Amsterdam, The Netherlands, 2004.
27. Nidhia, K.; Agarwala, N.; Yanga, S.; Purwadia, X.; Sheua, G.; Tsaib, J. Failure analysis of power mosfets based on multifinger configuration under unclamped inductive switching (uis) stress condition. In Proceedings of the SISPAD 2012, Denver, CO, USA, 5–7 September 2012.

Proceeding Paper

Process and Device Simulation of SAW Temperature Sensors Compatible with 1 μm CMOS Technology [†]

Nabila Belkhelfa * and Rafik Serhane *

Centre de Développement des Technologies Avancées (CDTA), Baba Hassen, Algiers 16192, Algeria
* Correspondence: nbelkhelfa@cdta.dz (N.B.); rserhane@cdta.dz (R.S.)
† Presented at the 1st International Conference on Computational Engineering and Intelligent Systems, Online, 10–12 December 2021.

Abstract: Process and device simulation of a surface acoustics wave (SAW) temperature sensor based AlN material as piezoelectric film, grown on Si wafer and patterned with Al electrodes, is described. CMOS 1 μm process is the process used to simulate a SAW sensor with number of IDT electrodes pairs N_p = 16 using Silvaco software; fabrication steps inside the cleanroom are also described. The Athena Silvaco module is used for technological process simulation and the Atlas module is used to characterize the sensor in terms of electrical potential and electric field distribution under IDTs. IDS = f (VDS) simulation curves are compared to those issued from experimental characterizations performed on PMOS and NMOS transistors realized by 1 μm CMOS technology. The mask needed for SAW realization is designed. In order to choose the best sensor to manufacture, two SAW sensors with N_p = 16 are characterized using Comsol multiphysics. Their IDTs length "*a*" and spacing "*b*" are 2 μm for the first sensor and 3 μm for the second one, which corresponds to 600 MHz and 400 MHz resonance frequencies respectively. The mechanical displacement field at the center frequency of the 3 μm structure and the reflection coefficients (S_{11}) of both structures are determined to deduce the piezoelectric response. Afterwards, the SAW temperature sensors are studied in the temperature range extending from −25 °C to 200 °C; their sensitivities are evaluated at 19.10 ppm/°C and 23.53 ppm/°C for 600 MHz and 400 MHz devices respectively.

Keywords: SAW temperature sensor; CMOS 1 μm process; Silvaco; Comsol; S_{11} reflection coefficient; sensitivity

1. Introduction

For a long time, many types of sensors have been elaborated; these sensors have been developed by the means of various methods and techniques [1–4]. Compared to the other sensors, surface acoustic wave detectors (SAWs) have a lot of characteristics that make them more favorable. Among their numerous features we can mention reusability, higher sensitivity, reliability, multifunctionality and noninvasiveness.

SAW device principle is based on the conversion of an interrogative electromagnetic wave into an acoustic one by means of interdigital transducers (IDTs) fabricated over a piezoelectric crystal (Figure 1). During acoustic wave propagation over the piezo substrate, its velocity changes while the surrounding environment conditions change, the modified acoustic wave is transduced back into an electromagnetic signal that is transmitted for processing (determination of frequency shift or time delay according to the sensor type). The propagation properties (like wavelength and resonance frequency) of acoustic waves in piezoelectric media depend on the substrate material, the crystal cut and the structure of electrodes [5,6].

A typical SAW device in sensor applications consists in a transmitting IDT and a receiving one separated by few wavelengths, which constitutes the delay line configuration. IDTs with reflectors (called Bragg reflectors) form the resonator model and are mainly used in telecommunication circuits; they also can be used as sensors [7].

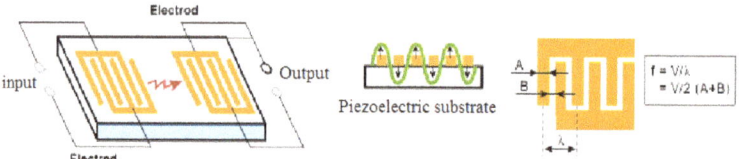

Figure 1. SAW devices working principle and geometrical parameters.

In this work, a SAW temperature sensor was designed using Silvaco TCAD Tools, Silvaco TCAD refers to technology computer-aided design. TCAD modules required for SAW simulation are Athena and Atlas [8]. The sensor was simulated using a specific fabrication process that is the CMOS 1 μm technology; this process was adopted because it is the process acquired by our fab. The necessary process steps needed for sensor realization were identified and simulated using Athena module, details about the realization steps inside the cleanroom were described. Characterizations using Atlas module were achieved to determine distribution of dopants, electrical potential and electric field under IDTs. The mask needed for IDTs realization, with different SAWs configurations and dimensions, was designed.

After that, a complementary study, following on from a previous one and performed in the Comsol multiphysics environment, was achieved on two sensors (2 μm and 3 μm IDTs width). The mechanical displacement field at the center frequency of the 3 μm IDTs structure was highlighted and (S_{11}) the variation of the reflection coefficient with temperature ranging from −25 °C to 200 °C was investigated for both structures; their sensitivities were evaluated and the adequate design for sensor realization was adopted.

2. Relevant Geometrical Parameters of SAW Sensors

Parameters such as IDTs width a, spacing between them b, their pairs number (N_p) and the acoustic aperture W are very important. The reason is that the SAW central frequency f_0 depends on them, and this central frequency has a direct effect on the sensor sensitivity, which is the first feature to focus on while designing a SAW device [5]. The sensitivity is related to the center frequency according to Equation (1) in the case of a resonator type sensor and according to Equation (2) in the case of a delay line type sensor:

$$S = \frac{1}{f_0}\frac{\partial f_0}{\partial T} = TCF \quad (1)$$

where δT is temperature variation and δf_0 is the resonance frequency shift, and:

$$s = \delta f/\delta T = 2\pi a f_0 \tau \quad (2)$$

where δf is the phase shift and τ is the delay.

3. Description of 1 μm CMOS Process

This technology realizes simultaneously on the same substrate MOS transistors with N channel and MOS transistors with P channel, for which the length of the gate is 1 μm. In our simulations, the SAW sensor is designed next to the N and P CMOS 1 μm transistors resulting from the simulation of the whole 1 μm process flow; it is simulated at the same time using the same flow. The aim is to check the possibility of fabricating the SAW sensor in the same chip with its electronic read out, which forms the integrated circuit later. We have chosen this approach because, in recent years, acoustic-sensor-based devices have become more and more important for sensing; which means SAW sensors can be applied as well as wired sensor elements in active circuits and as remote passive devices [4].

The 1 μm CMOS process's main characteristics are:

- P type substrate, orientation (100), resistivity 10 Ohm·cm;
- N-well/P-well;
- Double poly doped n$^+$;
- Double metal;
- Barrier metal Ti/TiN;
- 14 photolithography steps;
- 12 masques.

4. The 1 μm CMOS Process Steps for SAW Sensor Realization

The fabrication of circuits on silicon wafers is done with various layers, each with its own pattern, deposited on the surface by a specific order and over precise areas that are defined by the technological process. The several patterns used while depositing layers on the substrate (or during other realization steps such as doping or etching) are shaped by a process called lithography [9]. Some technological steps necessary to realize a surface acoustic wave sensor are described in Figures 2–5 resulting from Silvaco simulations (obviously during realization, all these processes take place inside the clean room). We have chosen 1 μm as the IDT length because the aim of this study is to list and understand the SAW realization steps and to have a representative idea of the behavior of the sensor after each one. The final IDT length will be adopted after Comsol characterizations achieved in Section 6.

Figure 2. AlN piezoelectric layer deposition.

The process flow steps needed for SAW sensor realization are:

Substrate initialization (definition), it is a silicon substrate-doped boron for which resistivity is 10 Ohm·cm (concentration 10^{15} e$^-$/cm^3) and orientation is (100). In the fab, the wafer is first cleaned using acetone and ethanol baths, agitated by ultrasound to eliminate most of the surface pollutions (grease, dust, etc. ...) [10]. The ethanol being extremely volatile, its use facilitates the drying of the substrate under dry nitrogen flow, which is done after a rinse with deionized water. It should be noted that the silicon substrates (100) undergo, before this standard cleaning, a hydrofluoric acid bath (HF at 5%) in order to eliminate the native SiO$_2$ layer present on their surface.

AlN piezoelectric layer deposition (Figure 2), its thickness is 1.5 μm; AlN thickness was deduced from a previous study which objective was the optimization of SAW technological parameters [11]. AlN was chosen as the piezoelectric layer because of its several properties and its compatibility with CMOS process [10]. In fact, in the cleanroom, AlN is deposited using a PVD process (physical vapor deposition) with a specific recipe [12] inside a PVD cluster tool called the MRC Star Eclipse. Sputtering is the technique used for AlN deposition. It is a relatively simple and industrialized technique, allowing the deposition of thin films on various substrates at relatively low temperatures (<400 °C) and therefore CMOS compatible. Thus, for the realization of the sensor's piezoelectric layer an aluminum target is placed in an atmosphere constituted of an inert gas (Argon Ar) and a reactive gas (Nitrogen N$_2$). The nitrogen molecules are split and the nitrogen atoms (N) react with the aluminum target to form AlN. Argon is then sprayed onto the AlN created on the surface of the target to form the thin film on the substrate that is attached to the anode [12].

First metal layer deposition (Figure 3), the first metal layer is titanium that is 0.115 nm thick (100 nm TiN + 15 nm Ti). Ti, TiN layer is a barrier used to prevent metal diffusion into Si and to improve its adhesion This Ti layer has the characteristic of being very adhesive to Si and SiO2. In the cleanroom, it is a PVD deposition using MRC Star Eclipse tool.

Second metal layer deposition, it is Al that is 500 nm-thick (Figure 3). Aluminum is the metal used in the 1 µm CMOS process (deposited by PVD technique in the cleanroom on the whole substrate surface).

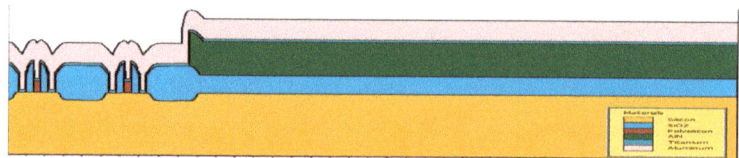

Figure 3. Metal layers deposition.

The following step is *metal etch for SAW sensor IDTs formation*. Such a process is done in two steps: first, the lithography step where we deposit a protection layer called photoresist and, second, etching step where only the open areas of the metal are etched. During simulations, the photolithographic step consists in photoresist deposition; its thickness in our process is 1.2 µm (Figure 4a), and the photoresist etch opens the areas of the metal to be etched (Figure 4b).

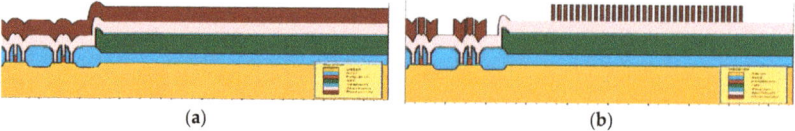

Figure 4. Photoresist deposition and etch.

Inside the cleanroom, these two steps are completed as follows: a layer of photoresist (PR) material is first spin-coated on the surface of the wafer using SVG 8800 tool. The resist layer is then selectively exposed to radiation such as ultraviolet light, with the exposed areas defined by the exposure tool mask which is UV i-line Stepper GCA, i.e., we use ultraviolet light to form patterns on the photoresist through printing. After exposure, the PR layer is subjected to development, which destroys unwanted areas of the PR layer, and allows exposing the corresponding underlying layer (the unwanted areas in the PR are dissolved by the developer SVG 8800 tool).

After that, *aluminum and titanium are dry etched* to get read of them between the covered IDTs (Figure 5). In the cleanroom, metal dry etch is achieved in the LAM 9600 tool, which is a reactive ion etching reactor (RIE) that allows, added to metal etch, in situ resist etching and metal rinsing and drying to avoid the metal corrosion phenomenon. This tool uses chlorine (Cl_2) and argon (Ar) plasma to achieve the metal etch, oxygen (O_2) to etch the photoresist inside the tool and azote (N_2) to dry the wafer. The accuracy of the metal etch is very important, because IDTs pitch etch accuracy influences the response signal and helps reducing the noise [13,14].

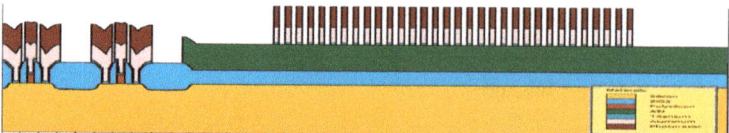

Figure 5. Titanium and aluminum etch.

The remaining *photoresist is etched later* (Figure 6). In the fab, photoresist for metal patterning is etched inside the LAM 9600 metal etcher but the photoresist used for other technological steps is etched in the Tepla 300 tool, which is a microwave, high-frequency reactor that uses oxygen plasma. The photoresist can also be etched through the wet etch process. In this case, liquid solutions (like HF) are used to remove the photoresist and other chemicals to clean the wafer, the chemicals used depend on the required etch selectivity. Many tools are employed, such as the Spray Cleaner Semitool. The wet etch process is also used in some technological steps where the anisotropy (etch directionality) is not a critical criterion.

Inside the cleanroom and for *metal passivation*, an oxide layer, namely silicon nitride (SiON) is deposited. Its thickness is 1.5 µm and it is later etched to open the bond pad.

The simulated sensor is a one-port resonator with number of IDT pairs N_p = 16; it is represented in Figure 6 next to the N and P transistors resulting from the 1 µm CMOS process flow simulation. The sensor was simulated using the 1 µm process steps that overlap with those necessary for its realization, i.e., within the 1 µm process flow; which gives a sensor on the same substrate (in the same die) with the N and P transistors.

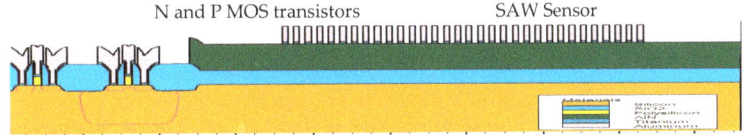

Figure 6. Athena results of CMOS process simulation (N and P transistors besides the SAW temperature sensor).

5. CMOS Process and Devices Validation

To validate our process simulation results, characterizations of the resulting PMOS and NMOS transistors were achieved in the Atlas tool to evaluate their IDS = f (VDS) curves. The latter were compared to curves issued from experimental characterizations performed on devices realized by 1 µm CMOS technology in ISIT fab (Experimental ISIT structures). The results are represented in Figure 7a,b, and they show a good agreement between experimental curves and those issued from simulations, for both N and PMOS structures.

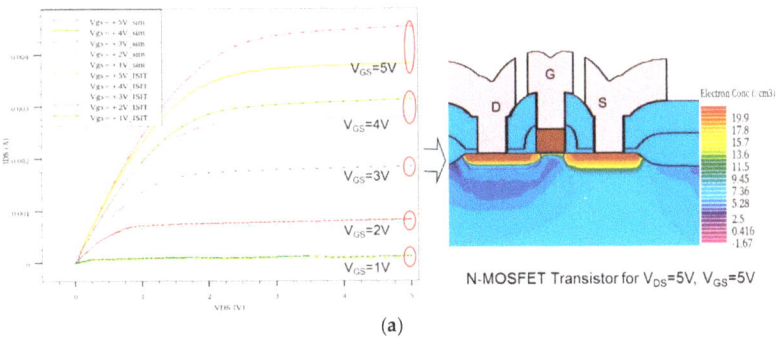

(a)

Figure 7. *Cont.*

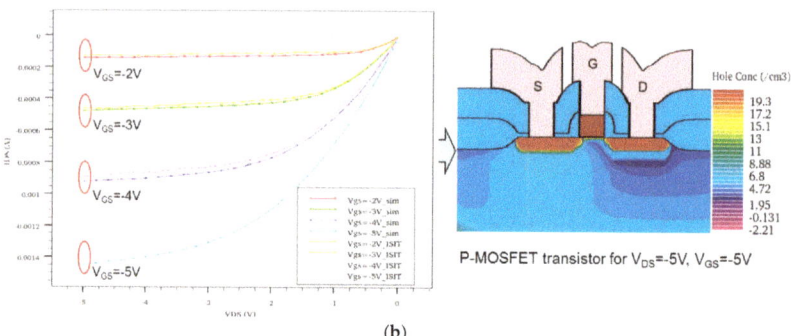

(b)

Figure 7. IDS = f (VDS) characteristics comparison between experimental and TCAD simulated data of NMOS (**a**) and PMOS (**b**) transistors, realized by 1 µm CMOS technology (ISIT).

Electrical characterizations in terms of dopant concentrations, electric potential and electric field distribution under IDT electrodes (Figure 8a–c) are achieved on the obtained SAW sensor using Atlas module. From Figure 8a, we deduce that the highest concentration is under the source and drain electrodes added to the poly-gate of the N and P transistors. It is around 10^{21} e$^-$/cm^3. In Figure 8b, we can see the electrical potential distribution under IDT electrodes after the application of 5V voltage. This electrical potential induces an electric field (Figure 8c) that launches, by reverse piezoelectric effect (Equation (3) [15]), a surface acoustic wave propagating over the AlN piezoelectric layer.

$$D_j = e_{jkl}S_{kl} + \varepsilon_{jk}^S E_k \text{ and } T_{ij} = c_{ijkl}^E S_{kl} - e_{kij}E_k \qquad (3)$$

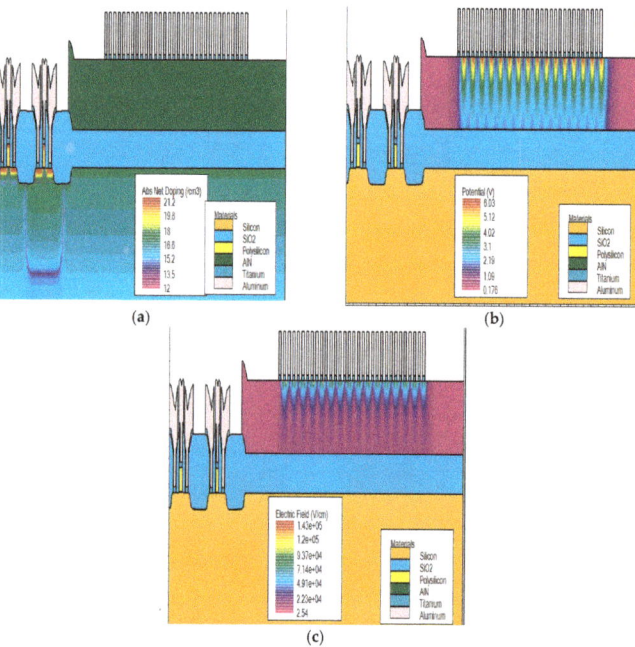

Figure 8. (**a**) Distribution of dopants concentration in the realized structure, (**b**) electrical potential distribution under IDT electrodes and (**c**) electric field distribution under IDTs.

6. The Designed Sensor Mask

A mask or "photomask" is a square glass sheet on which is patterned a mixture of metal film (on one side only). The mask is aligned with the wafer, so that the pattern can be reproduced faithfully onto its surface. An open-access design software was employed to design the mask used in the fabrication process. IDT masks designed have different electrodes lengths "a" and spacing "b" values (1 µm 2 µm, 3 µm, 4 µm, etc.) and different SAW configurations (one-port resonators, two-port resonators, delay lines). Figure 9 shows the layout of the designed mask.

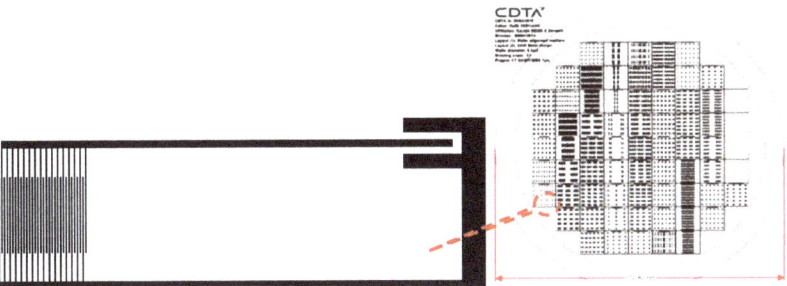

Figure 9. The designed SAW IDTs mask.

7. Multiphysics Simulation of the Designed SAW Sensor

A 2D finite element method (FEM) simulation using Comsol software was used to evaluate the physical and electrical behaviors of two SAW sensors. The sensors are one-port resonator type, they differ in the length of IDTs "a" and each of them has $N_p = 16$. The ongoing study follows on from a previous one [11] which the objective was the optimization of SAW geometrical parameters. The perspectives of the cited work were the investigation of 2 µm and 3 µm structures (corresponding to 8 µm and 12 µm wavelengths respectively) and the results presented in the current study concern their sensitivities, since the other characteristics (like velocity and reflectivity) have already been studied and were interesting [11].

When simulating SAW devices in Comsol, boundary conditions are imposed to the structure: the acoustic displacements and stresses are assumed continuous at the AlN-silicon interface and both top and bottom sides of the structure are assumed to be stress free surfaces. In order to avoid the slowness of the calculations, silicon depth is fixed at 3λ and a perfectly matched layer (*PML*) approximation is used to simulate the endless edges of the structure. Its thickness is 1.5λ [11].

The mechanical displacement field, of the 3 µm IDT length structure, is represented in Figure 10a; one can notice that this mechanical field is located in the interface between the Al and AlN layer, which is a characteristic of the Rayleigh mode surface acoustic wave.

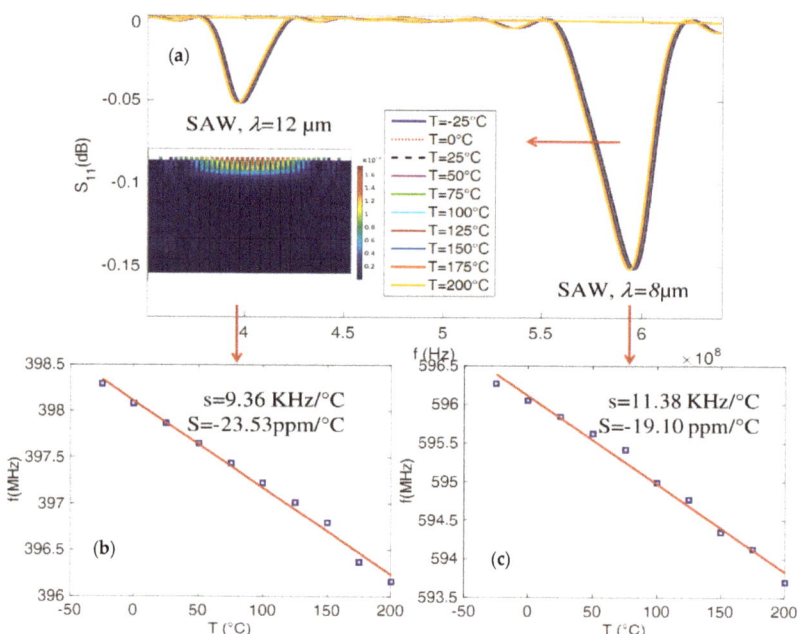

Figure 10. (a) Reflection coefficient (S_{11}) and (b) frequency shift variation, versus temperature for structures with (b) 12 μm and (c) 8 μm wavelengths.

Simulation of the SAW Sensors Sensitivity to Temperature

The variation of the reflection coefficient (S_{11}) parameter is computed for different values of the temperature ranging from −25 °C to 200 °C with a step of 25 °C; it is plotted in Figure 10a for structures with 8 μm and 12 μm wavelengths respectively.

We can notice that the resonance frequency of the sensor (f_0) shifts toward low values and that (S_{11}) magnitude increases slightly for both structures, when temperature rises. For the study of (S_{11}) variation with temperature, we used a theoretical temperature model coupled to FEM model, this model was developed in a previous work [16].

The calculated sensitivities, resulting from the determination of the slope of the lines obtained in Figure 10b,c and using Equation (1), are 19.10 ppm/°C and 23.53 ppm/°C for 600 MHz and 400 MHz devices respectively (corresponding to 8 and 12 μm wavelength, respectively). This sensitivity was evaluated at S = 8.53 ppm/°C for a structure of 1 μm IDTs length (f_0 = 1.16 GHz), which means that the structure with 3 μm-long IDTs gives the best sensitivity and acceptable other characteristics, as deduced from [11].

8. Conclusions

In the past, researchers depended on experiments to design and develop SAW devices but, nowadays, the design of SAW devices is enhanced by the use of modeling techniques such as TCAD and FEM, which helps the study of all their characteristics. In this paper, SAW temperature sensors were designed and simulated using Silvaco TCAD tools and Comsol Multiphysics software. The simulated SAW temperature sensors consist in a silicon substrate on which an AlN piezoelectric layer has been deposited; AlN was chosen for its compatibility with the 1 μm CMOS process available in our cleanroom. The electrodes are made of aluminum. The process steps for SAW realization are described by indicating their course inside the cleanroom; electrical properties like potential and electric field distribution were extracted using Atlas Silvaco module.

We performed FEM analysis of acoustic waves propagating on two SAW devices (8 μm and 12 μm wavelengths working at 600 and 400 MHz frequency respectively). Mechanical characterizations in terms of mechanical displacement field and electrical characterizations in terms of electrical power reflection coefficient (S_{11}) were performed while temperature was varied. S_{11} variation with temperature showed a shift toward low frequencies when temperature increased whereas its magnitude rose. The sensor-calculated sensitivities were $S = 19.10$ ppm/°C and $S = 23.53$ ppm/°C for 600 MHz and 400 MHz devices respectively. Knowing that this sensitivity was evaluated at $S = 8.53$ ppm/°C for the structure of 1 μm IDTs ($f_0 = 1.16$ GHz, previous work), we deduce that the structure with 3 μm IDTs length gives the best sensitivity added to acceptable other characteristics, which makes it a good candidate for the manufacture of our SAW temperature sensor.

Author Contributions: Conceptualization, N.B. and R.S.; methodology, N.B. and R.S.; software, N.B. and R.S.; validation, N.B. and R.S.; formal analysis, N.B. and R.S.; investigation, N.B.; resources, N.B. and R.S.; data curation, N.B. and R.S.; writing—original draft preparation, N.B.; writing—review and editing, N.B.; visualization, N.B.; supervision, N.B.; project administration, R.S.; funding acquisition, R.S. All authors have read and agreed to the published version of the manuscript.

Funding: This research was supported by Ministère de l'enseignement supèrieur et de la recherche scientifque and funded by Direction Générale de la Recherche Scientifique et du Développement Technologique (DGRSDT), Algeria, grant number: 05/CDTA/DGRSDT/2017, CT-SAW/CMOS 1 μm project. The funders had no role in the design of the study; in the collection, analyses, or interpretation of data; in the writing of the manuscript, or in the decision to publish the results.

Institutional Review Board Statement: Not applicable.

Informed Consent Statement: Not applicable.

Data Availability Statement: Experimental data provided by Fraunhofer ISIT Institute in Itzehoe, Germany and available at CDTA.

Conflicts of Interest: The authors declare no conflict of interest.

References

1. Amendola, G.; Poulichet, P.; Sevely, L.; Valbin, L. *Les Capteurs MEMS: Généralités, Principes de Fonctionnement et Procédés de Fabrication, Techniques de L'Ingénieur*; Editions T.I: Saint-Denix, France, 10 March 2011.
2. Bayart, M.; Conrrard, B.; Chovin, A.; Robert, M. *Capteurs et Actionneurs Intelligents, Techniques de L'ingénieur*; Editions T.I: Saint-Denix, France, 10 March 2005.
3. Wise, K.D.; Najafi, K. Microfabrication Techniques for Integrated Sensors and Microsystems. *Science* **1991**, *254*, 1335–1342. [CrossRef]
4. Sivadas, T.K. *Development of Sensors and Measurement Techniques and Their Implementation for Oceanographic Observations*; IEEE Underw. Technology (UT): Chennai, India, 2015.
5. Kannan, T. Finite Element Analysis of Surface Acoustic Wave Resonators. Master's Thesis, University of Saskatchewan, Saskatoon, SK, Canada, 2006.
6. Serhane, R.; Belkhelfa, N.; Hadj-Larbi, F.; Merah, S.; Bakha, Y. Electrical Performances of a Surface Acoustic Wave Device With Inter Digital Transducers Electrodes in Local Resonances. *J. Vib. Acoust. AMSE* **2021**, *143*, 011009. [CrossRef]
7. Tanski, W.J. UHF SAW Resonators and Applications. In Proceedings of the 34th Annual Symposium on Frequency Control, Philadelphia, PA, USA, 28–30 May 1980; pp. 278–285.
8. Goel, A.K.; Merry, M.; Arkenberg, K. Optimization of Device Performance Using Semiconductor TCAD Tools. 3 May 2001. Available online: https://silvaco.com.cn/tech_info/academiccoursematerials/pdf/UMichigan_TCAD.pdf (accessed on 15 October 2021).
9. Cardinale, G.F.; Skinner, J.L.; Talin, A.A. Fabrication of a surface acoustic wave-based correlator using step-and-flash imprint lithography. *J. Vac. Sci. Technol.* **2004**, *22*, 3265–3270. [CrossRef]
10. Champeaux, C. Films Minces et Multicouches de Matériaux Piézoélectriques: Synthèse par Ablation Laser; Caractérisation Microstructurale et Intégration Dans des Dispositifs SAW. Ph.D. Thesis, Limoge Uniersity Perrine Dutheil, Limoges, France, 2012.
11. Belkhelfa, N.; Serhane, R. Silicon SAW parameters extraction and optimization using finite elements analysis. In Proceedings of the International Conference on Advanced Electrical Engineering (ICAEE 2019), Algiers, Algeria, 19–21 November 2019.
12. Mammeri, A.Z. Dépôt par Pulvérisation Magnétron de Couches Minces de Nitrure D'aluminium à axe c Incliné en vue de la Réalisation des Dispositifs a Ondes Acoustiques Vibrant en Mode de Cisaillement. Ph.D. Thesis, Abou Bekr Belkaid University, Tlemcen, Algeria, 2009.

13. Weinheim, E.Z. *Introduction to Solid State Physics for Materials Engineers*; Wiley-VCH: Weinheim, Germany, 2021.
14. Devkota, J.; Ohodnicki, P.R.; Greve, D.W. SAW Sensors for Chemical Vapors and Gases. *Sensors* **2017**, *17*, 801. [CrossRef]
15. Serhane, R.; Boutkedjirt, T.; Bey, A.H. Electromechanical response Simulation of film bulk Acoustic wave resonator. In Proceedings of the 2012 24th International Conference on Microelectronics (ICM), Algiers, Algeria, 17–20 December 2012; pp. 1–4.
16. Belkhelfa, N.; Serhane, R. Design optimization of SAW temperature sensor based one port resonator using FEM simulation. *J. New Technol. Mater.* **2021**, *11*, 24–32.

Proceeding Paper

Design of an LDMOS Transistor Based on the 1 µm CMOS Process for High/Low Power Applications [†]

Ali Houadef [1,*] and Boualem Djezzar [2]

1. Signals and Systems Laboratory (LSS), Institute of Electrical and Electronic Engineering (IGEE), M'Hamed Bouguerra University of Boumerdés (UMBB), Boumerdés 35000, Algeria
2. Reliability of Semiconductor Components Team (FCS), Microelectronics and Nanotechnology Division (DMN), Centre de Développement des Technologies Avancées (CDTA), Algiers 16000, Algeria; bdjezzar@cdta.dz
* Correspondence: a.houadef@univ-boumerdes.dz
† Presented at the 1st International Conference on Computational Engineering and Intelligent Systems, Online, 10–12 December 2021.

Abstract: In this paper we investigate the performance of an integrated n-type laterally-diffused metal oxide semiconductor (nLDMOS) transistor, using 2D TCAD simulations. This work is based on the 1 µm CMOS technology node at CDTAs clean room. The nLDMOS process uses the necessary steps extracted from logic-integrated circuits fabrication flow, which yields to local oxidation of silicon (LOCOS), single reduced surface field (RESURF)-based nLDMOS, without needing any additional masks or steps. The resulting device has a 22 V breakdown voltage (BV) and 272 mm^2 mΩ specific on-state resistance (R_{ON}). The analysis determined that the proposed device could be implemented in RF power amplifiers for wireless communications or automotive circuits as primary domains, provided experimental calibrations.

Keywords: LDMOS; TCAD; CMOS

1. Introduction

In many power, RF, and microwave electronic circuits, the laterally-diffused metal oxide semiconductor (LDMOS) transistor is widely adopted, which is due to its low cost and excellent performance [1,2]. LDMOS transistor design is also a mature, well-optimized practice [3]. The influence of each process step, region, and operating regime is well understood, especially when it is fabricated in complementary MOS (CMOS) technology [4]. Additionally, the basic LDMOS structure allows easy integration with the logic, low power circuits, opening more application possibilities, even with old technology nodes [5]. A good LDMOS for power/analog applications should have a relatively high breakdown voltage (BV), low on-state resistance (R_{ON}), and a large safe operating area (SOA). It also needs to take into account the characteristics of various parasitic BJTs and their influence on self-heating, the capacitors' impact on the linearity and resistors' temperature dependence, and how it affects the frequency response [6,7].

Based on the available equipment at CDTAs clean room, which uses the 1 µm CMOS technology node [8,9], we propose an nLDMOS transistor by TCAD simulations. The latter is designed to be integrated with the rest of the logic circuits, as it follows the extracted CMOS flow adopted at the facility. The proposed device uses a single-RESURF and adopts the LOCOS separation method as field oxide. The DC and RF behavior is consistent with what is reported in the literature [10]. The characteristics described in the following paragraphs, more precisely the breakdown voltage of 22 V, show that the proposed device is a good candidate as a power device, RF power amplifiers (PA) for wireless applications, automotive circuits, or similar domains [11,12].

2. Results and Discussion

The proposed LDMOS structure was generated using the Sprocess tool in Sentaurus simulator [13]. The process flow was extracted from a standard CMOS flow adopted at CDTA [8,9]. CDTA's process uses 14 masks for both the FEOL and BEOL. However, for our study of the FEOL of the LDMOS, the process used seven masks and six implants. Figure 1 shows the general steps.

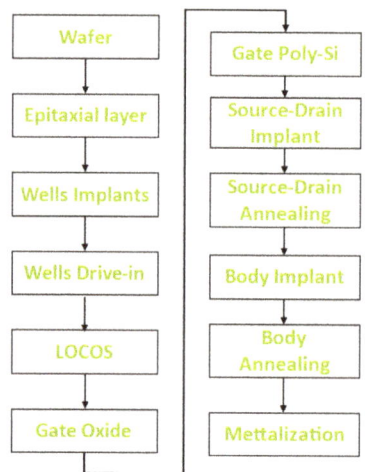

Figure 1. General process steps.

The substrate was boron-doped with a final resistivity of 10 Ω that corresponds to $N_{sub} = 5 \times 10^{14}$ cm^{-3}, <100> orientation, and 10 µm thickness. The transistor used an epitaxial layer, grown by diffusion at 1000 °C for 6 min, which gave a thickness of 12 µm; the same doping concentration as the substrate was chosen, thus the same resistivity. Next, the 2D mesh engine was triggered and we prepared the n-well, starting with a dry O_2 diffusion at 950 °C for 40 min, then photoresist deposition with a thickness of 1.2 µm. The implant used a phosphorus dose of 1.3×10^{13} cm^{-2}, at 150 KeV, tilting the substrate at 7°, using the Pearson distribution function.

After, we stripped the oxide. The same procedure was done to prepare the p-well implant, which used a boron dose of 3.7×10^{13} cm^{-2} at 160 KeV while adding a rotation of 22°. Before proceeding to other layers, we performed a well drive-in by diffusion in an N_2 environment at 1150 °C for 120 min.

The next step was to prepare the LOCOS separation, starting with stripping the previous oxide, diffusing dry O_2 at 950 °C for 20 min, then depositing a nitride isotropic layer of 150 nm thickness. We etched the nitride using the LOCOS mask anisotropically. Finally, a wet H_2O diffusion was performed at 960 °C for 240 min. The post-LOCOS steps included stripping the nitride and an isotropic oxide etch of 0.2 µm. For the threshold adjustment, we used a Boron implant with a dose of 2×10^{12} cm^{-2} at 25 KeV and a tilt of 7°.

The gate oxide used diffusion of dry O_2 at 900 °C for 40 min, followed by the poly-silicon layer, which used an isotropic deposition doped with phosphorus, with a concentration of 5×10^{19} cm^{-3} and a thickness of 0.5 µm. We etched 0.58 µm of poly-silicon using the gate mask anisotropically.

For the lightly doped drain step (LDD), the single implant found in the original process did not yield a good threshold voltage. V_{TH} was too high and it would be an issue for a full integration, thus it had to be changed. We used four consecutive implants of Boron with a dose of 1×10^{12} cm^{-2}, a tilt of 30°, and rotation by 90° for each implant. Then, we followed immediately with an arsenic implant for the n-type extension, at a dosage of 1×10^{15} cm^{-2}, and 0° tilt and no rotation. The annealing peaks were at 960 °C under N_2 and O_2.

Next, the spacers were grown at rate of 150 nm/s at 750 °C, which was etched back as well as 20 nm of silicon. After, we prepared for the source and drain implant by diffusing dry O_2 at 925 °C for 20 min, then deposited a 1.2 µm photoresist layer. The implant used an arsenic dose of 5×10^{15} cm^{-2} at 60 KeV, also using the Pearson distribution function.

After, we prepared for the source and drain implant by diffusing dry O_2 at 925 °C for 20 min then deposited a 1.2 µm photoresist layer. The implant used an arsenic dose of 5×10^{15} cm^{-2} at 60 KeV, also using the Pearson distribution function.

During the process, we noticed the necessity of two additional annealing steps, one for the source and drain implant and another for the body implant. Without these annealing steps, the low energy implant was not enough for the species to make them penetrate the device at the desired depth. These particular steps used an adequate temperature elevation using N_2 environment, and a mixture of N_2 and O_2 gas flow, for a total duration of 1.67 min in the temperature range 700–1050 °C. We can make sure the annealing did not affect the previous layers destructively by simply observing the before and after structure.

Finally, for the body implant, after a 1.2 µm photoresist deposition, we used a BF_2 dose of 3×10^{15} cm^{-2} at 80 KeV with 7° tilt. Then we stripped the photoresist and performed annealing for 1.57 min. This particular step is the source and drain implant of the PMOS transistors.

Although it is feasible to simulate the deposition and etching of aluminum and titanium, it is not possible to solve the transport equations coupled with temperature for metals in our simulator version. Solving for temperature is critical to accurately evaluate the self-heating effect and the breakdown voltage. Therefore, the metal layers were omitted in the final structure.

Figure 2 shows the resulting device. The gate oxide and LOCOS thicknesses are 15 and 787.4 nm respectively.

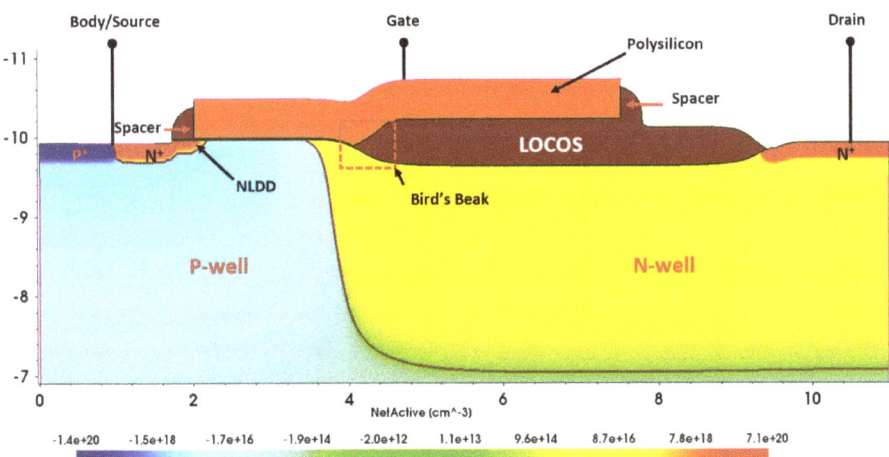

Figure 2. Final structure net doping profile.

The device simulation, conducted using the SDevice tool [14], will reflect the front-end of line (FEOL) behavior only. We used the area-factor function to simulate a device width of 100 µm without using an actual 3D mesh. We chose the hydrodynamic transport model with Fermi statistics and density quantization model for electrons, and mobility degradation using the "Inversion-Accumulation layer mobility model" coupled with the Hänsch model for high field saturation. Doping and temperature-dependent Shockley-Read-Hall (SRH),

Auger, and avalanche (UniBo) were used to model recombination and impact ionization. Finally, the "OldSlotboom" model was used for bandgap narrowing.

The transfer characteristic is plotted in Figure 3a, where the sweep is done for various V_{DS}, from 3 to 30 V with a 3 V step. The highest leakage current (I_{off}) is 1.3×10^{-11} A under $V_{DS} = 30$ V. The curves were then differentiated to show the transconductance (g_m), plotted in Figure 3b. g_m keeps increasing with increasing V_{GS} when V_{DS} is high, which is good for RF behavior, as the cut-off and maximum frequencies are directly proportional to g_m.

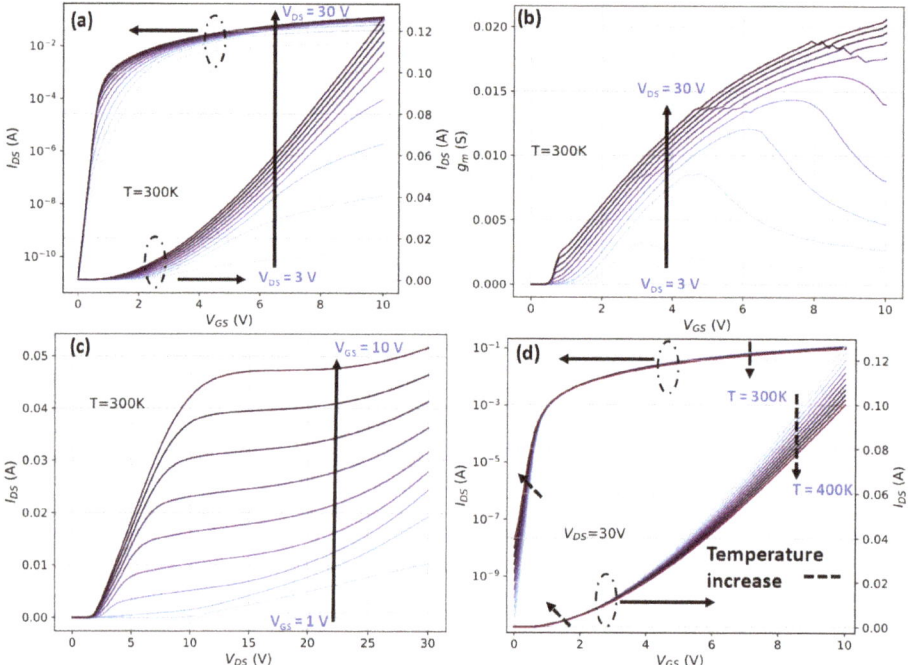

Figure 3. Various IV characteristics: (**a**,**d**) Transfer, (**b**) transconductance, (**c**) output.

Figure 3c shows the output characteristic plotted for various V_{GS} values. According to this electrothermal simulation, temperature rises, during this DC sweep, did not create the self-heating effect. Self-heating manifests as a dip in I_{DS} after saturation and causes a compression effect in the output characteristic due to the Kirk effect [15], which is practically absent in our device. Instead, this device suffers from a prolonged quasi-saturation regime at low V_{GS} as well as an early on-state breakdown.

We also plotted the transfer characteristic for various temperatures, as shown in Figure 3d, to extract the zero-temperature coefficient point (ZTC). The ZTC point is where the threshold voltage and mobility temperature dependencies are canceled. This point is useful for current referencing, a common practice in RF design [16]. The ZTC point occurs in our case at ~1.6 V. We also noticed a rise in I_{off}, where it reached 1.9×10^{-8} A at 400 K, which is a good value considering that we did not include any form of thermal dissipation of the backend of the process and the packaging.

As for the breakdown voltage (BV), it was extracted using the continuation method, while maintaining the gate voltage, V_{GS} at 0. BV occurs at $V_{DS} = 22$ V and approximately 10^{-11} A, the result is plotted in Figure 4. If we leave a 30% safe operating area, which is a standard value in LDMOS designs, the limit will be 15.4 V for an off-state drain bias.

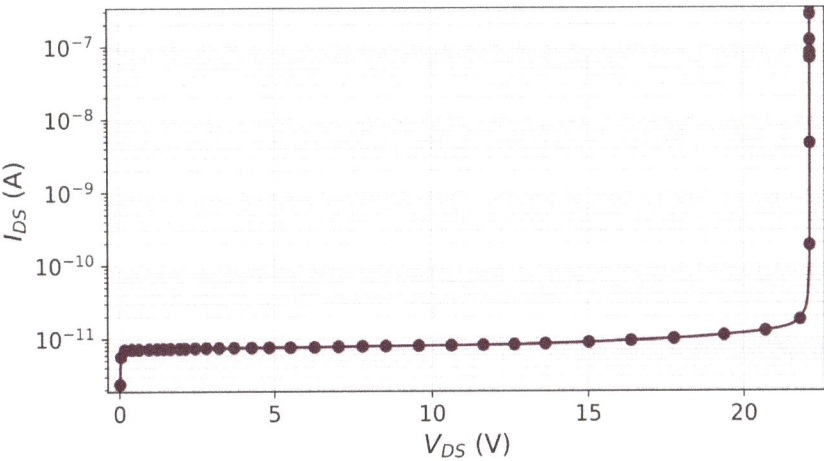

Figure 4. Off-state breakdown characteristic of the LDMOS.

Figure 5 shows the 2D scalar distribution of the absolute value of the electric field and with its extracted maximum path. The bird's beak and near areas have the highest values, and we reported that it triggers noticeable degradation under hot carrier injection [17,18].

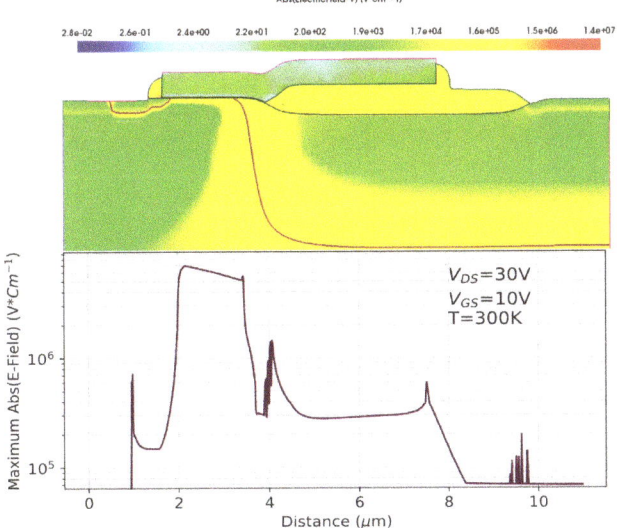

Figure 5. Electric-field scalar distribution and its maximum value along the LDMOS.

As mentioned earlier, the LDMOS operates in RF modes, thus it is important to determine its frequency response. The AC sweep simulation saves all possible combinations of capacitances and admittances between the electrodes. The saved data were used in the Svisual tool, which relies on a two-port network configuration to extract the RF parameters. The resistances 150 and 1 kΩ were used for stability at the source and substrate, respectively, as well as using a 100 kΩ resistance for the gate to drain feedback to reduce low-frequency gains. This setup was intended as a first approximation for the LDMOS response, not a final configuration, as further impedance matching will be in SPICE circuit level simulations.

First, we extracted the maximum oscillation frequency (f_{max}) and the cut-off frequency (f_T), using the admittance and hybrid parameters, respectively, with the unit-gain-point method. The results are plotted in Figure 6a,b. Next, we examined the transistor gain as a function of frequency for multiple gate voltages, using Mason's unilateral gain (MUG) approach. MUG simulation results are plotted in Figure 6c. Stable gains occur if $V_G \leq 6$ V and under 10^9 Hz frequencies, thus strong inversion regimes must be avoided; it also causes hot carrier injection degradations.

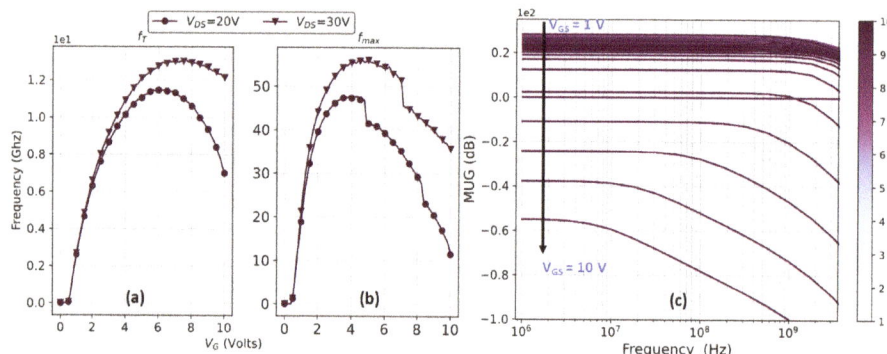

Figure 6. Maximum and cut-off frequency extracted from a two-port network simulation (a,b), respectively. (c) Mason's unilateral gain (MUG) as a function of gate voltage.

A recapitulation of the DC and RF parameters is presented in Table 1. This simulation showed that integrating RF and/or power modules is possible using the 1 µm CMOS process flow at CDTA, and the results show overall acceptable electrothermal behavior under DC and RF regimes, provided further studies. However, to take full advantage of the RESURF principle, which can enhance BV up to 120 V, a slight change in the process flow (like implant energies) and using a double-gate design are more fitting to our targeted applications.

Table 1. Main electric parameters from DC and RF characteristics.

Parameter	Value
Off-state current (I_{off}) @V_{DS} = 30 V	1.7×10^{-11} (A)
ON-state current (I_{ON}) @ V_{DS} = 30 V	0.126 (A)
Threshold voltage (V_{TH}) @ V_{DS} = 30 V	0.44 (V)
Peak transconductance	0.136 (S)
Zero-temperature coefficient (ZTC)	1.6 (V)
Subthreshold swing (SS)	105 mV/dec
On-state resistance (R_{ON})	272 (mm² mΩ)
Breakdown voltage (BV)	22 (V)
Figure of merit (FoM) (FoM = BV^2/R_{ON})	1.77 (V/mm² mΩ)
Maximum oscillation frequency (f_{max})-PeakdB-	56.07 (GHz)
Cut-off frequency (f_T)-Peak0-	13.14 (GHz)

3. Conclusions

The DC and RF performances of an integrated LDMOS were investigated in this paper. The 2D process simulation was based on the 1 µm CMOS technology node, available at CDTA. The extracted process flow yielded a 22 V BV and 272 mm² mΩ R_{ON}. The temperature effect and the stability in various bias conditions and frequencies are presented. According to the extracted data, the proposed nLDMOS could be used for power amplifiers in wireless communications, automotive, and similar domains.

Author Contributions: A.H. created the scripts of the TCAD simulations, extracted and visualized the results, and wrote the paper. B.D. provided the necessary process parameters, examined the numerical values of the results, and assisted in the paper's correction. All authors have read and agreed to the published version of the manuscript.

Funding: This work was supported by the Directorate-General for Scientific Research and Technological Development/Ministry of High Education and Scientific Research of Algeria (DGRSDT/MESRS).

Institutional Review Board Statement: Not applicable.

Informed Consent Statement: Not applicable.

Data Availability Statement: Not applicable.

Conflicts of Interest: The authors declare no conflict of interest.

References

1. Ma, G.; Burger, W.; Dragon, C.; Gillenwater, T. High efficiency LDMOS power FET for low voltage wireless communications. In Proceedings of the International Electron Devices Meeting, Technical Digest, San Francisco, CA, USA, 8–11 December 1996; pp. 91–94.
2. Houadef, A.; Djezzar, B. Process and performance optimization of Triple-RESURF LDMOS with Trenched-Gate. *Int. J. RF Microw. Comput.-Aided Eng.* **2021**, *31*, e22755. [CrossRef]
3. Golio, M. *RF and Microwave Semiconductor Device Handbook*; CRC Press: Boca Raton, FL, USA, 2017.
4. Kwon, O.K.; Ng, W.T. Others An optimized RESURF LDMOS power device module compatible with advanced logic processes. In Proceedings of the 1992 International Technical Digest on Electron Devices Meeting, San Francisco, CA, USA, 13–16 December 1992; pp. 237–240.
5. Tan, Y.; Kumar, M.; Sin, J.K.; Cai, J.; Lau, J. A LDMOS technology compatible with CMOS and passive components for integrated RF power amplifiers. *IEEE Electron Device Lett.* **2000**, *21*, 82–84. [CrossRef]
6. Fu, Y.; Li, Z.; Ng, W.T.; Sin, J.K. *Integrated Power Devices and TCAD Simulation*; CRC Press: Boca Raton, FL, USA, 2014.
7. Houadef, A.; Djezzar, B. Hot Carrier Degradation in Triple-RESURF LDMOS with Trenched-Gate. In Proceedings of the 2021 IEEE 32nd International Conference on Microelectronics (MIEL), Nis, Serbia, 12–14 September 2021; pp. 141–144.
8. Djezzar, B.; Bellaroussi, M.T. Process and Device Simulation of 1.2 µm- Channel N- well C-MOS Technology. In Proceedings of the 5th International Conference on Microelectronics (ICM'93), Dhahran, Saudi Arabia, 14–16 December 1993; pp. 28–32.
9. Boubaaya, M.; Larbi, F.H.H.; Oussalah, S. Simulation of Ion Implantation for CMOS 1 µm Using SILVACO Tools. In Proceedings of the 2012 24th International Conference on Microelectronics (ICM), Algiers, Algeria, 16–20 December 2012.
10. Whiston, S.; Bain, D.; Deignan, A.; Pollard, J.; Chleirigh, C.N.; O'Neill, C.M.M. Complementary LDMOS transistors for a CMOS/BiCMOS process. In Proceedings of the 12th International Symposium on Power Semiconductor Devices and ICs. Proceedings (Cat. No. 00CH37094), Toulouse, France, 22–25 May 2000; pp. 51–54.
11. Ma, G.; Burger, W.; Shields, M. High efficiency 0.4/spl mu/m gate LDMOS power FET for low voltage wireless communications. In Proceedings of the 1999 IEEE MTT-S International Microwave Symposium Digest (Cat. No. 99CH36282), Anaheim, CA, USA, 13–19 June 1999; Volume 3, pp. 1195–1198.
12. Gray, P.R.; Meyer, R.G. Future directions in silicon ICs for RF personal communications. In Proceedings of the Proceedings of the IEEE 1995 Custom Integrated Circuits Conference, Santa Clara, CA, USA, 1–4 May 1995; pp. 83–90.
13. *SentaurusTM Process User Guide 2017*; Synopsys: Mountain View, CA, USA, 2017.
14. *SentaurusTM Device User Guide 2017*; Synopsys: Mountain View, CA, USA, 2017.
15. Hower, P.; Lin, J.; Pendharkar, S.; Hu, B.; Arch, J.; Smith, J.; Efland, T. A rugged LDMOS for LBC5 technology. In Proceedings of the 17th International Symposium on Power Semiconductor Devices and ICs, Santa Barbara, CA, USA, 23–26 May 2005; pp. 327–330.
16. Najafizadeh, L.; Filanovsky, I.M. A simple voltage reference using transistor with ZTC point and PTAT current source. In Proceedings of the 2004 IEEE International Symposium on Circuits and Systems (IEEE Cat. No. 04CH37512), Vancouver, BC, Canada, 23–26 May 2004; Volume 1, pp. 1–909.
17. Houadef, A.; Djezzar, B. HCI Degradation of LOCOS-based LDMOS Transistor fabricated by 1 µm CMOS Process. In Proceedings of the 2020 International Conference on Electrical Engineering (ICEE), Istanbul, Turkey, 25–27 September 2020; pp. 1–6.
18. Houadef, A.; Djezzar, B. Evaluation of Hot Carrier Impact on Lateral-DMOS with LOCOS feature. *Alger. J. Signals Syst.* **2021**, *6*, 16–23.

MDPI
St. Alban-Anlage 66
4052 Basel
Switzerland
Tel. +41 61 683 77 34
Fax +41 61 302 89 18
www.mdpi.com

Engineering Proceedings Editorial Office
E-mail: engproc@mdpi.com
www.mdpi.com/journal/engproc

www.ingramcontent.com/pod-product-compliance
Lightning Source LLC
LaVergne TN
LVHW070358100526
838202LV00014B/1341